THE POSSIBILITY OF LANGUAGE

BENJAMINS TRANSLATION LIBRARY

The Benjamins Translation Library aims to stimulate academic research and training in translation studies, lexicography and terminology. The Library provides a forum for a variety of approaches (which may sometimes be conflicting) in a historical, theoretical, applied and pedagogical context. The Library includes scholarly works, reference books, post-graduate text books and readers in the English language.

Volume 14

Alan K. Melby with C. Terry Warner

The Possibility of Language
A discussion of the nature of language, with implications for human and machine translation

THE POSSIBILITY OF LANGUAGE

A DISCUSSION OF THE NATURE OF LANGUAGE, WITH IMPLICATIONS FOR HUMAN AND MACHINE TRANSLATION

ALAN K. MELBY

with

C. TERRY WARNER

JOHN BENJAMINS PUBLISHING COMPANY
AMSTERDAM/PHILADELPHIA

The paper used in this publication meets the minimum requirements of American National Standard for Information Sciences — Permanence of Paper for Printed Library Materials, ANSI Z39.48-1984.

Library of Congress Cataloging-in-Publication Data

Melby, Alan K.

The possibility of language : a discussion of the nature of language, with implications for human and machine translation / Alan K. Melby, with C. Terry Warner.

p. cm. -- (Benjamins translation library, ISSN 0929-7316 ; v. 14)

Includes bibliographical references (p.) and index.

1. Machine translating. 2. Translating and interpreting, 3. Language and languages--Philosophy. I. Warner, C. Terry. II. Title. III. Series.

P306.M44 1995

418'.02'0285--dc20 95-45373

ISBN 90 272 1614 2 (Eur.) / 1-55619-695-4 (US) (alk. paper) CIP

John Benjamins Publishing Co. • P.O.Box 75577 • 1070 AN Amsterdam • The Netherlands

John Benjamins North America • P.O.Box 27519 • Philadelphia PA 19118-0519 • USA

to Jean-Marie Zemb of the *Collège de France*
and to our parents

Contents

Abbreviations

(see also the glossary at the end of this book)

AI	Artificial Intelligence
ALPAC	Automated Language Processing Advisory Committee
ASCII	American Standard Code for Information Interchange
BYU	Brigham Young University (Provo, Utah, USA campus)
EC	European Commission
FAHQT	Fully Automatic High-Quality Translation
GG	Generative Grammar
LSP	Language for Special Purposes
LU	Lexical Unit
LTU	Lexical/Terminological Unit
MAT	Machine Assisted Translation
MIT	Massachusetts Institute of Technology
MT	Machine Translation
NLP	Natural Language Processing
SGML	Standard Generalized Markup Language
ST	Source Text
TT	Target Text
TU	Terminological Unit
UT	Unrestricted Text
UBW	Utterly Boring World

Acknowledgments

Extraordinary thanks from Alan K. Melby, the first author, to C. Terry Warner, the second author. Terry introduced me to his work in philosophical psychology, to its implications for the theory of language, and to some philosophers, particularly Emmanuel Levinas, whose writings reinforce and advance our approach to language. This book would not have happened were it not for our discussions. During the 1970s, we each experienced a turning point in our intellectual careers which would lead us to a reevaluation of mainstream thinking. Little did we suspect that during the 1990s those career paths would intersect briefly, bringing my radical ideas about translation and his radical ideas about psychology together through a particular approach to the philosophy of language.

Original thanks to the *Collège de France* for the invitation to present a series of lectures in Paris in 1990. These lectures have served as a basis for chapter 3. Particular thanks to Adam Makkai for the encouragement to present a paper on the possibility of language at the 1993 LACUS meeting and to expand the paper into a book. Public thanks to Bertie Kaal of John Benjamins for inviting me to submit a manuscript for a volume in the Translation Library and for valuable suggestions along the way. Multiple thanks to all those who have read portions or all of the draft and commented on it. Extended thanks to Daniel Hardman, who has helped with many research items and the final details of formatting and indexing. Essential thanks to BYU for a leave which allowed me to spend half time for one semester away from the Provo campus putting together the rough draft of the book during the fourth quarter of 1994 while I was in Neuchâtel, Switzerland, as a guest scholar attached to the University of Geneva. Warmest thanks to all members of my family, including extended family, for their unswerving support as I have been writing.

Foreword

The foreword to this book is divided into two sections, each focused toward readers with different interests and backgrounds. Marilyn Gaddis Rose situates the book for those who approach it from a background in literature and/or translation; John Hutchins introduces the discussion for linguists and machine translation developers and theorists.

Rapprochement and reconciliation

Marilyn Gaddis Rose [comparative literature and human translation]

For nearly a half century, linguistics and comparative literature have disputed the terrain of translation studies. The struggle arguably started when Harry Zohn brought Benjamin's "The Task of the Translator" into English in 1955. It became quite open when George Steiner divided translation studies between Walter Benjamin and Noam Chomsky in *After Babel* (1975). It became controversial when Jacques Derrida answered Steiner with a Deconstructionist reading of Benjamin in "Des Tours de Babel" in 1980.[1] Generally, the struggle has been civil and, in my opinion, has advanced translation studies. The civility usually surfaces in smiling, unbelieving face-to-face encounters. The linguist and comparatist, wearing dutiful smiles throughout, shake hands and go their *very* separate ways, each reconfirmed in the validity of his or her views and the wrongheadedness of the other's.

Linguist Alan Melby's *The Possibility of Language* changes that face-to-face encounter to the genuine smiles of mutual comprehension (or, perhaps, an open-minded apprehension). His is an essay comparatists can accept and learn from. This is because Melby relates what linguistics, especially computational linguistics and generative grammar, have done in, to, or with the traditional, speculative philosophies of language. The thinking of C. Terry Warner and the works of Emmanuel Levinas (1906—) appear to have been his bridge, although, of course, in his study of Chomsky and post-Chomsky linguistics, he had to study Chomsky's heritage from Descartes to Wittgenstein and beyond.

For practicing translators, who have belittled the dispute from a distance, now is the time to start reading—reading Melby.

For the smiling antagonists, now is the time to really mean it, for this essay will show how we can come together.

For the practicing translator any method of analysis is valid if it is personally useful. I would go further: any conceptual explanation that accounts for this usefulness is valid as well, if the user is personally satisfied. We judge translations by our notions of accuracy and style,[2] not by either the currency or the idiosyncrasy of whatever theories, if any, their translators espouse.

A translator's theoretical base remains relevant, however. If we admire a translation—and we may find it difficult to explain our admiration—we may repeat the translator's methodology in the hope of repeating some of his or her success. We judge a speculation in theory by different criteria. We look not only for internal coherence and articulation with tradition which a translation may share if its model does, but we look also for originality, something that would never have occurred to us but which imposes its own logic upon us. This logic imposes partly because we can test it for replicability and applicability.

For example, we would not deny Burton Raffel the brilliance of his many achievements. Consider his *Beowulf*, *Gargantua and Pantagruel*, and *Don Quixote*. Still we may find *The Forked Tongue*, *The Art of Translating Poetry*, and *The Art of Translating Prose* a restatement of the often thought and nearly as well expressed.[3] On the other hand, Benjamin's translations of Baudelaire follow his own dicta to an absurd extent. It is one thing to let the French echo through the German. Another, to force a reader to back-translate to understand Baudelaire's reputation as a major modern poet.[4] Nevertheless, when he wrote "The Task of the Translator" (1923), he gave us new spaces to think in, terrains that re-explorations have yet to contain.

Thus, speculation on what translating is, what a translation represents, how the two or more languages relate, is a value in itself, even when, perhaps especially when, speculations get emended, discarded, or superseded. Such speculations on the nature of translation lure us into thinking we have sighted something about the nature of language. Probably we have, but exactly what that something is will likely always elude us. Generally, the act itself of speculation becomes the value. Melby in *The Possibility of Language* has taken the speculative spaces opened by Levinas and shown where it elucidates dynamic general language, which has eluded computational linguistics and generative grammar.

For many years, Melby, long recognized as one of the most knowledgeable advisers on machine-aided translation in the U.S., was engaged in one of the longest-running and best-funded speculations: the *pour voir*, the "what if," of machine translation. Rather than lament the money and time invested, we would do well to classify the explorations of machine translation and artificial intelligence with all other costly explorations that advance human knowledge considerably ahead of human utilization, for instance, the Mars landing and space stations. Melby does not offer an apologia for his determined pursuit of machine translation (MT) and machine-aided translation (MAT). He does, however, provide here a concise, unbiased account of the MT waves of enthusiasm and discouragement from the immediate post World War II years to the present.

In reading *The Possibility of Language*, we sense that Melby was sorry to give up his belief in the coming conquest of dynamic general language by human-programmed machines. On the other hand, he has compensated for this loss with a belief in the continuing creativity of and in language. Texts in a specific, controllable domain belong to the "Utterly Boring World," as he puts it. When they must be translated, they often respond well to an electronic program. Their lexical terminology units can be updated and inputted. As a trained linguist, Melby is sorry also that linguistics can describe language but not explain it, above all, not predict it. The conceptually complicated matter of MT gave way to MAT, and genuine aid in MAT is limited to the extent of specific domain language in the text.

In the covert autobiographical narrative of *The Possibility of Language*, we sense that this shortcoming of linguistics was disheartening for Melby. Even his appealing sense of humor cannot mask the sinking feeling—which a reader shares—when he recognized that general language is erratic and ambiguous in its formation. Translating from one natural language to another can just as easily compound or reduce the randomness and ambiguity. The unpredictable collectivity of usage in historical settings can destabilize both the first text and the translation.

Did the MT mystique turn out to be a kind of Babel? Should we draw similar morals from the respective situations? Certainly the MT limitations pointed up the vitality and autonomy of natural languages. That vitality and autonomy might have led me back to Benjamin.

For Melby, who traces the history of language in the modern (post-Renaissance) era, the way around the Tower led to Levinas, who stresses the ethical implications of social interactions. Although a Lithuanian who studied in Germany and made his career in France, so we might assume that his expression involves constant semi-conscious translation, Levinas does not deal with translation qua translation. Melby and Warner extrapolate that when we communicate with and for other people, we accommodate our language usage to theirs. They in turn accommodate ours. This process may be most obvious in conversation, but it occurs in any text in any media. We are especially aware of such accommodations when we translate or study translations.[5] Any time we accommodate our listener or reader, even in solipsistic lyrics we hope no one ever discovers, we are incorporating language change and exploiting ambiguity. Any time as listeners or readers we struggle to follow the implicit dialogue being conducted with us, we incorporate such change and ambiguity while adding our own.

Is it any wonder that God struck down the Tower of Babel or that MT has had to fall back on MAT? The limitlessness of language expands with each limit crossed.

While it is amazing that usage is as stable as it is, it is gratifying, even exhilarating, that it defeats entropy. Melby, if disappointed in some early hopes, has been heartened by that realization. Always resourceful, he engages us here in the ethical face-to-face of communication between users of different languages. He supports and enhances such communication with the expertise and experience of exhaustive and inspired service in the MT vanguard.

Notes

[1] First delivered as a lecture at Binghamton University in October 1980, the essay was widely circulated before being published in an anthology by Cornell University in 1985 (Joseph Graham, ed., *Difference in Translation*).

[2] What leads us to find a translation stylish, to use Kurt Gingold's turn of phrase, (ATA *Series* 1, p. 119) is subjective and only intentionally stay at a remove from the latest usage.

[3] I am grateful for having had the opportunity of reviewing each, but I find his discussions helpful chiefly for explaining my own taste. For example, his observation that "the logic we associate with prose is linear and the logic we more often than not associate with poetry is nonlinear" (*The Art of Translating Prose*, Pennsylvania State Press, 1993, p. 16).

[4] Harry Zohn, trans. *Illuminations* (New York: Harcourt, Brace, and World, 1955) and *Gesammelte Schriften* 4 (Frankfurt am Main: Surhkamp, 1972). See my "Walter Benjamin as Translation Theorist: a Reconsideration," *Dispositio* 7 (1982): pp. 163-175.

[5] Prime examples would be stereoscopic handling of texts in humanities classes.

Languages and machines
John Hutchins [linguistics and machine translation]

It was under this title that the Automated Language Processing Advisory Committee (ALPAC) of the U.S. National Academy of Sciences reported in 1966 on the prospects for machine translation (MT). The first suggestion that automatic translation was an appropriate task for computers had been made by Warren Weaver of the Rockefeller Foundation some twenty years earlier, but research began in earnest on a large scale only after a demonstration of a small Russian-English translation program in 1954 had impressed the general public with the possibilities and encouraged substantial funding from U.S. governmental agencies. After ten years, however, there were no MT systems in operation producing translations of a quality comparable with those of human translators. The ALPAC report concluded that progress on MT had been unsatisfactory, and it recommended the cessation of funding for MT in the United States; instead, it recommended the support of fundamental research in computational linguistics and the development of computer-based aids for translators.

This report was interpreted as a definitive judgment of the 'failure' of MT. To this day, it is widely believed (not just by the general public but by linguists, translators and computer scientists) that MT failed. But what ALPAC announced was not the failure of MT as such but the failure of the excessively ambitious and unrealistic ideal of fully automatic translation of texts on any subject. Even at the time of ALPAC there were working MT systems producing useful (by no means perfect) translations which in unedited rough form were serving the needs of information gatherers and evaluators, or which after appropriate human revision ('post-editing') could be used as the basis for adequate publishable translations.

After the ALPAC report, research continued on MT with markedly less ambitious aims. There have been four main strands. Firstly the development of computer-based tools for translators (as recommended by ALPAC), e.g., multilingual word processing, concordances, glossaries, terminology management facilities, and now the successfully marketed translation workstations. In this sphere Alan Melby has himself been an influential advocate and active developer for many years.

The second strand has been the continued development of MT systems with post-editing facilities for large organisations: e.g., the European Communities, multinational companies such as General Motors and Aerospatiale. The major systems in this sphere have included Systran and Logos, building upon MT expertise going back to the pre-ALPAC period. From these systems are now produced millions of translated pages every year, and the numbers are increasing.[1]

The third major strand has grown primarily since the mid 1960s. This is the design or adaptation of MT systems to operate within specific sublanguages or domains, or with controlled language input. The earliest success was the METEO system for translating weather reports in Canada from English into French. Another early significant example was the use of Systran by the Xerox company for the translation of technical manuals written in a controlled subset of English. As Melby illustrates in this book, controlled domain-specific MT is capable of good quality output with little or no human revision or interaction. In recent years, many MT systems have been specifically designed to take advantage of this feature. And we are now seeing research specifically on controlled-language MT, e.g., systems for business people ignorant of target languages who want to communicate 'standard' messages, and (more ambitiously) systems for translating spoken telephone messages to make conference registrations and hotel bookings.

The final strand is the appearance of systems for dealing with unrestricted input of colloquial language. With the increasing use of global telecommunications (e.g., the Internet) there is clearly a huge need for the translation of short electronic messages on almost any topic. (On CompuServe, such a service is already available.) In addition, the appearance on the market of cheap PC-based translation software has stimulated a latent demand for 'occasional' personal and business translation by monolinguals and non-translators. Furthermore, there is the continuing need to translate documents for information purposes. For reasons which Melby explains, the MT of unrestricted text is much more difficult and less successful than the MT of controlled texts. In this area, then, MT is providing a crude tool with many imperfections which is nevertheless satisfying identifiable needs.

Alongside these clear demonstrations of the practical everyday usefulness of MT, there continues to be research on MT with the clear and obvious aim of improving the quality of MT in general. It is here that the idealism of the early period still has echoes, and it is this field of activity which is the main focus of Melby's book. The first efforts in MT research were necessarily constrained by limitations in hardware, inadequate storage facilities and the lack of suitable programming languages. More crucially there was no help from the language experts: syntax was a relatively neglected area of linguistic research and semantics was virtually ignored in the United States thanks to the behaviourist inclinations of the leading scholars. However, within a few years there were dramatic improvements in hardware and software and there were exciting developments in linguistic theory which gave rise to the belief that good quality output comparable to that of human translators was achievable within a matter of a few years. It became widely assumed that the goal of MT must be the development of fully automatic systems producing high quality translations. The use of human assistance was regarded as an interim arrangement: post-editing ought to wither away as systems improved. The emphasis of research was therefore on the search for theories and methods for the achievement of 'perfect' translations.

Although the effect of ALPAC was to encourage more realistic objectives (with the successes outlined above), MT research continued on much the same lines as before. There was a firm belief that the systems developed during the "first generation" (before ALPAC) and which were now being brought into operation (Systran, Logos, etc.) were inherently incapable of further improvement. They were considered to be deficient from the perspective of theoretical linguistics. Thus arose after ALPAC the "second generation" architectures in which source languages were analyzed into abstract representations of the meaning of sentences, from which target texts were generated. The systems were explicit applications of models, rules and formalisms derived directly or indirectly from linguistics. Some argued that the representations should be interlingual language-neutral or language-independent representations, in order that new language pairs could be readily added to the system architecture. Others held that representations should be disambiguated abstractions of source sentences, and that they should then be transformed first into similar unambiguous representations of the target language before generation into target sentences. In this case, lexical items (root forms) and basic structures were converted by a bilingual 'transfer' module of relatively simple form. Both approaches assumed that lexical and structural equivalences can be formulated in computationally appropriate rules.

Many models of linguistic formalism have been explored in MT (Transformational Generative Grammar, Categorial Grammar, Lexical-Functional Grammar, Head-Driven Phrase Structure Grammar, Principles-and-Parameters Grammar, etc.); indeed from one perspective it can be argued that MT has often served as a testbed for theories developed elsewhere—for the simple reason that whether a translation succeeds or not is relatively easy to evaluate. It is of course quite another and more complex matter to judge the quality and appropriateness of translations for specific needs; but, as far as the theorists are concerned, the production of any reasonable translation is acceptable—improvements, they would contend, can come over time with greater sophistication and elaboration of the rules.

However, it is precisely this last assumption that has proved to be mistaken time and again; beyond a certain level of quality, it has been found that rule-based systems become increasingly more complex and more difficult to improve. The solution of one outstanding problem tends to degrade some other aspect of the system previously working satisfactorily. In this respect the linguistics-based systems of the second generation appear to be no more capable of improvement than those of the first generation.

In recent years, MT researchers have looked to other methodologies. First, knowledge-based methods familiar in AI research were adopted; but ultimately, this variant of the rule-based approach showed similar problematic aspects; in particular, generalisability from relatively small-scale systems has proved difficult. It is notable that the best known group using this approach (at Carnegie Mellon University) is now developing a controlled-language domain-specific system in collaboration with the Caterpillar Corporation.

More significantly, however, there have emerged in the last five years corpus-based methods which explicitly reject the rule-based methods of the linguistic systems. There are two main directions: the statistical methods developed by an IBM group on the basis of the vast Canadian Hansard corpus of English and French texts; and the example-based methods adopted by many Japanese research groups which use aligned bilingual corpora of (usually human) translated text to match segments of source sentences against possible target outputs. In neither case is there any linguistic analysis in the traditional sense (i.e., morphological, syntactic, semantic analysis) of the source texts.[2]

Nevertheless, few MT researchers believe that these corpus-based methods will supersede completely the rule-based methods. Since systems would have to be 'trained' on specific text corpora, it would seem on the face of it that corpus-based approaches will be most appropriate in restricted domains; and that they will be no more (and perhaps less) successful with unrestricted general language corpora than rule-based systems. Most believe that future MT research systems will be hybrids, selecting the best and most effective aspects from both rule-based and corpus-based methods.

Whatever the future development of MT research, there remains the fundamental question which Alan Melby addresses in this book. Is it possible in principle to design and construct a fully automatic system to translate unrestricted general language at a performance level comparable to that of human translators? We know that it cannot be done at present, but is it perhaps just a matter of time (perhaps a very long time) before methods are developed to deal with everyday language? And if not, then why not?[3]

Melby's answer begins by marshalling the major objections (some well known, some less known) to the 'universalist' theoretical linguists who believe that they are investigating the very foundations of all human language. By focusing on the universals of language they have neglected the variability and differences of languages and the communicative contexts of language itself. By seeking models of linguistic competence and language acquisition they have neglected models of linguistic performance. In brief, they have developed theories of language which are divorced from languages in use. Consequently linguistic theory is of little value to the processing of texts and to the treatment of bilingual and multilingual communication essential for translation.[4] Indeed, Melby contends that linguistic theory is irrelevant to human translation because it cannot account for ordinary normal language and communication. And it is relevant in MT only for those systems which deal with regularised and controlled 'artificial' special languages.

Of course, not all linguists share universalist aims; many are more concerned with the social, psychological and pragmatic dimensions of languages in action. It is in fact arguable that these other aspects of language, which are probably more relevant to translation, are in principle unformalisable—at least, not reducible to rules and procedures suitable for computational treatment. It is, however, the computationally attractive formalisations of the 'universalist' linguistic theories which have had and continue to have such influence on many MT researchers. In this book, Melby directs his argument mainly towards the Chomskyan brand of linguistic theory, but his criticisms are equally valid for many of the varieties of formal linguistics which have been applied and adopted in MT, since the issues concern the basic assumptions of these theories about the nature of language, meaning and communication.

Melby's argument is relevant specifically to the rule-based linguistics-inspired MT research. Its relevance to the newer corpus-based approaches is more indirect. It is a basic assumption of MT that it is possible for any given text to produce the 'correct' translation (or at least the 'best possible' translation) if the equivalences between source and target vocabularies and structures are correctly defined and recorded, and if the relevant contextual factors can be identified and brought into play appropriately. The assumption is as relevant to the statistically derived (probabilistic) equivalences and contexts of the corpus-based approaches as it is (more obviously) to the rule-specified equivalences and contexts of the linguistics-based systems. Melby's thesis is that underlying this assumption is a belief in objective 'meanings' independent of human communication.

If the computer modelling or implementation of a theory can be regarded as proof of the validity of its assumptions (although this itself is disputable), then the automatic translation of ordinary unrestricted language as good as human translation would be proof of the 'objectivist' view of meaning which lies at the root of much of linguistics, science and philosophy. However, it does have to be translation from and into languages which are not restricted in any way to specific domains or sublanguages; automatic translation of 'unnatural' (standardised, homogenised, normalised, etc.) language is not sufficient.

On the other hand, if it can be proved that unrestricted MT is impossible, then (as Melby stresses) there are significant ramifications and implications, not just for translation both human and automatic, but also for linguistic theory, computer science and the philosophy of language. With such a thesis it will be a surprise if readers agree with everything Melby writes. Some will want to reject his main argument, others will dispute particular details or inferences. No readers are going to be neutral or indifferent. Melby's arguments deserve the most careful consideration by all those concerned with the fundamental aims and the future prospects of both human and machine translation.

Notes

[1] The rapid growth in the use of MT systems is reported in a survey by Muriel Vasconcellos: 'The present state of machine translation usage technology, or: How do I use thee? Let me count the ways!' in *MT Summit IV*: International Cooperation for Global Communication, July 20-22, 1993, Kobe, Japan, pp.35-46. Also published in *MT News International 6* (September 1993), pp.12-17.

[2] For a critical review of recent developments in MT research see Harold Somers: 'Current research in machine translation' *Machine Translation 7*(4), 1993, pp.231-246. A general overview of current research can be found in John Hutchins: 'Latest developments in machine translation technology' in *MT Summit IV*, July 20-22 1993, Kobe, Japan, pp.11-34; and in John Hutchins: 'A new era in machine translation research' in *Translating and the Computer 16*...10-11 November 1994 (London: Aslib, 1994), pp.1-13.

[3] The conundrum is akin to that faced by researchers in Artificial Intelligence where it has been found that systems can cope with formalised, rule-specifiable expert knowledge but that ordinary common sense has so far defied all attempts at computational treatment. Is this too impossible in principle? And if so, why? The answer may well be related to Melby's thesis in this book.

[4] In this respect the title of the ALPAC report had an aptness which the authors were perhaps only dimly aware of: in the context of MT, computers must deal with the variations and differences of living *languages* in use and not with the generalities and universals of *language* in the abstract.

Preface

It is not the purpose of this book to replace a general introduction to machine translation, such as Hutchins and Somers (1992) or Arnold et al. (1994), nor to replace a general introduction to translation theory. Rather, it is to explore the “open questions” of machine translation. In the preface to Hutchins and Somers (1992), Martin Kay comments on the status and future of machine translation:

> Certainly, even when applied to texts on very limited subjects by authors with no literary pretensions, machine translation still generally produces results that would not be acceptable from a human translator under any circumstances. Just what would improve the quality of the result, and even whether any substantial improvement is possible, are open questions.... [The authors] clearly both have opinions on the open questions of machine translation, but they are not the subject of this book.

We attempt to address these open issues by examining the intellectual tradition of mainstream linguistics and philosophy and to identify why this tradition has failed to provide an adequate theoretical framework for some of the goals of machine translation. In the course of this investigation, we present an alternative view of how human language is possible. We then trace some of the implications of this view for the shape of translation theories, the practice of human translation, and the future of translation technology, including both machine translation and computer-based tools for human translators.

If this book is convincing or even just troubling, the interested reader can go on to consult publications on machine translation (with ammunition to perform a careful analysis of assumptions), publications on translation theory (again, to look for underlying assumptions about language), or writings in philosophy (to explore the original sources mentioned in chapter 4). We hope that some readers will be so intrigued by the topic that they will choose to investigate what makes human language possible and how such an understanding can be applied.

Depending on the background of the reader, some of the material in chapters 1 (which includes a brief introduction to human translation) and 2 (which includes a brief introduction to machine translation) can be covered quickly. However, the arguments in chapters 3 ("The Wall") and 4 ("Possibilities") should be new to everyone except those who have read our recent papers.

We recognize that the title of this book could have been *The Limits of Machine Translation*. Only chapter 4 deals directly with the question of why language as a tool for communication between humans is possible without relying on the assumptions, which we will call *objectivism*, underlying mainstream linguistics. However, we hope that our exploration of the possibility of language is worth further effort by ourselves and others. We dismiss radical relativism as a basis for explaining human communication because it excludes any grounding of our concepts in reality. We also reject objectivism as a basis for explaining dynamic general language. We are therefore obliged to present a third alternative. One of many unfinished tasks for us is to further examine approaches to language that claim to handle dynamic metaphor to see if they have completely abandoned objectivism. We invite dialogue with colleagues.

Apologies are given in advance for the bias toward French examples. The first author is a French-English translator. Some readers will also be uncomfortable with the use of personal pronouns. Sometimes, when the first-person plural is used in this book, it is Melby and Warner, but other times 'we' is used to avoid the more formal third-person singular 'one' and to alternate with the informal 'I'. Though I (Melby) as first author take responsibility for everything in the book, including errors that certainly remain, I happily share that responsibility with Warner for the parts on which we collaborated.

A few further notes on style are in order. Bold is used to mark the first use of a term that is defined in the glossary at the end of the book. This book is unashamedly and unavoidably American in some respects of which I am aware (such as the references to Generative Grammar as mainstream linguistics), and in many respects of which I am not aware, because they are still invisible to me. However, some stylebook details are intentionally British, such as the placement of punctuation relative to quotations and conventions of number ('type of apple' versus 'type of apples'), which I find more logical than American usage. I am told my attempts at humor are neither British nor American, being more akin to Alien.

Alan K. Melby
Provo, August 1995

1 Limits in Search of a Cause

1.1 An answer

What are the limits of **machine translation**? Within the field of translation, attitudes concerning this question have changed significantly since the early 1980s. Answers used to be extreme and contradictory. Some would claim that there were no limits except the speed and memory capacity of computers and that most human translators would soon be replaced by computers. Others would claim that machine translation is necessarily so limited as to be useless and that all development efforts should be abandoned. Thus these incompatible stances characterized machine translation as either nearly trivial or outright impossible. Gradually, more people have taken a more moderate and pragmatic position, acknowledging that machine translation certainly has limits but that within those limits it can be very useful. High-quality machine translation is currently feasible only when the text to be translated is highly restricted. It must be restricted to the vocabulary of some narrow domain of knowledge, such as a particular brand of photocopiers, and it must be straightforward in style and grammar. This type of text is often called a controlled-language text.

Thus we have an answer to the question about the limits of machine translation. The answer is that fully automatic high-quality machine translation requiring little or no revision is feasible only for highly controlled language. But do we have a cause? It is obvious that computers can be more easily programmed to process controlled-language texts than general-language texts. There is less ambiguity and more regularity. What is *not* obvious is why computers do so poorly on general-language texts. A human translator can adapt to various types of text. A computer may do well on a controlled-language text and very poorly on a slightly more general text. Why do computers behave so differently on different types of text? Why can't we generalize and extend the approaches that work on controlled-language texts? Why can't computers be more like humans? Perhaps the way computers process language creates artificial limits which do not apply to human translators. It is generally agreed that speed and memory capacity are no longer the cause of the limits and that the limits are not likely to be lifted in the near future. We have an answer to the question of what are the limits of machine translation, but the answer is still in search of a cause. There has been insufficient effort expended in understanding the cause, or basis, of the failure of machine translation to approach the range of performance of human translators.

This book is an account of a search for underlying causes for the generally accepted limits of machine translation. The search led first to the suspicion that controlled-language texts from a single domain of knowledge are radically different from general-language texts. The search also led to an examination of the assumptions on which current techniques in machine translation are based. This examination then demanded an exploration of alternative assumptions.

The assumptions that this search has called into question are not unique to machine translation but are part of the paradigm of mainstream linguistics. What the search has suggested is that mainstream linguistics has overstepped its bounds by making claims about general language that are only true for restricted types of texts. Mainstream linguists assume that the meaning of a sentence is built up from the meanings of its parts by a mechanical process, independent of the speaker or hearer or any human. But I will argue in this book that meaning is not always built up in this way. Machine translation systems analyze the text to be translated and somehow make a jump into the syntax of another language. But this syntax jump falls short of dealing with the problem of how to transfer meaning from one language to another. Even if there is a universal grammar that ties the two languages together, and even if that grammar can be programmed on a computer, what ties the words of one language to the words of another language? Nearly everyone assumes that words have meaning, and the natural progression of this idea is to assume that meaning is shared between languages. So, do a word and its equivalent in another language share a single unit of meaning? This brings us to another question. Where does meaning come from?

The unacknowledged, underlying philosophical framework that supports mainstream linguistics responds that meanings exist independently of people, words, and languages. Because of this, it should be possible to maneuver between the meanings of words in different languages. To get from one language to another, one moves from a word in one language to its language-independent meaning to a word in another language. These meanings are assumed to be reflections of reality. Language is therefore computable. It should be possible to program a computer to translate perfectly.

So why is the current success of machine translation so limited? When dealing with more dynamic language which is not restricted to any particular domain, words take on nuances of meaning as needed. We discover that meaning does not exist independently of people. As we think more about the ramifications of this new "framework" (perhaps better called an approach), it is no longer clear how to maneuver between languages. If there is no word-meaning independent of people, we even begin to wonder how people can communicate in the same language. What is there to grab onto?

Join us in an account of an exploration of the nature of language. Surprisingly the exploration will lead us to a reconsideration of what makes human language possible—a suspicion that language in humans and machines may not flow from the same source and that this difference may be a major cause of the difference between humans and today's machines.

We will eventually come to conclusions which have implications for the appropriate division of labor in the field of machine translation among three tasks: developing machine translation systems based on current techniques, searching for entirely new techniques that overcome current limitations, and providing practical tools for human translators. If we attempt to apply current techniques to all texts we will waste resources which should be available for other tasks.

The account is personal, and I am only one of many to have concerns about the limits of machine translation (see, for example, Nagao 1989), but hopefully the conclusions presented here will be helpful to others. The reader is invited to participate in the journey and even to enjoy it as we explore human translation, machine translation, and linguistic/psychological theory. The next section is completely useless from the perspective of pure logic, but we are convinced that language is incomplete if restricted to logic. Damasio (1994) argues convincingly that effective reasoning requires an integration with emotion. If we are to persevere for several hundred pages in our search for a cause behind the limits of machine translation, we need something to encourage us to go on. How about a mascot?

1.2 A mascot for translation

If human translators were to choose an animal as their mascot, what would it be? Some might choose a bumblebee. Engineers have stated that theoretically a bumblebee can't fly, its body being too heavy for its wings; and philosophers have stated that theoretically one language cannot be translated into another, yet bumblebees fly around and people translate every day. Some might choose a mythical animal such as a two-headed lion, symbolizing the translator's ability in two languages. But anyone who is a fan of Douglas Adams would probably choose the Babel fish. For the benefit of the reader who has not enjoyed *The Hitchhiker's Guide to the Galaxy* (Adams 1979), the Babel fish is

> small, yellow, and leechlike, and probably the oddest thing in the Universe. It feeds on brainwave energy received not from its own carrier but from those around it. It absorbs all unconscious mental frequencies from this brainwave energy to nourish itself with. It then excretes into the mind of its carrier a telepathic matrix formed by combining the conscious thought frequencies with nerve signals picked up from the speech centers of the brain which has supplied them.

The practical result of placing a Babel fish deep in your ear canal is that thereafter you can understand anything said to you in any language. The Babel fish is an obvious choice of mascot for a translator who appreciates British humor since the very lack of such a fish justifies the translation profession. Of course, the Babel fish is named after the Tower of Babel, which the Bible connects to the origin of multiple human languages. Thus the Babel fish represents both the origin of translation and the need for human translators in the absence of an alternative.

The mascot for those more interested in machine translation than human translation would probably be the talking computer named HAL in *2001: A Space Odyssey*.

If the proposals we will be developing in this book are valid, then fundamental differences between human and machine translation justify separate mascots because they render translation difficult to analyze monolithically.

Although translation has been practiced for thousands of years, there are still conflicting theories about how it should be done. Translation is fascinating partly because even though it has been around so long, we still do not understand it. How should one begin to study translation? Perhaps by looking at a few specific difficulties in translation.

1.3 Some difficulties in translation

A common translation difficulty for someone who is just beginning to study two related languages is to be tricked by a false cognate. For example, consider the English word 'menu', which is spelled the same as the French word *menu* but whose French cognate is not identical in meaning. If an American in Paris asks for the *menu*, he or she may receive a set meal, also called a *formule*, including appetizer (usually called the *entrée*), main course (never called the *entrée* in French, even though it may be called the 'entree' in English), and dessert. In order to receive a menu, that is, a list of everything that can be ordered, one should ask for the *carte* in French. To further complicate matters, the usage of *menu* varies regionally in France.

Other difficulties in translation are less easily avoided than false cognates and can have more serious consequences. Consider the role of translation in the following event in the long-term relationship between the United States and Haiti.[1] In an effort to restore democratically elected but then exiled President Aristide to power in Haiti, a deal was made with General Cédras for him to step down in the fall of 1993. Terms of the deal allowed for U.S. military personnel to enter Haiti carrying side arms. "Somehow in translating from English to French to Creole, 'side arms' turned out as 'pistols'." However, some of the Americans were carrying M-16 assault rifles as side arms. As a U.S. warship steamed toward Haiti for a landing at Port-au-Prince, Secretary of State Les Aspin was being interviewed on national television by Sam Donaldson, who asked Aspin whether the 600 Americans would be unarmed. Aspin replied that they would have M-16s. Within an hour, a report of Aspin's comment had made its way to General Cédras, who cried "double cross". When the U.S. warship arrived, several dozen thugs were waiting at the dock to oppose the arrival of the Americans. The warship returned to the U.S. without docking, and the deal with Cédras fell through until the next attempt a year later. Although the reasoning behind the retreat has not been made public, it may have been influenced by the embarrassment over the translation problem.

How could M-16s become pistols in an important political document? One possibility is that 'side arm' was translated into French as *arme de poing* (literally, 'fist arm'). The English expression describes a weapon carried at one's side, while the French expression describes a weapon that can be fired while held in one's fist or hand. It seems that the French expression is equivalent to the English 'handgun', which is usually translated into French as *pistolet*, and which may be translated back into English as 'pistol'. The above scenario would account for a side arm becoming a pistol and explain the misunderstanding. But how could the misunderstanding have been avoided? There is no easy answer, since there is no context-independent French equivalent for 'side arm'. The French expression *arme de poing* is usually a good translation of 'side arm', since side arms are usually handguns, but not in every situation, since the English expression is a little more comprehensive than the closest French one. This could be called an instance of asymmetry between English and French. Asymmetry is rampant between languages and is therefore a major source of difficulty in translation.

Later on, we will examine many other examples of asymmetry between languages involving expressions consisting of one or more words, and we will discuss at length the distinction between general vocabulary, which is familiar to most adult native speakers of a language, and specialized terminology, which has a precise meaning within a particular domain of knowledge. For example, the word 'bus' can be an item of general vocabulary referring to a public transportation vehicle or an item of specialized terminology referring to a component in a computer that has several slots into which cards can be placed. These cards may perform functions such as adding more memory or connecting to a CD-ROM drive. The same three letters (b-u-s) can thus be either an item of general vocabulary, in which case we will call it a lexical unit (LU), or it can be an item of specialized terminology, in which case we will call it a terminological unit (TU). An LU or a TU can consist of several words; for example, 'open up' can be an LU, and 'removable cartridge drive' can be a TU.

When we want a cover term which includes both lexical unit and terminological unit—for example, in speaking of a word or expression that may be an item of general vocabulary in some contexts and an item of specialized terminology in other contexts (i.e., 'bus')—we will use the term lexical/terminological unit (LTU). So if we speak of the LTU 'bus', we are including both its vehicle and computer usages. We will see later that the distinction between general vocabulary and specialized terminology is very important. Since specialized terminology is associated with particular domains, we will speak of the **general/domain distinction**.

Now that we have introduced the general/domain distinction, we can discuss some options for handling problems such as the translation of 'side arm'. In the particular case of an international agreement, where precision is very important and one encounters an asymmetrical LTU, one could list (perhaps in a footnote or appendix) the specific types of side arms that would be allowed. Then one could choose a rather general translation for 'side arm' since it would be restricted by the list of specific weapons. Alternatively, one could define a shared domain of military concepts to be used in agreements. Then a TU such as Class B Personal Weapon (CBPW) and some corresponding term in the other language could be used instead of 'side arm'. It is not obvious which solution is better. In a novel, one might encounter 'side arm' and appropriately translate it as 'pistol' because the context makes it clear what was intended by the author.

Asymmetry between LTUs is not the only difficulty encountered when translating. One additional problem is grammatical and rhetorical differences between languages. Larson (1984) provides a rich set of examples of grammatical and rhetorical differences between various languages. English has both active and passive constructions ("a car struck him" versus "he was struck by a car"). Should an active English sentence always be translated into the active and the passive into the passive? In Thai, the passive is used to suggest unpleasantness (Larson 1984:225). Therefore, most English passives would be rendered as actives in Thai. In Aguaruna (a language of Peru), the passive is used mainly in introductory and concluding sections of a text (Larson 1984:220), so a passive in the body of a text could mislead the reader into thinking the summary had been reached. Another kind of problem in translation is how to deal with culturally specific items. Suppose we are translating a children's story about a boy who steals a piece of fruit from a neighbor's tree and later decides to tell the neighbor and try to make amends. Further suppose that the original story is from Tahiti, that the fruit is a mango, and that the translation is intended for children in Wisconsin where mangos are not grown. Should the reference to mango be changed to a common local fruit, such as an apple? This question is part of a larger question of naturalness: should a translation read like an original text?

Making a translation read like an original can involve considerable adjustment. In the case of the story of the stolen fruit, it must be decided where the action is taking place. If the desire is to present the action as occurring in Wisconsin, then all references to anything specific to Tahiti must be changed. This might involve the name of the boy, the name of the fruit, and any incidental references to cultural items not shared between Wisconsin and Tahiti, such as articles of clothing, animals, and construction of houses. Some would object to moving the setting of the story. However, if the action is left in Tahiti and the main character is a French-speaking native boy, then it will be difficult to translate the story into English and make it sound like an original text. Why would the boy be speaking English? Perhaps the translation could be about an English-speaking boy living in Tahiti, but this may also involve considerable adjustment. Making a translation read like an original with no hint that it is a translation may be possible, but often not without substantial adjustment to the events described in the text. It is perhaps not obvious that a translation should always read like an original, especially when naturalness conflicts with faithfulness.

The play *West Side Story* can be thought of as a translation of *Romeo and Juliet* from sixteenth-century Shakespearean English to twentieth-century American English with a change of place and the requirement that the translation read like an original. This raises several additional questions, such as whether the period of language of a document should be maintained. Should a sixteenth-century French text be translated into sixteenth-century English or twentieth-century English?

Sometimes even so-called universal gestures differ from culture to culture. In the country of Albania, which was isolated from the Western world for over forty years, and even isolated from other Communist countries after 1978, the typical way to indicate 'no' with a movement of the head is to move it up and down in a way that would be interpreted by most people in the Western hemisphere as indicating a 'yes'. Agreement is indicated by a movement of the head from side to side (in a manner that is not identical to the typical Western gesture for disagreement, but close enough to cause confusion). In translating an Albanian text which includes a statement that a woman nodded her head up and down in disagreement, it will be difficult to make the translation sound like an original without changing the facts about how she moved her head. Is such a change justified?

1.4 Some issues in translation theories

One might expect to find in a theory of translation some guidance on how translation should be done, including how to deal with some of the difficulties mentioned in the previous section. Over the past two thousand years, translation theories have been concerned mainly with the tension between **literal translation** and **free translation**.[2]

A literal translation stays as close as possible to the text being translated (often called the **source text** (ST)). Where possible, for each word in the source text there is a corresponding word in the translation, often called the **target text** (TT). Also, in a literal translation, the syntax (that is, the grammatical structure) of the source text is carried over into the target text insofar as it is possible to use the same grammatical constructions in the target language. Usually, the word order of the source text is not expected to carry over to a literal translation. This extreme type of translation (word for word in the same order) is often called an **interlinear translation**. A major difficulty of literal translations is that they are almost always rather unnatural and difficult to understand in the target language. However, such translations can be extremely helpful for linguistic and rhetorical analysis.

A free translation, on the other hand, is expected to somehow mean the same thing as the original; there is no attempt to follow the source text word for word, but rather to translate meaning for meaning. A major difficulty of free translation is that it is far from obvious how to determine the meaning of a text, and therefore it is unclear how to determine whether two units of text have the same meaning.

Of course, literal and free translations are extremes which are seldom encountered. Most translations are a mixture of literal and free. Nevertheless, there are tendencies toward one extreme or the other. Over the years, the pendulum has swung back and forth many times, sometimes favoring advocates of free translation (who accuse literal translations of violating the target language), and sometimes favoring advocates of literal translation (which these advocates often call *faithful* to imply that free translation is somehow unfaithful to the source text).

In an important 1923 essay, "The Task of the Translator" (in Schulte 1992), Walter Benjamin argued for a more literal approach. Eugene Nida, in his influential 1947 essay "Principles of translation as exemplified by Bible translating..." (in Brower 1959), argued for cultural adaptation in Bible translations, which nudged thinking toward the free side, with the translator attempting to be *invisible* in the sense that the translation appears to the reader to have been written in the target language. Venuti, in his essay "The Translator's Invisibility" (1986), argues that invisibility is not necessarily desirable.

Given such a long history of heated debate over the literal/free dichotomy, it seems likely that the dispute will never be settled. Marilyn Gaddis Rose (1993), speaking of the tension between proponents of literal versus free translation, agrees: “What we can count on is that the debate will go on”. Perhaps there is some way to look at translation theory other than as an attempt to decide whether translation in general should be literal or free. Perhaps from some other perspective there is no need to decide the question once and for all, if from *that* vantage point some circumstances call for a free translation and others for a more literal one.

Nida and Taber (1969) suggest that the **analysis-transfer-synthesis** approach is an alternative to previous approaches to translation. The first step is an analysis of the source text to show its structure. The second step (transfer) involves replacing source language words with target language words and making other adjustments for incompatibilities between languages. The third step (synthesis) involves making the target text more natural according to the target language. This approach is new to human translation in that it makes translation into an explicit process. As we will see in the next chapter, these same steps are often used when programming a computer to translate from one language to another. It is open to discussion how directly these steps apply to human translation and unlikely that they provide the larger perspective we are seeking.

Snell-Hornby (1988) claims that one reason there has been so much debate about how to translate is that each theory treats only one type of text, and that instead an integrated approach is needed. This claim seems reasonable. An approach to translation that is based on the translation of poetry would likely be very different from an approach based on the translation of technical documentation for complex machines. Bible translation has its own tradition, which may not apply to all other types of texts.

Robinson (1991) suggests that the entire literal/free debate is misguided because it is trapped within a long-standing tradition of treating meaning as transcendent and disembodied. He suggests a *somatic* approach as a true alternative to continuing the literal/free debate. The term somatic is used by Robinson to refer to the human body and human feelings. He emphasizes the anti-somatic influence of Augustine, who describes the meaning of a word as something pure and stable that comes from God, exists independently of humans and human bodies (that is, it transcends or goes beyond human experience), and thus is transcendent and disembodied. In the Augustinian approach, which is a fifth-century mixture of Greek philosophy and early Christian thinking, a transcendent unit of meaning is somehow linked to a sign (the written or spoken word) that humans use to refer to the meaning. As Robinson points out, Saussure[3] continued this tradition of transcendent meaning in the distinction between *langue* and *parole*. But as many have pointed out, in Saussure's approach meaning is destabilized since it no longer has a divine basis. Each meaning is defined only in terms of other meanings, with no external starting point. For Robinson, the human body is the starting point for meaning, and human feelings are a continuing basis for translation; hence he proposes a somatic approach. Saussure and Robinson have irreconcilable differences.

Implicit in this chapter's discussion has been the presupposition that meaning is relevant to translation. It seems obvious that a source text and its translation should somehow mean the same thing. But what is meaning? Is it created by humans or does it exist independently? Is it a property of a text, independent of the reader, or does it exist only in the mind of the reader and not at all in the text?

The literal/free debate seems to be based on the assumption that there is just one correct translation of a given text and one correct way to translate and that we should discover that one correct way. Much of the recent work in translation studies suggests that it is fruitless to try to decide whether translation (in general) should be literal or free (see, for example, Neubert and Shreve 1992, in addition to Robinson and Snell-Hornby, already cited). Some circumstances can make a more literal translation appropriate and other circumstances can make a freer translation appropriate, possibly for the same text. But such flexibility seems to contradict the notion of transcendental meaning. This generates the need to clarify basic theoretical issues in order to provide a solid basis for translation studies. If meaning is transcendental, then why would there not be one correct translation, the one that most closely encodes the meaning? And if meaning is not transcendental, then what is it, where is it, and how is it even possible to communicate through language? This question of the possibility of communication through human language is the central question of this book, as indicated in the title. But before discussing further what makes human language possible, we will look at nonhuman translation. If computers could produce translations indistinguishable from those of humans, would that ability be evidence for transcendental meaning? Conversely, if computers are limited in their ability to translate, could those limitations teach us something about the nature of meaning?

On the belief that the successes and failures of computers applied to translation are indeed relevant to an understanding of meaning, we will next look briefly at the history of machine translation and eventually (by chapter 5) draw some conclusions that will bear on the questions we have left unanswered in this tiny introduction to the enormously rich topic of human translation. We will resolve the literal/free tension through a multidimensional approach. We will even suggest how meaning originates in domain-specific and general language.

2 Machine Translation

2.1 The fascination of machine translation

In the television science fiction series *Star Trek*, staged in the distant future, the difficulties of translation have been solved. There is no need for human translators aboard the starship Enterprise because the ship's main computer can translate anything from any language to any other language while doing a thousand other things at the same time. In the movie *Star Wars* the robot C3PO specializes in translation. Both of these science fiction stories assume that by and large translation is possible through mechanical procedures, without the help of a human.

One might suppose that such thinking is relatively recent and is the result of the availability of computers in the 1950s, but the idea that translation can be mechanistic goes back centuries. The idea lay dormant only because of the difficulty of constructing machines sophisticated enough to perform the operations that people imagined. It is natural, then, that as soon as general-purpose electronic digital computers became available, people tried using them for machine translation, that is, translation by a machine rather than by a human translator. As we shall see in the next section, the 1950s in the United States was a period of intense research in machine translation and great optimism concerning its eventual success.

Even though the dream of machine translation was not fulfilled in the 1950s and 1960s, it has not died, as evidenced by the commonplace nature of machine translation in recent futuristic science fiction stories. Why is the idea of machine translation so fascinating? Perhaps the answer is to be found in an understanding of why people were so optimistic in the 1950s that the problem of machine translation would soon be solved.

One reason for optimism in the early stages of research in machine translation was a general feeling of optimism in the United States, Canada, and Western Europe. The Allied Forces had just experienced a decisive victory in ending World War II. The German code for secret messages had been broken.

In the United States, at least, many thought that the use of the atom bomb to hasten the end of the war in the Pacific contributed substantially to the overall victory of the Allies. The atom bomb seemed at that time a particularly visible example of the triumph of modern science.

In contemplating the deep respect in which science was held by most people in the 1950s, we should remember the significance of the first atomic explosions. Einstein predicted that matter could literally be converted into massive amounts of energy. For most people, it seemed highly unlikely that such a prediction would come true. The atom bomb was an extremely public and impressive test of his complex theory. One did not need a degree in physics to appreciate the power that was unleashed in a nuclear explosion. The massive mushroom-shaped cloud, visually unlike any previous man-made explosion, spoke for itself.

The power of modern science was evident in the middle of the twentieth century, but some of the problems of the end of the twentieth century that resist the efforts of science were not yet widely observed. For example, the still unsolved problem of nuclear waste disposal troubled few people. No one had yet made a connection between a high incidence of cancer and residing downwind from above-ground nuclear test sites. But there was a justified euphoria over the success of antibiotics in treating infections which had been killing and maiming for thousands of years.

Dr. Salk was a public hero for discovering a vaccine against polio in the mid-1950s. No one had heard of antibiotic-resistant strains of pneumonia or, even worse, the modern plague of AIDS caused by the so far unconquered HIV virus. Scientific agriculture made possible tremendous increases in the productivity of farmlands, and the opponents of chemical pesticides and fertilizers had not yet gained public attention. Indeed, it seemed that the world's problems of hunger and disease were being solved by modern technology, based on modern science, and the limitations of science and technology had not yet become apparent. The only highly visible enemy to the West was the Soviet Union. The United States and the Soviet Union were engaged in the cold war, and the battleground was technology.

I clearly remember the day (October 4) in 1957 when the Soviets announced the successful launch of the first satellite to orbit the earth. This satellite, called Sputnik, symbolized a major victory on the part of the Soviets in the cold war. Khrushchev later said before the entire world that the Soviet Union would "bury" the United States (although he later denied that he intended "bury" in reference to the United States in the sense of "burying a dead body"). I was acutely aware that the United States space program was also attempting to launch a satellite but that the Soviets had won this round.

When President Kennedy announced his intent to begin a program that would place a man on the moon, it brought cheers from many who viewed the effort as the one remaining dramatic opportunity to demonstrate to the world that the United States was able to surpass the Soviets in the space race area of the cold war. Recently, I was listening to a radio talk show on which the host was discussing the twenty-fifth anniversary of the first moon landing. The talk show host was arguing that the results of placing a man on the moon have not justified the tremendous cost of the effort. He discounted the importance of the accomplishment as a demonstration of technological superiority. However, if one remembers the public mood at the time, it becomes clear that it was not important to cost-justify the effort; it was simply important to show technological superiority.

The first general-purpose digital computers began to operate in the late 1940s. Although not very powerful when compared with today's typical home computer, they evoked considerable awe in the 1950s. They were huge machines that used vacuum tubes, since the transistor was still an experiment at Bell Laboratories and would not be ready for commercial use in computers for years to come. Even when transistors replaced vacuum tubes in computers, computers were still large machines because integrated circuits had not yet been developed. The result was that in their early years, computers were not just physically large, they were also very expensive to build and maintain and they were inaccessible to the general public. This cost and inaccessibility, which contrasts with today's relatively inexpensive and accessible personal computers, added to the mystique of the early computers.

In the 1950s, a computer was often referred to as an *electronic brain*. This popular name reflected the belief that computers could or soon would be able to perform any mental operation that humans are capable of. This belief is tied to the general cultural presupposition (discussed at the end of the previous chapter) that meaning exists independently of people. If there is nothing particularly specific to the human body in human language, then why couldn't an electronic brain translate just as well as a human brain? There was an additional connection between early efforts in machine translation and world events in the 1950s and 1960s. One of the main justifications for using U.S. government funds for research in machine translation was that U.S. scientists needed to know what Soviet scientists were up to. Therefore, most early projects worked toward Russian-to-English systems. Although the question did not arise in exactly this form, if someone had asked whether it would be harder to solve the problem of machine translation or to place a man on the moon, most people in the 1950s would probably have responded that, given the availability of electronic brains, the moon landing would obviously be more challenging. The reader might analyze his or her present view of language by reflecting on what would be more difficult, a manned visit to a planet of another star or the development of a machine translation system that produces translations indistinguishable from those of a competent human translator. This question is complicated by the issue of whether faster-than-light travel is possible. We will later return to this question after discussing the nature of human language.

In light of these attitudes in the 1950s, it should be understandable that early researchers started machine translation projects with gusto, fully confident that with sufficient effort, the problem would be solved within a few years. Science had already solved apparently more difficult problems, and electronic brains had by then become available. These electronic brains could perform complex mathematical calculations many times faster than a team of the most brilliant mathematical minds. Not many humans can master advanced mathematics, but any human child with modest intelligence, when raised in a bilingual environment, can learn two languages and translate easily between them. Surely, some must have reasoned, machine translation is an easier problem than placing a man on the moon, let alone on a planet outside the solar system.

The next section will provide a brief history of machine translation, describe typical techniques, and show how attitudes changed as the difficulty of the task became apparent. However, I note in passing a certain phenomenon that seems to repeat itself even today. A researcher who starts out in machine translation, aware of past failures, often has the feeling that the problem should not be that hard, that somehow everyone else who has worked on the problem was either incompetent or unable to find the right mechanical procedures to finally solve the problem. And the attempt to find the key to perfect machine translation begins again.

2.2 A brief history of machine translation

As evidence that machine translation was an idea waiting for its time to come, we note that in the 1930s two patents were granted for mechanical translation procedures. One was for a device which used a paper tape that could look up a foreign-language word that corresponded to a source-language word.

The other patent, by a Russian named Troyanskii, described a more comprehensive process for mechanical translation. The source text would first be analyzed by finding the base form of each word and identifying its grammatical function in the sentence it was part of. Then, in a second stage, which would now be called transfer, the base forms and grammatical functions would be converted to corresponding base forms and grammatical functions in the target language. Finally, in a third stage which would now be called synthesis or generation, the sequence of base forms and grammatical functions would be made into acceptable sentences in the target language.

Troyanskii's patent described a machine that would perform the processing of the middle stage. Initially, the first stage of processing would be done by someone who spoke only the source language—in other words, a source-language monolingual—and the third stage would be done by a target-language monolingual. In this way, there would be human involvement, but neither human would need to know both languages; thus the system was intended to replace the human translator completely. Troyanskii anticipated that the process would later be further automated to reduce or eliminate the need for even the human monolinguals.

The stages of processing proposed by Troyanskii are remarkably similar to what actually happens in current machine translation systems. And many systems do try to make the steps of analysis, transfer, and generation fully automatic, that is, requiring no human involvement, even though human translators are needed for dictionary maintenance and for review of the raw output. However, Troyanskii's patent was forgotten because of the difficulty of building the machine he described.

When computers became available about fifteen years later, some people immediately saw them as a tool for translating languages, without knowledge of the Russian patent. The time to try out the idea of machine translation had come. Warren Weaver of the Rockefeller Foundation wrote a particularly influential memo in July 1949 (in Locke and Booth 1955). In the memo, Weaver suggests that there is a universal basis for language and that if we could find it, we would be able to use it as an interlingua, that is, something which is neutral and in between various languages. Weaver also suggested that techniques in cryptography, which had proven so successful during World War II in deciphering Nazi military messages, could now be applied to machine translation. Essentially, he was suggesting that a text in a human language is the result of encoding the message behind the text. The message is the same for all languages; only the encoding system differs.

This thinking is in line with the widespread Western assumption discussed in chapter 1 that meaning exists in a realm separate from people. Weaver gives an example of someone who was able to decode a message without knowing what language it was written in and suggests that machine translation could be approached as a process of deciphering an encoded message. To a professional human translator this suggestion may seem ludicrous, but the Weaver memo was not sent to human translators. Indeed, professional translators were apparently not involved in early machine translation projects. This is perhaps not too surprising when it is considered that the intent of the early projects was to replace human translators.

Weaver's underlying assumptions about the similarity between humans and computers are revealed by his discussion of ambiguity. He admits, as does everyone, that there will not always be just one possible translation for a word of the source text. What is interesting is his proposal for resolving ambiguity. He notes that if one covers up a page except for one word, then a human may not be sure what the word means but that if the human is allowed to see the preceding word or two and the following word or two, it is often possible to figure out what the word means. Weaver suggests, therefore, that showing the computer two or three words preceding and following the word in question, that is, the immediate context or co-text, should allow the computer to figure out how to translate the word. Ignoring for the moment the obvious counter-examples of cases in which a human translator agonizes over an entire book in trying to decide how to translate one crucial word, let us admit that with a straightforward text, a human can often propose a reasonable translation for a word by seeing only that word and a few words of context. Weaver's assumption seems to be that a computer is similar enough to a human that it can arrive at the same conclusion from the same starting point, namely a sequence of up to seven words. The question here is how a human resolves ambiguity and whether that process, if indeed it is a process, can be formulated as a series of steps that can be programmed on a computer.

The issue of whether Weaver's assumptions about ambiguity are valid can be explored empirically by testing Weaver's thesis in the following way. First a list of words is chosen. For each word in the list, a procedure is developed to determine how to translate that word. For some words, such as 'electricity', there will be just one translation that works most of the time. For other words, such as 'cut', there will probably be several possible translations. In the case of 'cut' there will probably be one translation which applies when it is a verb, as in 'to cut off a piece of cheese', and another translation for when it is a noun, as in 'the cut on his finger got infected'.

The question then becomes how to decide when 'cut' is a noun and when it is a verb. The procedure for clearing up this particular kind of ambiguity is called homograph resolution. For the decision procedure to be useful in machine translation, it must be extremely explicit and precise, so that it can be programmed. For example, if the preceding word is a personal pronoun, such as 'she', then *cut* is probably a verb, while if the preceding word is a possessive pronoun, such as 'his', then 'cut' is probably a noun. But what about the sentence 'her knife cut well but his cut poorly, since it was dull'? The word 'cut' is clearly a verb even though it is preceded by a possessive pronoun. Unfortunately, the more one works on such problems, the more complex they appear. However, Weaver had not actually tried to develop a machine translation system when he wrote his memo; therefore, he had not yet encountered such difficulties.

2.3 Problems with tuning in early systems

Weaver's widely circulated memo generated considerable enthusiasm for trying machine translation. This is evidence that the underlying assumptions on which it is based did not seem too shocking to people. Within a few years from the time Weaver wrote his memo several machine translation projects were underway, including projects at MIT, the University of Texas at Austin, and Georgetown University. In 1954, the Georgetown project, in cooperation with IBM, gave the first public demonstration of machine translation. The demonstration showed a computer translating a set of preselected sentences that had been worked on for some time and for which the computer produced reasonably good translations.

The apparent success of this demonstration led to considerable additional funding for machine translation projects. But the results of that first demonstration were misleading. The computer produced reasonably good translations of the demonstration sentences, but that did not mean that the computer was ready to translate large quantities of text. First, the dictionary inside the computer was very small, so introducing new sentences would often result in the computer being unable to find some of the words in its dictionary. And second, a process of *tuning* occurs when a set of sentences is worked on laboriously until the computer can translate them well. This manipulation of the system to respond to particular sentences gave the appearance of success.

To improve reception on a radio, we 'tune', or adjust, the radio receiver. In much the same way, when a machine translation system is tuned to a set of sentences, various aspects of the machine translation system are adjusted in order to make the sentences translate the way the researcher wants them to. Dictionary entries are modified so that the words in the translation will be the ones desired. Grammar rules are adjusted so that the test sentences will receive the desired analysis and generation. All these adjustments together constitute the tuning of the system to the needs of the test sentences.

The problem occurs when another set of test sentences is fed into the machine translation system. Often, the new sentences produce horrible output. Then the system must be tuned to the new set of sentences. After working on several sets of sentences, one then tries the first set of sentences, which worked fine before, and it is discovered that they do not translate properly any more. The adjustments for the subsequent sentences invalidated the processing of the first ones. When a radio is tuned to one station, that station is received well. If the radio is then tuned to another station, that station is received well but the first station is no longer received. This phenomenon of tuning applies to most, if not all, machine translation systems, and I too have experienced it while working on a machine translation project. Tuning is desirable in a radio but undesirable in a machine translation system (unless, as we will discuss later, it is tuning to a particular domain rather than to a particular text). A radio should receive only one station at a time, but a machine translation system should be prepared to handle more than one text without re-tuning. If re-tuning in a machine translation system were as simple and fast as turning a dial on a radio, tuning would not be such a problem in machine translation, but in fact it may take longer to tune a machine translation system to a new text than a human translator would spend translating the text by traditional methods.

It is often assumed that the problem of tuning a machine to a particular set of sentences, at least in the early stages of development when the dictionaries are small, is unavoidable. Large quantities of new text cannot be tested in the system because many of the words will not be found in the computer dictionary. The hope is that eventually the system can be made to work on new material without having to re-tune it. Later on, however, when the dictionaries are bigger, it is too late to change the system in a fundamental way, since dictionary format and other basics have already been decided on. The system does not work well unless it is tuned to the material being translated, but constant tuning is of course out of the question for a commercial system.

Nevertheless, there is an alternative to excessively tuning a system in its early development and thereby generating false hopes. The answer is to use an alternative testing method which I developed in response to a request to evaluate the potential of a new approach to machine translation.

This method requires the involvement of a separate person, whom we will call the word-list provider, for the selection of the words to be placed in the dictionary when it is still small. Several small test passages, each consisting of one or more sentences, are selected by the word-list provider. These test passages must fall within the guidelines of the developer if the system is to be restricted to a single domain. Then each sentence is split into words, each word is reduced to its base form, and all the words are arranged in an alphabetical list, with duplicates removed. In order to avoid the dangers of tuning to a specific set of sentences, the alphabetical list is further processed to make it more difficult to reconstruct the source sentences from the alphabetical list. This is done by adding to the list other words that are not in the test sentences. These should consist of both a range of all the common function words (such as articles, conjunctions, and prepositions) that might need to be handled by the system and a selection of nouns, verbs, and adjectives. The final list could be as short as a hundred words or as long as a thousand words.

When the alphabetical list of base forms has been completed, it is presented to the machine translation developer. The test sentences, of course, are kept secret. The developer is then asked to build a system which can handle any text which can be made out of sentences from the list. Then an evaluation can be made using sentences from the original set of sentences or using sentences constructed from the list. In either case, the translations are evaluated the first time the sentences are put into the machine translation system. Since the developer had the word list in advance, no words should be missing from the dictionary. However, the developer may not have thought of all the ways a word from the list can be used. Thus, the output may contain target-language equivalents which are inappropriate for the test passages. If the dictionary builders had been given the test passages in advance, the dictionary entries would naturally have been tailored to those passages. By not giving the test passages until the dictionary is updated, everyone can get a much more accurate picture of how the system will respond to real text in a production mode.

One wonders what would have been the course of MT research and development in the 1950s and 1960s if the preceding approach had been used instead of giving demonstrations of sentences to which the systems had been tuned in advance. However, tuning was performed and funding was provided and unwise promises were made of large-scale practical systems that were to appear within six months or so. A year or more later, the systems were still not forthcoming. It was argued that a little more work was needed because of unforeseen problems but that the system would be operational within another six months or so. This cycle of unfulfilled promises was repeated for years and finally came to a head in the mid-1960s with the publication of the ALPAC report, which brutally stopped the cycle. But we will come back to this report after describing the current incarnation of the one system which has survived the work done in the 1950s and 1960s in the United States, namely, the Systran system. Much of the information here presented on Systran has been obtained from Hutchins and Somers (1992).

2.4 The Systran machine translation system

Systran was developed by Peter Toma, based on work done in the late 1950s and early 1960s at Georgetown University. He developed a Russian to English version for the United States Air Force, and it has been in use there since 1970. A version was purchased by the Commission of the European Communities in 1975 and has been used there since 1981. Most of the rights to Systran, other than those purchased by the Commission, have since been purchased by a company called Gachot, named after its founder. Until recently, Systran ran only on an IBM mainframe computer, but now it has been rewritten in the C++ programming language and runs as a Windows™ application on a personal computer. It is even available as an **on-line** information service of Minitel.

Systran translates from one language to another in the following stages:[4]

1. The source text is read in, and elements such as titles, paragraphs, and sentences are identified. In Systran, as in most machine translation systems, a sentence is the basic unit of text that is processed. A title is usually treated much the same as a sentence, but there are obvious differences, such as the fact that a title need not be a complete sentence. Any indications of how sentences (and other units) fit together into paragraphs, sections, chapters, etc, are called **markup**. It is desirable to preserve the markup in a text and use it to put together the translations of the sentences and other units into a target text that has the same markup as the source text. Otherwise, this markup has to be inserted manually, which can be very expensive. We will return to the question of markup later.

2. A dictionary of invariant expressions is consulted (that is, expressions which do not inflect or change in any way), and any such expressions in the

text are treated as if they were a single word. For example, *à la mode* might be treated as an adjective indicating that some food is served with ice cream. The information that this expression is actually a prepositional phrase is lost. An advantage of this approach is that it avoids the need to try to represent the internal structure of such expressions. On the other hand, even supposedly fixed expressions can sometimes be used with internal changes. Someone who wants a certain kind of ice cream with a piece of pie, say Ben and Jerry brand ice cream, might ask for pie "à la Ben and Jerry mode". This dynamic use of a normally fixed expression would be understandable to a human, but Systran would not be able to process it properly.

3. The main dictionary is then consulted for words that are not part of fixed expressions. Information about the word found in the main dictionary is retrieved for later use.

4. Inflected forms of words may not be found in the dictionary. If a word is not found, analysis is used to reduce it to its base form. For example, in English, 'wished' could be reduced to 'wish', 'ran' could be reduced to 'run', and 'dishes' could be reduced to 'dish'. A base form, such as 'wish', when acting as a verb, may take a past tense inflection to become the inflected form 'wished'. So inflection and analysis are opposite processes. In many languages, one base form can become several hundred inflected forms, thus making analysis to the base form, often called **morphological analysis**, much more complex than in English. In fact, English morphology is so simple that the main Systran dictionary contains all the inflected forms of English words, whereas this approach becomes impractical for more highly inflected languages such as Spanish or German.

5. Next, **compound nouns**, which consist of two or more nouns separated by a space and which form a unit, are identified by looking in a dictionary that lists compounds. For example, 'yard stick' is a measuring device. However, there can be false identifications, as in the sentence "toward the back of your yard stick three lanterns in the ground". Here the sequence of words 'yard' and 'stick' does not form a compound which refers to a measuring device. Actually, this false identification would not occur if compounds were identified *after* grammatical categories were identified or if the words were separated by a comma. The word 'stick' can be a noun or a verb and the noun compound usage only applies when 'stick' is a noun, but at this stage of Systran processing, we do not yet know if 'stick' is a noun or a verb.

6. Next, homographs are resolved by examining adjacent words. As mentioned, a homograph is a word which can function as more than one grammatical category without changing form. Thus, 'stick' is a homograph.

1. Identify segments (sentences) in source text
2. Identify invariant expressions
3. Look up remaining words in main dictionary
4. Reduce inflected words to base forms
5. Identify potential compound nouns
6. Resolve homographs by examining immediate context
7. Find clausal components of sentence
8. Map syntactic relationships (adjective-modified noun, verb-object, etc.)
9. Make conjunctive relationships explicit
10. Identify subject and predicate, and classify clause as declarative, interrogative, or imperative
11. Construct logical relationships (e.g., logical object of passive verb)

12-15. Transfer to target-language words and adjust target structure as needed

16. Inflect target-language words
17. Order target-language words appropriately

Figure 1: Steps in Systran's translation process

In English, a rule might be applied that says a noun/verb homograph preceded by an adjective will be assumed to be a noun. For example, 'big hopes' will be assumed to contain a noun usage of 'hopes' while 'he hopes' will be assumed to be a verb usage of 'hopes'. Of course there are exceptions to this rule, such as the sentence "the pig that is big hopes to escape from the wolf".

7. Sentences are segmented into main and subordinate clauses based on punctuation and function words such as 'that' and 'because'. This step of analysis will also encounter exceptions.

8. Several syntactic relations within clauses are determined, such as between a noun and an adjective that modifies it, between a verb and its object, and between a clause and its main verb.

9. Conjunctions such as 'and' are analyzed to decide what is being joined together. For example, in 'a spill of diesel oil and algae' it must be decided whether the elements being conjoined are 'oil' and 'algae' or 'diesel oil' and 'algae'. If it is the first option, then 'diesel' applies to both 'oil' and 'algae', and the phrase may end up being erroneously translated in some language as 'a spill of oil of diesel and algae of diesel'.

10. The subject and predicate of a clause are identified, and clauses are identified as declarative, interrogative, or imperative. This information is later used in some languages for such tasks as making a verb agree with the gender of the subject. For example, in many languages, a sentence such as "she is happy" would require a feminine form of the translation of 'happy', while "he is happy" would require a masculine form.

11. Further relations are identified, such as the **logical object** of a passive. For example, in "the order was filled the same day", the logical object of 'filled' is 'order'. This becomes important if the passive is later converted to an active sentence such as "we filled the order the same day".

Note that steps 6-11 involve what is often called **parsing**, that is, syntactic analysis or identifying the relations among the elements of a sentence. In more recent systems, the parsing process and the result of parsing are quite different from what is found in Systran. Many recent systems use a set of **phrase structure rules**. A very simple grammar might consist of the following three rules:

S → NP VP
NP → (Det) (Adj) N
VP → V (NP)

Roughly, the first line says that a sentence (S) consists of a noun phrase (NP), the subject, followed by a verb phrase (VP). The second line says that a noun phrase consists of an optional determiner (Det) such as a definite or indefinite article ('a' or 'the'), followed by an optional adjective (Adj), followed by a common noun (N). The third line says that a verb phrase consists of a core verb (V) followed by an optional noun phrase (the direct object). The expansion of the noun phrase is given in the second line, serving as the expansion of a noun phrase whether in the subject or direct object position. Obviously, this grammar is extremely limited, but it is intended only to give the flavor of phrase structure rules.

Modern techniques can overcome many of the problems of Systran's approach to parsing by exploring multiple paths of analysis to see which one allows the entire sentence to fit together, but those techniques assume that each sentence of the source text is fully grammatical. The result of parsing is a branching diagram that somewhat resembles a genealogical tree. On the other hand, the result of parsing in Systran is still a sequence of words in the original order with pointers back and forth. In the ideal case, where every word of a sentence fits into the possibilities implicit in the phrase structure rules, the modern approach is clearly superior in its ability to eliminate invalid options on a sentence-global rather than on local basis involving just a few words. However, when a sentence which does not fit the grammar is encountered, the modern approach may produce a bigger mess than the Systran approach.

12-15. In these stages, which roughly correspond to what is called the transfer stage in more recent systems, target language words are substituted for source language words, and structural adjustments are made based on differences between languages. For example, 'to attend a concert' becomes *assister à un concert* (literally, 'attend at a concert'); in the structural change a direct object becomes an indirect object.

The aspect of transfer that involves the substitution of target language words is usually called **lexical transfer**. In Systran, for a given grammatical category, there is just one basic translation per word for general usage in the main dictionary. However, that basic translation, often called the **default** translation (the one that is used when there is no specific reason to do otherwise), can be overridden if the source word appears in a specialized dictionary that is used because it applies to the domain of the source text.

The problem of lexical transfer—finding the appropriate target language words—is a huge one; we will discuss it in later chapters.

16. Words are inflected according to the grammar of the target language. Here structural information from analysis about what modifies what may be used to decide how to inflect a word.

17. Word order is rearranged according to the conventions of the target language. Here again the structural information from analysis is used. For example, in German, part of a verb phrase will normally be found at the end of a clause, as in:

Er mußte erkennen, daß sie völlig überfordert war, und so sagte er.

"He had to recognize that she was totally overwhelmed, and he said so".

Or more literally, using German word order:

"He had to recognize that she totally overwhelmed was, and so said he".

The routine which adjusts for German word order must move the verb 'was' from after the subject ('she') to the end of the clause, and therefore it is essential to have available a syntactic analysis which indicates the boundaries of clauses in the sentence.

The preceding description of the seventeen stages of processing applies directly to Systran during the 1970s. Systran, which has evolved beyond what are generally called *first-generation* systems, gives a flavor of the design of the early systems of the 1950s and 1960s. Much of the analysis in such systems was triggered by routines associated with specific LTUs in the various dictionaries rather than by some overall grammar.

2.5 Bar-Hillel

The performance of early systems was uneven because of the phenomenon of tuning to a specific text (discussed earlier in this chapter). Researchers chose a set of test sentences and tuned their system until it worked well on those sentences, generating considerable optimism. Then a new set of sentences was fed into the modified system, and the results were usually disappointing. However, since the system would then be re-tuned—adjusting dictionary routines and grammatical rules to produce acceptable translations of the new set of sentences—optimism was repeatedly rekindled. What did not occur to many of the early researchers was the possibility that the system would never reach a state where it would handle any set of sentences without further tuning. That possibility did, however, occur to Y. Bar-Hillel, an MIT scientist who was the first full-time researcher in machine translation.

In 1960, Bar-Hillel published an article which argued that fully automatic high-quality machine translation of unrestricted text (FAHQT) would remain out of reach. His unpronounceable initialism, FAHQT, has stuck, often with a modifier, FAHQT of UT, to indicate that it means translation of unrestricted text, that is, any text one cares to throw at it. This clarification is needed because FAHQT has indeed been achieved on highly restricted texts all from the same narrow domain, but such systems are not at all able to produce the same quality of translation on other types of text. A fundamental question is, What would it take to remove this limitation and produce FAHQT of UT?

Bar-Hillel's basic argument against the possibility of FAHQT of UT was that extensive real-world knowledge would have to be placed in the computer in order to identify the appropriate **sense** of some words. For now, we can think of a sense of a word as one of its definitions. Later, we will enter into rather intricate discussions of the nature of meaning. Bar-Hillel gave as an example of the need for real-world knowledge the now-famous sentence "The box is in the pen". The word 'pen' has at least two senses: 'enclosure for a small child to play in, a play pen' and 'writing instrument'. Bar-Hillel argued that even though a human would probably conclude that in the given sentence 'pen' refers to a play pen, this conclusion is based on real-world knowledge about the relative sizes of boxes and pens.

Real-world knowledge is usually considered not to be linguistic knowledge. Modern linguistics makes a distinction between syntactic, semantic, and pragmatic information, with pragmatic information being outside the realm of linguistics proper, although the boundaries are sometimes unclear. That the word 'pen' can be a noun is syntactic; that as a noun it can have the two senses listed above is semantic, as is the feature *animate*. The word 'child' (in the normal sense of human offspring) would have the feature animate, while the two senses of 'box' would not be considered animate. The identification of multiple senses of a word is a semantic task, but actually choosing which one is appropriate in a given situation is a pragmatic task. Also, interpretations of intent, such as the interpretation that the comment "It is cold in here with the window open" is actually a request to close the window, are considered to be part of pragmatics. However, sometimes semantic features are used in eliminating some readings as inconsistent, which makes some aspects of the selection of appropriate word senses a semantic, rather than pragmatic, task. Further confusion derives from the fact that semantic features are actually a limited form of real-world knowledge. For example, the feature 'animate' refers to the real-world question of whether something is alive, not to linguistic questions of grammatical category. The semantic/pragmatic distinction seems questionable at best.

As surprising and counterintuitive as it may seem, mainstream linguistics in the United States (commonly known as **Generative Grammar**) does not even claim to deal directly with the question of communication between real people (which is clearly part of language), but rather with syntactic and semantic properties of sentences in isolation. Thus, mainstream linguistics cannot be fully equated with the study of all aspects of language. Consequently, semantics does not include the study of all aspects of meaning.

Bar-Hillel's argument, cast in terms of modern mainstream linguistics, was basically as follows. In order to achieve FAHQT of UT, one must be able to adequately translate sentences such as "The box is in the pen". The word 'pen' (along with thousands of other words) is ambiguous, and in most target languages the various senses of 'pen' will be translated as different words which are not interchangeable. Therefore, an adequate translation requires the resolution of the word-sense ambiguity. But the ambiguity cannot be resolved using solely linguistic information. Syntactic features will not suffice since both senses of pen are nouns. Neither will typical semantic features such as whether a pen is animate and whether it is a physical object, since both senses are inanimate physical objects. Information about relative sizes of objects and reasoning about relative sizes as it applies to selecting the appropriate sense of a word in a given sentence go beyond semantics and into the realm of pragmatics and outside the realm of linguistics proper. Up to this point, Bar-Hillel's argument contains little which is controversial. Some may claim that pragmatics, including the representation and use of encyclopedic world knowledge, may eventually be considered part of linguistics proper, but few would argue that such sentences can be properly translated using purely syntactic and semantic techniques. To emphasize this, consider the sentence "The pen is in the box". Here the word 'pen', depending on the situation, may be interpreted as a writing instrument, as opposed to the play pen interpretation in "The box is in the pen". The next step in Bar-Hillel's argument is where the controversy comes in. He assumed that it was and would remain impossible to represent massive amounts of world knowledge in a computer for resolving ambiguities in sentences like his 'box-pen' examples. He then reasoned that without the resolution of such ambiguities, high-quality translation is impossible, and therefore FAHQT of UT is impossible.

Reactions to Bar-Hillel's argument have varied. Some have challenged his assumption that it is impossible to represent world knowledge in a computer, and they have set about to actually program encyclopedic knowledge into a computer or to build special-purpose machines that have knowledge and think like humans. These people are part of the **artificial intelligence** (AI) community. They would agree with Bar-Hillel that knowledge representation is necessary but would disagree that it is impossible. We will discuss later whether AI has yet accomplished its goals.

When Bar-Hillel presented the preceding argument he had already chosen to abandon machine translation rather than attempt to build world knowledge into a machine translation system. He may have been the first major player to leave the field on theoretical grounds. It is difficult to determine what other researchers thought about Bar-Hillel's argument during the 1960s. My personal contacts with other machine translation researchers did not begin until the early 1970s. The fact is that there was no mass exodus in the early 1960s. Perhaps Bar-Hillel's article was not widely read at that time. Perhaps some read it but felt that his example was contrived and that such problems would occur so rarely as to be unimportant, or at least that much additional progress could be made with a strictly linguistic approach, and it would make sense to plow ahead and see how far linguistic techniques could take machine translation. Whatever the reasoning at the time, machine translation research and development was in full swing without Bar-Hillel in the mid-1960s when the ALPAC report appeared.

2.6 A government report and its aftermath

The Automatic Language Processing Advisory Committee (ALPAC) was formed in 1965 by the National Science Foundation to investigate the status of machine translation. The ALPAC report evaluated the quality of the output of various MT systems and found it to be very poor, especially when a new text was presented without allowing any tuning to the text. The report noted that it was expensive to post-edit raw machine translation output so that it became indistinguishable from human translation. The report also looked at the field of human translation, mainly the translation of Russian scientific articles into English, and found no shortage of human translators. The report concluded that since there was no shortage of human translators and no cost advantage in machine translation after fifteen years of hard work, there was no justification for further government funding of machine translation for the purpose of developing commercial systems to compete directly with human translators.

Actually, the ALPAC report was not entirely negative. It contained positive recommendations at the end, including suggestions for funding pure research into the nature of language and the development of computer-based tools for human translators. Unfortunately, however, these recommendations were not included in the executive summary at the beginning and were consequently not seen by most executives who made funding decisions. The result was an immediate stop to government funding of MT research in the United States and a black cloud that spread over the field of MT worldwide. The late 1960s saw the continuation of MT research in just a few centers, notably the University of Montréal in Canada and the University of Grenoble in France. Peter Toma, the original designer of Systran, pursued his work in Germany rather than in the U.S. during the late 1960s. However, the black cloud began to lift in the 1970s, and interest in machine translation has increased over the past twenty years. Recently U.S. government funding for machine translation has been resumed.

2.7 Personal encounters with machine translation

My introduction to machine translation came about the time of the publication of the ALPAC report but I did not run into the dreaded report until years later. My first contact with MT was a short newspaper article about a machine translation system developed at IBM that used a *photoscopic disk* to store a fifty-thousand word Russian-English dictionary. The article did not mention the ALPAC report or any failings in the MT output, which I, probably along with most other readers, assumed to be of high quality. I was a university student majoring in mathematics at the time and the article captured my imagination, but the seed planted by that glowing description of the IBM system lay dormant for several years while I was living in Europe and speaking French daily. The seed sprouted in 1970 when I returned to the Provo campus of Brigham Young University (BYU) to finish my degree in mathematics. That semester I took my first linguistics class to try to combine mathematics with language. One day the instructor, Eldon Lytle, a brilliant syntactician, shared with me a letter he had just received from Daryl Gibb, a former graduate student who had applied Lytle's model of language (which was later called Junction Grammar) to the problem of Russian-English machine translation. Gibb, who was teaching English in Finland at the time, proposed in his letter that if Lytle could put together some funding, he would return in the fall to participate in a project to build on the encouraging results of his thesis. We put together some initial funding from several sources, including a governmental agency which had apparently not read or not believed the ALPAC report. By September 1970 we had begun the project in earnest. Within a year or two we settled on an approach we called **interactive** translation, going from English into several target languages. The interaction was between the computer and the human during the analysis phase; the goal was to resolve syntactic and word-sense ambiguities that the computer programs were not able to resolve automatically.

During the 1970s we met most of the other people who worked in the field of machine translation. They could be divided into the academic researchers and the first-generation commercial developers left over from the pre-ALPAC days. The academics in turn could be divided into the AI (Artificial Intelligence) camp and the linguistic theory camp (which included our project). The linguistic theory camp firmly believed that in order to obtain high-quality translation it is essential for the analysis phases to build a complete syntactic representation based on some coherent model of syntax. The various linguistic projects, such as Montréal, Grenoble, and Provo (BYU), may not have agreed with each other on which syntactic model was best, but they were united in their belief that it was necessary to base analysis on some coherent and comprehensive model of syntax.

The AI camp, typified by Roger Schank and Yorick Wilks, was rather anti-syntax at the time. Perhaps in order to distance themselves from the linguistic camp and the negative image of previous efforts in machine translation, they claimed they had no syntactic representation at all but rather a conceptual representation. Schank generally based each project on a narrow domain (a **microworld**) such as the task of replacing a washer in a particular type of water faucet. In this microworld, only the faucet and a few tools exist. There is no oven or toaster, no bathroom or bedroom, no cars or trees; only the faucet exists. This naturally resulted in a closed system which could be described with a small number of core concepts and a very small dictionary of LTUs, most of which took only one meaning in the microworld. Schank's MT project did not even call its output a translation but rather a paraphrase that happened to be in another language. He claimed that their conceptual representation of the meaning of a sentence was language independent so they could just as well generate output in one language as in another.

This claim of language independence was intriguing. If the basic elements of their conceptual representation were not dependent on any human language, then what were they dependent on? If they were arbitrary, simply based on the current whim of the researcher, one would wonder whether they would be adequate beyond a microworld. If they were not arbitrary, then they must be based on a non-arbitrary categorization of the universe, and one would wonder how to be sure to have found the one and only correct set of universal conceptual primitives. These are essentially the same questions that were raised in the previous chapter in connection with issues in translation theory, and we will return to them in the next chapter.

The commercial systems, typified by Systran and Logos, were eclectic and ad hoc rather than being based on a particular model of language. They used an empirical approach in which syntactic and semantic rules were added to the system as needed in order to fix specific errors in translating specific sentences, which amounted to constant tuning, rather than referring to a unified model that claimed to account for all major aspects of syntax and semantics.

Each of the three camps generally looked down its nose at the other two. The commercial camp viewed the academic projects as too *ivory tower* to accomplish anything worthwhile. The AI camp criticized the linguistic camp for its dependence on syntax. And the linguistic camp criticized the AI camp for ignoring syntax.

The reader who is not familiar with the history of machine translation might be curious to know which camp has won, that is, which approach has finally, after more than three decades of effort since Bar-Hillel said it couldn't be done, attained the original goal of FAHQT of UT. The answer is that no one has reached the original goal (we will begin to explore why in the next chapter), but several groups have nevertheless claimed a measure of success by redefining the goal. One way to categorize current approaches is to divide the original goal of FAHQT of UT into three components, namely, FA (fully automatic), HQ (high-quality), and UT (unrestricted text), and to drop one component at a time, as follows.

2.8 Giving up fully automatic translation

If you drop the requirement that the system be fully automatic, then you have some kind of human-machine interaction. Several projects have tried an interactive approach, with the computer asking questions and the human answering them. It turns out that it makes a big difference whether the human with whom the machine is interacting must be a translator (in other words, a bilingual) or whether the questions can be answered by a monolingual. It is inefficient to have the computer ask questions that require a bilingual human to give answers. These questions usually concern how a particular word or phrase should be translated. In order to answer the questions properly, the human must go through much of the same mental analysis of the source text that is necessary to translate the text without the computer. Obviously, much depends on how many questions the machine asks during the translation of a text. If the computer only needed to ask one question for every ten pages of text; and if the questions were straightforward for a human bilingual to answer accurately without reading the entire source text; and if the human did not need to wait for more than a few seconds for the next question to be presented; and if the resulting translation were of high quality (indistinguishable from that of an experienced human translator), then obviously the computer and a human translator would make an excellent team. However, no one has even come close to this kind of interactive system.

An alternative to interaction during the translation process is to let the machine go ahead and finish the translation, making errors along the way. Then a human translator revises the output to bring it up to required standards. This type of after-the-fact interaction is called **post-editing** and is not usually considered to be interactive translation. The term interactive translation is normally used for human-machine interaction during the translation process that draws on human intelligence to avert errors in the machine translation output, rather than applying to processes that use humans to fix errors after they have already appeared.

Another kind of interaction requires only a monolingual of the source language. This type of interaction, which is typically part of the analysis phase, is intended to resolve ambiguities in the source text that the computer is unable to resolve by itself. This is the type of interaction that we were doing in the BYU project in the early 1970s. In 1978, the design changed to include interaction that required a bilingual. We will come back to this change in design because the reasons for it turn out to be germane to important questions about the nature of language. As of this writing, no widely used machine translation systems feature interaction, but there is renewed interest in source-language monolingual interaction during analysis.

One project that uses interaction is being done at the Center for Machine Translation (CMT) at Carnegie Mellon University (CMU). Here a pre-processing tool called ClearCheck™ interacts with the author of the source text to resolve ambiguities and eliminate disallowed structures.

Another project involving interaction is being conducted at the University of Grenoble. They call their approach **dialogue-based machine translation (DBMT)** and it is intended to allow a monolingual or a native speaker of a language with limited ability in the target language to produce a useful translation by interacting with the computer only in the source language. One environment in which DBMT could be used is **e-mail** (electronic mail). When you send an e-mail message you are already at the computer. Immediately after (or even during) the composition of the message, you could use an interactive machine translation system to produce a message in the language of the other person.

Questions about syntax often involve ambiguities about what a prepositional phrase or other element of a sentence modifies. The main challenges are to avoid asking too many questions, to avoid asking questions which require the human monolingual to go through extensive training in the syntactic theory being used by the system, and to avoid asking questions in a manner which makes them hard for the human to answer. Questions about lexical transfer involve making sufficient distinctions to allow the choice of the appropriate target language lexical items. In the case of the Bar-Hillel example ("The box is in the pen") it is easy to formulate a source language question that asks whether the pen is a writing instrument or an enclosure for a child to play in. However, a pen may also be an enclosure for animals, and in some languages, a play pen and an animal pen may not be the same word. Therefore, a further distinction must be made in the question to the source language monolingual. Also, though more rarely, a pen may refer to a female swan. An additional complication is that the writing instrument sense of pen can refer to a ballpoint pen or a fountain pen. Will each target language have a single word that covers both senses? If not, then that distinction must also be made in the monolingual interaction. Then what about metonymical usage, such as when a pen is intended to refer to the writer (as in "She is a good pen") even if she is using a typewriter or a word processor? At this point, the English monolingual must choose among six noun senses. Of course, 'pen' is a rather straightforward case. Many words, as we will see in chapter 3, cause much stiffer challenges to those who design monolingual questions that are intended to allow the computer to select the appropriate target LTU.

The whole idea of giving up on fully automatic machine translation is to improve the quality of the final translation through some kind of human involvement, either interaction during the translation process or post-editing of raw machine translation output. This combination of machine translation and human involvement is often called **machine-assisted translation (MAT)** or

computer-assisted translation (CAT). As we have seen, two types of human involvement are currently being pursued: post-editing of raw output and monolingual interaction during or preceding analysis. In a commercial setting, the combination of machine translation and human involvement must obviously bring some advantage over purely human translation, or else it will be abandoned. Some of the advantages that have been claimed or projected are lower cost, higher speed, and increased quality through consistent use of terminology. The validity of cost claims is hard to establish, especially when one must decide whether to include only operational costs of MT or to also include a share of maintenance and development costs. We will later examine other ways to achieve consistency in translation, especially through the use of computer-based tools for human translators. Nevertheless, many people believe that a reasonable approach for some time to come will be a combination of machine translation and human involvement in order to achieve a desired level of quality.

2.9 Giving up high-quality translation

The second aspect of FAHQT of UT that could be given up is HQ (high quality). At first this may seem ridiculous. Who would want a low-quality translation? The answer is that low-quality translation can be quite useful in certain environments. The most famous such environment is the information gathering needs of the U.S. Air Force. At Rome Air Force Base in New York, scientists are expected to study relevant scientific articles written in Russian and other languages.

Most of these scientists do not read Russian, so they must rely on translation. However, despite the conclusions of the ALPAC report, it is not economically feasible to translate everything that is published in Russian, at least not at the publishing rate that was maintained in the 1970s and 1980s. Instead, these scientists select for translation a small subset of the Russian articles that seem most likely to be relevant. Sometimes one article can be a gold mine. For example, an obscure Russian article on theoretical aspects of radar that was studied by a U.S. scientist led to the idea of building a military airplane that could avoid radar detection because of its shape. The implementation in the form of the Stealth military aircraft has been enormously successful. The question is how to identify relevant documents. Sometimes a document has an abstract, and a human translation of the abstract is sufficient to decide whether the article is relevant. But often, no English abstract exists, or it is insufficient. In those cases, a scientist will frequently request raw machine translation of several promising articles. The texts are sent to Systran for fully automatic translation into English. No one claims that the output is of high quality, but with a little practice, the low-quality output can be scanned rather quickly to get an idea of whether an article is relevant. If so, a higher quality, but more expensive and slower, human translation can be requested.

This type of translation, which is not intended for publication or other broad dissemination but rather for an individual to get an indication of the content of a document, is sometimes called **indicative translation**. A related type of low-quality machine translation, using **rapid post-editing**, has been tried with some success in the **EC (European Commission)** of the **EU (European Union)**. Some translators have been able to curb their instincts for quality and instead learn to go over a raw machine translation output quickly, correcting only the most glaring errors.

Another use for indicative translation, besides getting an indication of the content of a document before deciding whether to have it translated by a human, is to help people engage in a conversation or an exchange of memos even though they do not speak the same language. Here the assumption is that both parties are highly cooperative and forgiving and that they would rather try to figure out a low-quality translation than try to figure out the other language. The use of indicative translation is quite feasible today over e-mail even if only one party has access to a machine translation system. In the United States, anyone with a modem can become a subscriber to Systran. One simply prepares a text as an electronic **file**, transmits it by modem to Systran headquarters in California, and receives the raw machine translation back a few minutes later. Other machine translation systems are available as an on-line service alongside e-mail. Another option is to install a machine translation system on your personal computer. Several low-cost personal machine translation systems are on the market. Two of them, Globalink™ and Language Assistant™, have each sold many thousands of copies.[5]

In one possible scenario, an American girl who is just beginning to learn German is trying to communicate with a German boy who knows very little English. Suppose the German has a machine translation system installed on his computer. Before sending an e-mail message, the German puts the German text file through the machine translation system and attaches the low-quality English output to the German original. The American reads the machine-translated English version, referring to the German original as desired, and replies in English. The German, upon receiving the reply in English, puts the file through the machine translation system on his **PC** and tries to decipher the low-quality German output, referring to the English original as desired. The e-mail conversation thus continues all in English from the point of view of the girl and all in German from the point of view of the boy. The machine translation output could be of such low quality as to be totally unacceptable to a professional human translator yet acceptable to the boy and girl communicating by e-mail, especially since hiring a professional translator is not an alternative to machine translation for them. We assume here that they are highly motivated to communicate (despite the language barrier); perhaps they met while she was touring Europe and they hit it off. An exchange of letters using indicative machine translation is found in Appendix A.2.

These personal machine translation systems will run on a low-end PC, and such computers are becoming more and more portable. This raises the possibility of carrying around a small computer and using it to communicate by translating messages you type in. The other person must then read the screen and type in the reply to be translated back. Obviously, this approach does not make for a lively conversation. However, if there is sufficient motivation, it could be better than not communicating at all. There is an anecdote about a man whose parents had immigrated from Italy. He spoke only English and his grandmother in Italy spoke only Italian. When his parents died, he visited his grandmother and was able to communicate with her thanks to the machine translation system on his portable computer. The grandmother was probably very forgiving of low quality in the translation, but it is unclear how forgiving people would be in a business environment.

The two compromises to FAHQT of UT, human involvement and indicative quality, are not mutually exclusive. In an e-mail environment, one could start with essentially raw machine translation, and there could be a user-controlled option to increase the level of interaction, hopefully with a corresponding increase in quality of raw output. The receiver could request that the sender increase the level of interaction if the quality of the output is so low as to make understanding it slow and painful or nearly impossible. In an information service of a large organization, promising results have been obtained by allowing the user to request raw machine translation, rapidly post-edited MT, or high-quality human translation, with each successive option having a higher price tag and a longer delivery time.

2.10 Living with restricted text

So far, we have been talking about systems that are designed to accept any text one cares to put into it, that is, unrestricted text (UT) systems. We will now look at the third option for backing off from the ideal, namely restricting the type of text the system is expected to translate. Normally, this means requiring that the source texts apply to a well-defined domain of knowledge. The classic success story in domain-specific translation is the **METEO** system developed at the University of Montréal. In the early 1970s, the TAUM project had a general-purpose approach to machine translation based on Q-systems, a programming language designed by Alain Colmerauer while he was a visiting professor in Montréal. Colmerauer returned to France and further developed his ideas, resulting in the programming language now known as **Prolog**. Prolog and LISP are the most widely used programming languages in the AI community.

The TAUM project had good technology, but no one, including those who worked on the project, had achieved FAHQT of UT. However, instead of backing down on FA or HQ, the TAUM project found a particularly useful way to back down on UT by finding naturally restricted source texts (Canadian government weather bulletins) and customizing the machine translation system for the translation of those texts from English to French. The government was having trouble with turnover in the staff of weather bulletin translators. The bulletins came hourly and were very consistent in their style. Unhappily for the translators, they quickly became bored and dissatisfied, but happily for the TAUM project, the weather bulletins formed a naturally occurring **sublanguage**[6] in the extremely limited domain of weather bulletins. A sublanguage is not just a subset of the words of general language, but rather a particular set of terms and syntactic constructions which are confined in their meanings and style to one particular narrow domain. Some of the terms of a sublanguage may look like words of general language but they are typically not used in the full range of senses that occur in general language. In the sublanguage of a technical domain, many terms may not even be part of a typical person's vocabulary, and are clearly not a subset of general vocabulary. In the weather bulletin sublanguage, even the syntax is not a subset of standard syntax. For example, in the sentence "Windy, with increasing chances of rain", there is no main verb and no article on 'chances'. A sublanguage consists of a particular syntax, semantics, and pragmatics within a well-defined domain.

The Canadian weather bulletins turned out to be a good example of a sublanguage, and the TAUM project developed a machine translation system for that sublanguage which produced fully automatic high-quality translations of texts from that sublanguage. There were still a few errors in the output, but they were mostly due to typographical errors in the input. A few human translators were retained to review and correct the machine translation output before sending it electronically to the news services, and they found this work more enjoyable than translating the bulletins. The METEO system has been in operation since 1977. It has since been moved from a mainframe computer to a microcomputer, using a programming language called **GramR** instead of the Q-systems, and it is still considered to be one of the primary examples of the success of machine translation. Other attempts have been made to duplicate the success of METEO in other domains, but naturally occurring sublanguages are hard to come by, especially with large quantities of machine-readable text. Stock market reports may seem at first to be a likely candidate for a sublanguage, but the sublanguage of the movements and status of stocks is mixed with general-language commentary on possible reasons for changes in the stock market. These general-language commentaries can mention everything from presidential elections to crop conditions to terrorist attacks on the other side of the globe.

An alternative to looking for naturally occurring sublanguages is defining a **controlled language**. A controlled language is essentially an artificially defined sublanguage in which authors learn to constrain their writing to conform to a set of rules about syntax and semantics when writing texts within a certain pragmatics (that is, for a given purpose, to a particular audience, and within a particular domain).

A success story for the controlled-language approach is the translation of photocopier maintenance and repair manuals within Xerox Corporation. Using Systran for machine translation, preprocessing software that checks for new vocabulary, and in-house authors who are trained to write in a style that improves raw machine translation output (that style being determined experimentally), machine translation output can be used with little or no post-editing. But it should be recalled that the translations are used only by Xerox technicians. Those technicians work for Xerox and can be required to adapt to using machine translation. The general public may not be as accommodating.

Other success stories can be told concerning the controlled-language approach, despite the difficulties of getting authors to conform their writing to the rules of the sublanguage in question and despite the fact that a system that has been customized for one sublanguage must be re-customized to work with another sublanguage. Some would say that controlled-language machine translation is not really fully automatic, since the process of obtaining controlled-language source texts can be viewed as a form of **pre-editing**. But all would agree that in some environments, controlled-language machine translation is successful in that it produces translations with consistent use of terminology, of acceptable quality, cost effectively, and with an overall shorter production time than traditional human-only methods.

2.11 Some recent events in machine translation

Much has happened in machine translation since the 1970s. A major European effort in machine translation, the **Eurotra** project, has come and gone. A major Japanese effort called the **Fifth Generation Computer** project, which was originally scheduled to include machine translation, has come and gone. A very substantial effort is still being made in Japan. We have seen several new commercial systems, including expensive ones such as **METAL** from Siemens Corporation (now from the Sietec division) and inexpensive ones such as Globalink. We have seen approaches based on large corpora of texts with an emphasis on statistics and on finding a previously translated sentence similar to the one to be translated next.

We have also seen a mellowing of the original optimism of machine translation researchers. Until recently, many people in the field firmly believed that most human translators would shortly be replaced by computers. Now, it is widely accepted within the machine translation community that current systems are not capable of FAHQT of UT and that the approach most likely to bring high-quality output is to select a domain, control the input language, and customize the system.

There has also been a softening of the lines between the commercial, linguistic, and AI camps. A conference on machine translation had as its theme technology partnerships between academic research and commercial users of machine translation.[7] And AI researchers are now willing to admit the need for syntactic information as well as conceptual information in machine translation.

However, despite the very real successes of machine translation, it is sobering to consider what portion of the text that is translated commercially each year is done using machine translation, either as indicative translation or as high-quality translation using controlled-language or post-editing or both.

The commercial translation market is estimated to be approximately fifteen **billion** U.S. dollars worldwide (where a billion is a thousand millions). This does not count the emerging personal machine translation market mentioned above, where non-translators use machine translation in conjunction with e-mail or portable computers. This market does not compete with the commercial market but rather fills a dormant need that has not been filled by the commercial market. It is generally agreed that machine translation is used for less than five percent of the text that is translated commercially, and many believe the figure is less than three percent.

What are we doing for the majority of the text that is translated commercially (at least ninety-five percent)?

2.12 Some issues in machine translation

Some questions remain unanswered: Why, after so many years and so much effort, has the original goal of FAHQT of UT been so resistant? Will the successes in controlled-language systems for a particular domain eventually apply to unrestricted text? Why do current techniques work well within a well-defined, narrow domain, and can they be gradually extended to larger and larger domains with less and less control over the source text without sacrificing quality? This last question is a philosophical question with economic implications. A convincing answer could influence the direction of future research and development and its funding. Some people have suggested that since machine translation has only had an impact on about five percent of the text that is translated commercially, more efforts should be directed toward developing computer-based tools for human translators, that is, solutions that involve computers but not machine translation proper. This becomes a hot topic of debate at any gathering of the machine translation community. When pressed, some in the MT community still believe that FAHQT of UT is not too far away (maybe twenty or thirty years). Is that belief justified?

The next chapter will return to the BYU project of the 1970s. It traces the evolution of my answer to the questions of why machine translation works so much better in a specific domain than on general-language texts and whether current techniques can in principle be extended to work well on unrestricted text.

3 The Wall

3.1 The fascination of universal sememes

As mentioned in the previous chapter, I was part of a machine translation project that began in 1970. We were part of the linguistic camp that believed in the importance of using a comprehensive model of syntax, and our model was Junction Grammar, developed by Eldon Lytle, the project director. In fact, the project was at least in part a test of Junction Grammar. As we saw in the previous chapter, by 1960 people like Bar-Hillel were claiming that there is a wall between human translation and machine translation; and in terms of performance on unrestricted text, there is now general agreement that such a wall exists. But what kind of wall is it? Where does it come from? Can it be taken down? Throughout the rest of the book, the wall metaphor will evolve as we discuss language. I will begin by discussing my personal encounter with the wall during the 1970s. The wall has turned out, to my surprise, to be more durable than the Berlin Wall.

When our machine translation project began, I was blissfully ignorant of any wall between human and machine translation. We were still using punched cards on an IBM mainframe, and I was focused on the hill we carried our cards up each morning to get to the computer center. Tired of returning in the evening to see the results of our daily computer run, we soon discovered an alternative, the VM/CMS operating system, which allowed us to interact directly with the mainframe using video display terminals. Not only did this allow us to be much more efficient in programming, it also opened up the possibility of on-line interaction with computer programs, which is familiar to everyone today who uses a personal computer, as opposed to the previous **batch** mode. We were translating from English into several target languages, so the cost of analyzing the English source text could be shared over several target languages. By then we had already bumped up against the wall, but we did not recognize its importance and hoped that on-line interaction would get us over the difficulties.

The interactive process of analysis consisted in running a computer program that attempted to analyze the source text but paused whenever an ambiguity was detected, displaying a question on the computer terminal and waiting for a human to answer it. The human answering the questions was an English monolingual with some training in Junction Grammar; therefore, no questions requiring any knowledge of the target language were permitted. The questions were of two types, syntactic and word-sense.

Syntactic questions involved aspects of Junction Grammar. Some ambiguities were easy to state and to answer, such as where a prepositional phrase attaches in a sentence (e.g., in the sentence "I saw the girl with a telescope" the prepositional phrase can attach to 'girl' or to 'saw', depending on whether the girl has a telescope or someone used a telescope to see the girl). Other interactions were more subtle, such as the possibility of attaching a modifier to several different points within a noun phrase or verb phrase, with point of attachment having semantic implications.

Word-sense interactions were of an entirely different nature. Here Junction Grammar gave us no clear guidance. Neither did we have much guidance from other machine translation projects. All machine translation projects, from the early 1950s on, recognized the importance of resolving categorial ambiguity. As indicated in the previous chapter, this process has traditionally been called homograph resolution in machine translation circles. For example, the LTU 'open' can function as a verb or an adjective ("We will open the case of oil" versus "We will keep the open case"). Clearly, resolving ambiguities of grammatical category is necessary in machine translation, but just as clearly, this simple categorial resolution is not always sufficient to determine the proper target language word. For example, the word 'beam' has several distinct noun senses, such as "beam of light" and "a beam of wood". It is not likely that these senses will translate as the same word in all target languages; thus, categorial resolution is insufficient, and the computer cannot simply look at the next few words since an ambiguous word such as 'beam' will often be used without a prepositional phrase. When a word with multiple senses was encountered, the machine translation system attempted to resolve the categorial ambiguity automatically, but when a word had multiple senses within a category, the program presented a list of definitions to the English monolingual to choose from and waited for a reply.

Other machine translation projects had of course encountered these same problems, but the other projects were different in design and objectives from ours. They were usually translating technical documents. In order to increase the chances of the computer making the right choice, the designers allowed the user to select among several technical dictionaries when a text was translated, with each dictionary tailored to a particular subject matter domain, such as chemical engineering or nuclear physics. Within each technical dictionary, a term was given just one translation, the one most likely to apply to documents specific to the domain in question. In case a document dealt with several domains, the user could even specify that several technical dictionaries should be consulted in a particular order. As we saw in the previous chapter, the Systran system had only one general translation for each word, but it was only used when the word was not found in any of the technical dictionaries specified for use during the translation of that text. This method was surprisingly effective when applied to documents within a very narrow domain. In contrast, we were translating rather general documents, often ranging over several topics within a single text, so we did not have the luxury of using a domain-specific approach. Also, most other projects were committed to a design in which the machine translation phase was automatic and produced translations that were as good as was feasible under that constraint, with the hope that their quality would gradually improve and the assumption that post-editing would be used as needed. Again in contrast, we were committed to producing high-quality output, even if this required a large number of interactions at first, with the hope that the number of interactions per sentence would gradually be reduced without sacrificing quality.

At first we thought we were alone in using the interactive approach, but soon we ran across an article by Martin Kay (1973) which reported on his implementation of interactive translation in a small system. With this and other encouragement, we pursued our attempt to develop a large-scale system for producing interactive high-quality machine translation of unrestricted text. Little did we know what awaited us.

Preparing a dictionary for interactively resolving word-sense ambiguities seemed at first to be a well-defined task, at least as well defined as the senses listed in a good dictionary. But questions quickly arose. For a given word and a given grammatical category, which word senses should be listed as options? Should they be tailored to the various translation equivalents in the target language? Tailoring was not acceptable since there were several target languages in our system, with the possibility of adding more at any time. Here I must mention an additional design requirement based on economics. Since we anticipated that interaction during analysis would be expensive, we wanted to be able to do it once for a given text and then re-use the results of analysis, sometimes much later, to translate automatically into several target languages, including target languages that were not yet part of the system. Therefore, the obvious approach was to identify all the possible concepts onto which a given word can be mapped. In order to build analysis dictionary entries that would not have to be redone (except to add new concepts as the language evolves) and to avoid having to re-analyze an old text even in that case, we decided to use only language-independent concepts and to assign a unique number to each of them. Then, we could map each universal, language-independent concept, which we called a **sememe**, onto just one word (or a small cluster of grammatically conditioned words) in any target language we chose to translate into.

Although the search for language-independent concept numbers now sounds to me misguided, twenty years ago we were extremely serious about the endeavor and convinced of its eventual success. So we embarked on more than five years of concerted effort to write an interactive Junction Grammar analyzer, to build up an analysis dictionary that incorporated many word senses which we hoped came from the language-independent universal set of sememes, and to write transfer/synthesis programs into several languages. Although we believed that the syntactic relations in Junction Grammar were rich enough to represent the structure of any sentence in any language, we did not pretend that our syntactic diagrams were language independent. Therefore, we did not have a true **interlingua**, that is, a language-independent intermediate representation, yet we did not find it strange to expect our sememe numbers to be language independent.

I remember a conversation with Richard Kittredge during this period (the mid-1970s). Kittredge was the director of the machine translation project at the University of Montréal, the TAUM project, and he suggested that our project was overly ambitious. I assured him that thanks to the power of Junction Grammar and the technique of using human interaction for the moment (with the goal of gradually reducing it to a negligible level or better yet, eventually eliminating it through intelligent programming), we were guaranteed to achieve success. I am now embarrassed when I recall this conversation.

Why did it seem so natural to me and to others who were working on the BYU project to attempt to write definitions which corresponded directly to both word senses and universal sememes? Recall from chapter 1 that the Western belief in a stable transcendental meaning, which is the basis for universal sememes, can be traced back many centuries, and that the shift away from stable transcendental meaning began only in this century with Saussure. Since Saussure and his contemporaries we have been in a confusing period of abandoning old ideas while not being satisfied with new ones, and often holding contradictory views simultaneously. Perhaps I can explain my willingness to believe in universal sememes by noting that Descartes, a great mathematician as well as a philosopher, found it worthwhile to try to do exactly what we were attempting to do with our dictionary of correspondences between words and sememes. Karen Sparck Jones (1986:211) cites Descartes who, in a letter to Pierre Mersenne dated November 20, 1629, described a proposed universal language built up from a basic set of "clear and simple ideas". Each basic idea would receive a unique numeric code; texts written in these codes would supposedly be understandable to anyone possessing a code book for the language. Later, in a well-known effort, Leibniz continued the search for a universal language. If minds as great as Descartes and Leibniz believed in what we were attempting, why should I be ashamed of our efforts?

3.2 Hitting the wall surrounding domain-specific machine translation

The syntactic side of our project went well. Junction Grammar developed into a coherent, fairly comprehensive model of the syntactic structure of language (Lytle 1974 and 1980; Melby 1980 and 1985), and many Junction Grammar insights have since occurred to others and have been incorporated into mainstream syntactic theory. The word-sense side was a disaster. As the dictionary got bigger and bigger and we ran more and more texts through the analyzer, it became harder and harder for native speakers of English to decide among the word-sense options listed for a given word. Often, they would say that a word was used with a sense somewhere between two listed senses but not right on either one. Often, they would say that an entirely new sense was needed, not like any on the list. And often, even if they chose a word sense from the list, the transfer/synthesis program would not produce an appropriate target-language word. The transfer/synthesis designers would complain that the analysis people were not choosing word senses consistently; the analysis people would complain that the dictionary writers were not doing their job; and the dictionary writers would explain that they were doing their best. It was a frustrating time, because no one could come up with a single example of a sentence that could not be handled perfectly—in hindsight, that is. Let me explain. Given a sentence that did not translate correctly the first time through the machine translation system, a diagnosis was made to identify the nature of the problem. Sometimes the sentence had been assigned an incorrect syntactic structure, and the analysis grammar team fixed the problem. Sometimes a sememe was mapped onto the wrong word in the target language, and the transfer/synthesis team fixed the problem. Sometimes there was a word in the

English source sentence for which there was no definition in the analysis dictionary that corresponded exactly to the meaning of the word in that sentence of the source text, and the analysis dictionary team fixed the problem. Every problem could be fixed, but the system usually failed on the next sentence presented to it. We did not know it at the time, but it was a form of the tuning problem that has been encountered by most, if not all, machine translation projects. There is no problem that cannot be fixed, yet you are never sure you have finally got it right.

By 1978, we had reached a crisis. We had hit a wall we could not get over. The system was not working (that is, the unfortunate need for heavy post-editing was recognized) and drastic action was in order. Some favored adding interaction to the transfer phase. But this was not an acceptable solution to me, since it required a bilingual human (actually, a qualified translator) for each target language (creating an economic problem) and since it did not answer the question of how to identify language-independent universal sememes (sidestepping a theoretical problem). This was when it suddenly occurred to me that although concepts certainly exist in some way, the real problem could be that the *language-independent universal sememes* we were looking for do not exist! Seldom in a person's career does such a complete change in world view take place. I had a degree in mathematics. The world was supposed to be a nice, tidy place. It was hard for me to admit that our approach to word senses was dead wrong. It was not just a matter of trying harder. I eventually became convinced that no amount of effort would patch up the system as we had designed it. The universal sememe search had reached a dead end.

My view of language and the world had changed. I had become convinced that what we had been looking for, *the* universal, language-independent set of sememes, did not exist. I started asking myself about the status of sememes. What was the justification for believing in them? It seemed to be an unsupported generalization: just because some terms could be reduced to a limited set of clearly distinguishable language-independent senses, we had supposed that all words could be. But pushed to the extreme, this generalization entails the doctrine of total reducibility of meaning to language-independent atoms, which we had called sememes. When we map all language, not just a few terms, onto sememes, supposing that there are a limited number of sememes that each word can map onto, we leave true creativity behind. All meaning becomes mechanical combinations of atomic word senses. Once this work is completed, we would *theoretically* arrive at the single correct, language-independent, all-encompassing basis for viewing, that is, categorizing the world, one universal view from which all individual views would be derived. This position has implications which, upon later reflection, I have found horrifying. In the early 1970s, I scoffed at the Whorf-Sapir hypothesis that one's world view is influenced by one's language. Now I have read some of Whorf's writing with interest and respect.

I emphasize that at the time, my objection to the view I abandoned included no high-flying reasoning. What brought down my naive faith was an *intuitive* realization that the search for the final determinate set of sememes was futile, obviously in practice but, I suspected, also in principle. I was beginning to sense that language is more dynamic and ambiguous in a deeper way than I had ever supposed and that there is not just one built-in, correct way to view the world. With no universal world view and thus no universal set of sememes, the basis for all lexical transfer in our machine translation system had disappeared.

The futility of searching for universal, language-independent sememes could explain the failure of *our* project. However, certain other machine translation projects had been successful. Why were they successful? I had already noted differences in approach. Upon comparing their design and objectives with ours, I observed the following that our project had the following design requirements: (1) it must produce high-quality translations (indistinguishable from competent human translations) of general texts; (2) human interaction in analysis was allowed, but little or no post-editing was permissible; and (3) all interaction with the computer must assume an English monolingual human operator. It turned out that no other project anywhere in the world was at that time able to satisfy those requirements; therefore, successful projects must have other design requirements. The crucial difference in design between our project and other projects was that we were not able to restrict the source text to the sublanguage of a single, well-defined domain. There was some kind of wall between sublanguage machine translation and general-language machine translation, but I did not at the time understand the nature of that wall.

3.3 The nature of the wall: two kinds of language

By 1981, the machine translation project had moved off campus, I had decided to stay on campus, and I had begun studying human translation. I was suddenly fascinated by human translation in its own right, since skilled human translators were doing, and had been doing for thousands of years, something which no machine translation project had been able to do—produce high-quality translations of a variety of general-language texts. I decided to try an inside-out approach. I became a translator, at least in the sense that I passed the accreditation exam (for French into English) and became a member of the American Translators Association. I even did some translation of articles on linguistic theory and contracted with a company to supervise the translation of a software manual into French. I also became very much engaged in the task of designing and programming productivity tools for human translators. The last few years of the BYU project, in addition to working on interactive machine translation (but of a basically different design once interaction in transfer was added in 1978), we also worked on various computer-based tools for translators. The development of these tools, along with interactive machine translation, was pursued off campus at ALPS (later ALPNET) by a group whose core consisted of former members of the BYU project. Another thread of development was pursued on campus and off campus (at LinguaTech) by myself and others. Once again, we ran into an insightful paper by Martin Kay (1980) that showed he was thinking along the same lines we were, and further.

Having been deeply committed to a certain view of machine translation and having been humbled by admitting that that view was in error but not having embraced a new view, I was prepared to see language in new ways. All through this period of the 1980s, in the midst of everyday activities of teaching, research, and software development, I yearned for a better understanding of what was wrong with the idea of a list of universal, language-independent sememes. Gradually, it dawned on me that within a well-defined domain—and I want to emphasize this restriction—one can get away with ignoring questions of universality. Each concept of a domain is normally associated with just one technical term per language. And in a standardized terminology file, each concept often has been assigned a unique number. This was exactly what we were trying to do for general language. So what was the difference? An answer struck me forcefully! *The concepts of a narrow domain and the concepts of general language are of a fundamentally different nature.* At first, this seemed too strange to be true. Technical terms and other specialized terms were thought to be just a subset of general vocabulary. However, on this new view, the general vocabulary of a language would form a language-specific semantic network, and each well-defined domain would have its own network, separate from the general-language network, which may be shared across various languages. In other words, there would be two fundamentally different kinds of network: general-language networks and domain-specific networks. This insight had overwhelmed me by 1989. If correct, it might explain much about when machine translation succeeds and when it fails. The next few years became a time to look for evidence for or against this general/domain distinction and to explore its consequences. The wall we had encountered between controlled-language MT and general-language MT turned out to be the wall around a domain that defines its boundaries.

3.4 The search for a term to cover both sides

Immediately, I realized that most texts consist of mixtures of general and domain-specific items. I say *item* because *word* does not quite fit technical terms, especially noun-noun compounds, that consist of more than one word. One piece of indirect evidence for a distinction between these two kinds of item came through the innocent search for a cover term for the two kinds. I have colleagues in the world of professional lexicography (makers of general dictionaries) and colleagues in the world of professional terminology research (translators and terminologists), and so I thought it would be a simple matter to talk with both groups to come up with a cover term that could refer to both expressions of general vocabulary (outside all walls) and terms from a specialized domain (inside a wall), that is, items on both sides of the walls around various domains. Not only was it not a simple matter, but in the unsuccessful process of trying to find a cover term acceptable to both, I discovered how different the two traditions are. Lexicographers use 'word', 'headword', 'compound', and 'expression', but terminologists do not. Terminologists use 'term', but lexicographers do not. The terms 'lexical unit' and 'lexeme' were proposed, but were rejected by the terminologists, who view their work as concept-oriented and the work of lexicographers as lexically oriented. I even considered using the neologism 'lexiconcept' suggested by a colleague.[8] I finally gave up and started using Lexical/Terminological Unit (LTU), as introduced in chapter 1. Unhappily, LTU is not a true cover term but rather a composite term. Looking for cover terms for similar items is not too difficult. A cover term for 'rose' and 'tulip' and similar plants is obviously 'flower'. But a cover term for 'rose' and 'hammer' that is not so general as to let in all kinds of other items ('object' would clearly be too general) might end up being a composite (such as 'flower/tool'). Thus, the lack of a cover term for lexical units of general vocabulary and terminological units of a specialized domain (other than a composite cover term such as LTU) suggests a substantial distinction.

An additional piece of evidence for a substantial distinction is the fact that terms are not just a subset of the words of general vocabulary. An unabridged English dictionary, which lists headwords from general vocabulary as well as many specialized terms, may have half a million entries, but there are several million specialized terms in English, many of which consist of two or more words that take on a new meaning as a terminological unit. Given just one hundred thousand words that can be used as one element of a two-word term, there are ten billion potential combinations. Even if only one percent of these potential combinations ever become terms, that is still one hundred million terms. And, of course, terms often consist of more than two words and become acronyms, such as ROM (Read-Only Memory), which can then participate in other terms, such as CD-ROM, as if they were words themselves, making the potential number of terms built from the words of general vocabulary practically infinite. The point is that although many terms are derived from one or several words taken from general vocabulary, they take on a new life and are no longer part of general vocabulary. And some terms, such as the nautical term 'yaw' (to turn abruptly from a straight course), are not even part of general vocabulary. In any case, terms are not a subset of general vocabulary, and general vocabulary is not a subset of the terms of all domains. Lexical units and terminological units are both derived from sequences of characters from the same writing system, but neither is a subset of the other.

3.5 The clay/stone analogy

Before continuing, I must point out that when we look at texts, although we find a continuum, that does not imply the lack of a wall between general vocabulary and domain-specific terms. The wall is not between two radically different text types but between the two types of LTU. Texts contain various mixtures of lexical units and terminological units. Suppose we think of clay and stone as physical materials somewhat analogous to lexical and terminological units. For this analogy, I am thinking not of the kind of clay that hardens overnight but the kind that remains pliable. For stones, I am not thinking just of granite or sandstone but also of precious stones such as sapphires and rubies, all of which were formed out of other substances by various processes. A word is thus a chunk of pliable clay and a term is a hard stone. One can think of a stone as a blob of clay that has become transformed into a solid object through some chemical process, just as a terminological unit receives a fixed meaning within the context of a certain domain of knowledge. Starting with the extremes, a text that consisted solely of general vocabulary would be a sequence of pieces of clay all molded together. The particular sequence of shapes may never have occurred before, even if the same words occurred previously, since the words are dynamic and their meanings shift in different situations, just as the shape of a piece of clay changes as you work it. On the other hand, a text from a very narrow domain, such as the domain of weather bulletins mentioned in chapter 2, would be mostly a sequence of stones, consisting almost entirely of terms, with little general vocabulary, just enough to hold the stones together, and no dynamic usages. No literary creativity is needed, even if the particular weather bulletin has never been issued before. Each term has a fixed and consistent meaning. Granted, terms receive new meanings over time, but not for the purposes of literary effect in a single sentence. In the United States, **storm watch** and **storm warning** are used consistently from bulletin to bulletin, just as one would want them to be.[9] In the far extreme case, even prepositions and other function words can be considered terms when they are highly restricted in their allowed usage.

The two extreme cases, texts consisting solely of general vocabulary and texts consisting solely of terms, are rare. In between the two extremes, there is a vast territory of **LSP** (**Language for Special Purposes**) texts, which consist of a mixture of clay and stones. It is also clear that some LTUs are in between soft clay and hard stone, such as terms that are not yet stable and words that are *recycled* terms (such as 'interface'), just starting to be used in general language again but in new ways. But this state is relatively rare and, more important, *unstable* in that *in-between* LTUs tend to fall off the wall and become either words or terms rather than remain something in between. Thus the wall could also be viewed as a *zone* charged with some kind of force field that tends to push an item to one side or the other. However, a particular sequence of letters (such as *i-n-t-e-r-f-a-c-e*) can be a word in one situation (referring to the way people relate to each other) and a term in another situation (referring to a conversion of computer data between formats).

In my view, the continuum between a very general text and a highly domain-specific text is *not* a gray scale along which words gradually become terms and terms gradually become words (see figure 2). The ratio of the mix may change gradually, but usually words are words and terms are terms, and different processing applies to each. The two analogies, a gray scale versus a clay/stone mixture, have very different implications for the computer processing of language. A gray-scale analogy would imply that techniques applicable to terms can gradually be extended to apply to words. A clay/stone

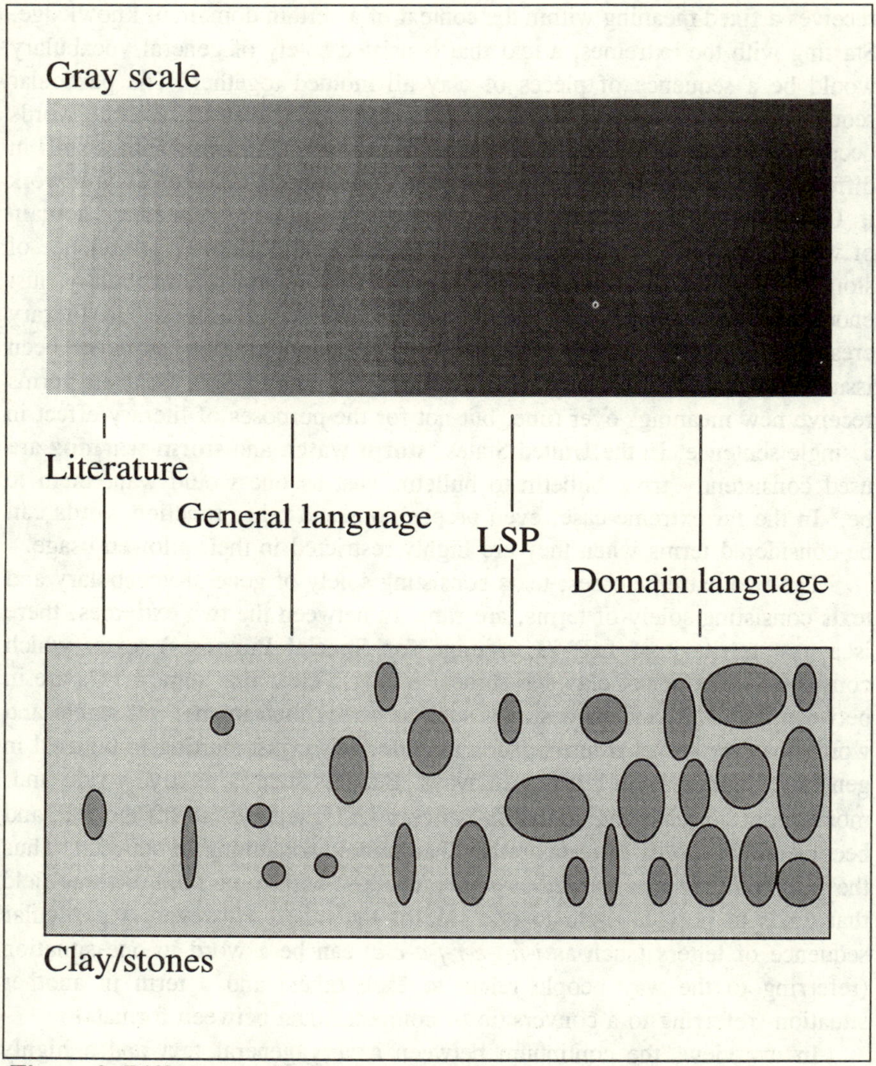

Figure 2: Different analogies for types of text

analogy, as proposed here, implies that techniques that apply to stones will never work for clay, and thus texts that contain more and more clay with fewer and fewer stones will be more and more resistant to stone techniques. New techniques will have to be developed that take into account the different natures of clay and stones. It will turn out that part of that difference is based on two types of ambiguity.

3.6 Fundamental ambiguity versus superficial ambiguity

In this book we will distinguish between superficial and fundamental ambiguity. Both types of ambiguity include the traditional notion of multiple word senses for the same string of characters. Terminological units (stones, according to the previous analogy) exhibit only *superficial ambiguity* because in a well-defined, narrow domain, a relatively stable, finite inventory of concepts are mapped to a given LTU, and in a given situation, the LTU means exactly one of those concepts (except for puns, a rarity in domain-specific text, where it means two simultaneously). Indeed, the normal and desired case for a terminological unit is for only one concept to be *mapped* onto it (that is, linked to it) so that there is a one-to-one correspondence between term and concept. On the other hand, when no stable, small inventory of concepts is associated with an LTU (that is, when dynamic, unpredictable meanings are created as needed in new situations thanks to the flexibility of the clay in the previous analogy), we will say the LTU exhibits *fundamental* ambiguity. Fundamental ambiguity involves three levels: (1) a superficial ambiguity between a given LTU and two or more concepts that map to it; (2) a second, deeper, dynamic ambiguity of *which* concepts and variations of concepts map to the LTU, and (3) a third, even deeper ambiguity between the world and the various concepts associated with an LTU such that no language-independent universal set of sememes exists. Fundamental ambiguity could also have been called *fluidity* (as suggested by John Hutchins) or *indeterminacy* (as suggested by Roy Harris). Clearly, arguments for or against fundamental ambiguity will involve basic philosophical issues.

This distinction between superficial and fundamental ambiguity is related to the issue of whether there is a stable comprehensive list of language-independent universal sememes. Within a narrow, well-organized domain, no fundamental ambiguity exists. The set of concepts is created and controlled by those who are influential in the domain. People decide what concepts belong to the domain and how they relate to the world. They use general language to define the domain, including its concepts and terms, and they can keep it stable until they choose to modify it and re-stabilize it. From within a domain, one cannot see beyond the human-maintained wall that surrounds it, so all ambiguity appears to be superficial. General language is the **metalanguage** for domains. However, for general language I have claimed that there is no stable, comprehensive list of sememes to map onto, and if I am right, there *may* be fundamental ambiguity in general language. There may well be a language-independent set of mathematical principles that very accurately describe the physical properties of matter at subatomic, atomic, and molecular levels (though even physics has a kind of ambiguity in the probabilistic aspects of quantum mechanics), but this does not *necessarily* imply that all concepts of human language are built up mechanically from physical principles. If *some* concepts are not built up mechanically from universal principles, then where might they come from? If *all* concepts are built up mechanically from atomistic concepts, then can we have a changing set of concepts associated with an LTU without requiring fundamental ambiguity? These questions will be explored more seriously later on. For now, we will merely give an informal introduction to the issue of whether there is fundamental ambiguity in language.

In our work on machine translation in the 1970s, we were able to maintain, over a period of several years of intensive work, our belief in a comprehensive list of language-independent sememes underlying general languages. If this presumed list does not actually exist, then how were we able to maintain a belief in it? One reason is that for any specific sentence in any specific text, one can, in retrospect, define a sememe that maps to each word. The problem is that for many words, the list of all possible sememes mapped to a word cannot be established in advance. This does not imply that meaning is random; meaning is dynamic and always motivated (at least in hindsight). And this dynamic aspect of meaning is the basis for fundamental ambiguity. For example, take the word 'dust'. Dust can be a noun or a verb. As a verb, it can mean to take off dust, as in 'dust the furniture' or 'dust the plants in the living room'. But in the fields, 'dust the crops' might mean to put pesticidal dust *on* the plants. In a novel or in an editorial, an author might create a new meaning for dust, such as 'to reduce to dust'. Each new verb meaning of 'dust' will have a syntactic paraphrase and will likely include 'dust' as a noun, but that does not mean that a complete list of possible meanings of 'dust' can be established in advance. A syntactic approach may be able to account for each meaning that turns up, after the fact, but there is no predetermined list of potential meanings for 'dust'.

Recently, I saw a bottle marked *tamper evident*. For an instant, I tried to figure out what it meant based on the expression *tamper proof*, and I wondered whether it meant that someone had evidently tampered with the bottle. Then I realized that it meant that it should be evident to the user whether the bottle (in this case, a bottle of medicine) had been tampered with prior to purchase. Suddenly, a new meaning had been created for me. Some seemingly similar ambiguities can be handled with Generative Grammar, for example, the two readings of 'electronic cat door': one in which the door is electronic, and the other in which the cat is electronic. The ambiguity in "tamper evident" is temporally based and is not easily handled structurally. Later, I saw another bottle which sported the phrase *body building*. Having worked as an instructor in a fitness center during high school, I immediately wondered what the bottle (in this case, a bottle of shampoo) had to do with weight lifting. Then I realized that it meant that the shampoo was claimed to increase the *body*, that is, the bulk, of ones hair. Not only is this a different sense of 'body', there is also a subtle shift in the meaning of 'build' in the two senses of 'body building'. Is there a finite, pre-determined list of possible nuances of meaning for 'build'?

Sometime later, I ran across a text by Pourtales (1966) that gives some background to Berlioz's writing of *La Symphonie fantastique*. Pourtales writes that Berlioz *buvait le temps comme les canards mâchent l'eau* (literally, "drank time like ducks chew water"). This introduces a new sense of drinking which is not likely to be in a dictionary.

Continuing with animals, we can imagine that an author could call an automobile a dog. In context, this could mean that it is unstable on slippery roads, essentially wagging its tail like a dog. Is there a limit to future metaphorical meanings of 'dog'?

All good literature is full of subtle new meanings created to give flavor to a particular text. And the further we go from concrete words like 'dog' toward abstract words like 'good', the harder it is to claim that a small list of well-defined concepts is associated with every word. If there is even one word for which there is no list of well-defined concepts, then there is something beyond superficial ambiguity.

Suppose there is a stable, finite set of atomistic building-block concepts from which all others are mechanically derived. Further suppose that some words do not have a well-defined list of senses but that as each new sense is dynamically created, it is a mechanical combination of the atomistic concepts. This state of affairs would certainly make machine translation challenging, but it would not fully qualify as allowing fundamental ambiguity, since all meanings would be derived from one system of categorizing the world. In this case, all possible viewpoints (categorizations) would be derived from the same underlying set of concepts, and with sufficient knowledge, one would expect to be able to completely understand anyone else's viewpoint. On the other hand, if there *is* fundamental ambiguity in language, there can be mutually incompatible viewpoints that are all consistent with the same physical world but that cannot be brought together under one coherent framework. Here we are touching on the issue of the **grounding** of language, which will be further explored later on. Is language grounded on anything at all? If not, then how do we communicate? If so, then on what?

The rest of this chapter will *not* attempt to demonstrate conclusively that there is fundamental ambiguity in general language. Instead, the next sections simply argue from several directions that there is a significant difference between domain-specific language and general language. In the background is the argument that a convincing general/domain distinction would make it more plausible to suppose that general language exhibits fundamental ambiguity. Later sections suggest connections between mainstream linguistics and the general/domain distinction. Eventually, we will consider preliminary implications for machine translation. A look at George Lakoff's recent work will suggest that the general/domain distinction may be related to **objectivism**, which underlies many linguistic theories.

Objectivism is a philosophical stance which implies that there is no fundamental ambiguity, so in the next chapter we will look at various traditions in Western philosophy in search of one that will allow for fundamental ambiguity without destabilizing language completely; in other words, we will look for an explanation of language that allows for the possibility of language as we feel it to be intuitively—fresh and alive, not tied down to any one view of the world, yet not so free floating as to disallow meaningful human communication. We will conclude our philosophical search with an introduction to an approach based on the work of Emmanuel Levinas, which allows for fundamental ambiguity without claiming that meaning is random. I realize I have not proven and will not prove the existence of fundamental ambiguity (since acceptance or rejection of fundamental ambiguity is a starting point rather than a conclusion), but I hope to suggest that it is plausible and that it provides a basis for the distinction between general and domain-specific language, which in turn explains the current status of machine translation and predicts its future. The final chapter will further explore some implications of our view of the general/domain distinction for translation theory and translator tools. With that preview, we now return to various arguments for the general/domain distinction.

3.7 Evidence for the general/domain distinction

To this point I have suggested that there is an important difference between general language and domain-specific language, or, otherwise put, between lexical units (words) and terminological units (terms). We have used the metaphor of a wall to describe the barrier (or zone of instability) that is built around the concepts and terms of a domain to distinguish the domain from general language. And I have claimed that most texts we encounter in real life consist of a mixture of lexical units and terminological units. So we will look at a few examples of text that will explain what I mean by the dynamic use of general vocabulary mixed with more static terms. Then we will look at two kinds of evidence for the importance of the general/domain distinction. The first kind of evidence will be words whose meaning (as evidenced by translations) is not reducible to a list of separate senses. If indeed such words exist, then they would be evidence that such LTUs differ significantly from domain-specific terms which display at most superficial ambiguity. The second kind of evidence will be facts from the history of computer processing of **natural language** that suggest that certain techniques apply only to domain-specific text.

3.7.1 Examples of dynamic versus static LTUs in LSP text

We will now consider a few examples of LSP (Language for Special Purposes) text and look for words, especially words that have dynamic meanings, to illustrate differences between the properties of words and terms.

LSP text is everywhere around us. In looking at a few pages of an old issue of *Byte* magazine,[10] I found the following examples of LSP text:

> The quality of IEF-developed systems is remarkable. In recent CASE research by the Gartner Group, application developers were asked to report the number of abends they had experienced.

The first sentence follows this pattern: The *x* of *y*-developed systems is *z*. Here *x* is 'quality' (a word of general vocabulary), *y* is 'IEF' (a term which expands to Information Engineering Facility™), and *z* is 'remarkable' (another word of general vocabulary).

The second sentence has a more complex syntactic pattern that contains four *stones* (terms): 'CASE' (a term that expands to Computer-Assisted Software Engineering), 'The Gartner Group' (a term that is a proper noun), 'application developer' (a term that means someone or some group who writes computer software application programs), and 'abend' (a software term which means abnormal termination).

In this two-sentence passage of LSP text, there are no truly creative uses of language. A very sophisticated **Natural Language Processing (NLP)** system could probably process it well.

Now consider another passage from the same magazine:

> "Double Your Clock Speed, Double Your Fun"
> Intel has developed a new technology for doubling the internal clock speed of its 486 and 486 SX processors. The clock doubler will boost the speed of the CPU (e.g., revving a 25 Mhz processor up to 50 Mhz) and this improves overall performance without requiring big changes in the rest of the system.

This passage of LSP text contains some units of dynamic general language. Granted, it contains several static technical terms (such as 'clock speed', '486 SX', 'CPU', and 'Mhz'). But consider the title, "Double Your Clock Speed, Double Your Fun". If understood and translated literally, it means that you will have twice as much fun if the clock in your computer runs twice as fast. Of course, this is false. Doubling clock speed does not necessarily double the amount of work accomplished overall or make work twice as fun, and even if it did, your boss would probably not let you leave work early to have more fun just because your computer runs faster and you get more work done. A literal translation, which lets the reader figure out what it might mean, may or may not be acceptable. An intelligent human translator who does not know the pun behind this title (pun explained below) would probably interpret the title in a reasonable way and translate it as something like "faster clock speed makes work more enjoyable". A standard machine translation system, on the other hand, has no way to decide when a passage should be translated literally and when it should be adapted, let alone decide how to adapt it. In addition, this title cannot be fully processed unless it is identified as a variant of an advertising slogan for an American chewing gum. The original slogan was "Double your pleasure, double your fun, with Double Mint ... gum". The knowledge domain of microcomputers does not include information about chewing gum. And although only one small piece of information is relevant to the interpretation, it is impossible to predict in advance (i.e., before seeing the passage) that chewing gum will be relevant. And even when that piece of information is accessed, it is still not obvious how the title should be translated into a language environment that does not know about the American chewing gum advertisement.

Another difficulty is the term 'clock doubler', introduced about the time the article was written to describe this technology. An NLP system for LSP texts must include a mechanism for quickly and easily adding to its lexicon new terms that are found in the text being processed. This becomes especially difficult for terms like 'clock doubler' in which both components of the LTU might already be in the lexicon with individual senses. The problem of accurately recognizing multi-item terms has been worked on for years and remains unsolved.

The verbal phrase 'to rev up' (to increase the number of *rev*olutions per minute), borrowed from the domain of automobile engines, is dynamically applied to **CPU**s. It is not obvious that the corresponding automotive phrase in another language will work well in this situation. This is where a human translator uses judgment and creates a new metaphor in another language, selecting expressions in the target language that are equivalent in sense and pleasing to the speaker of the target language.

Another item of general language that could cause problems is the word 'big'. It is being used in the sense of *significant* rather than *large*, but it is not obvious how this is to be determined by an NLP system.

We could continue indefinitely with examples of dynamic general language in LSP and general texts. They are found in almost any magazine or book, except perhaps the most boring and predictable. Some people might be satisfied with such examples as evidence that terms are basically different from words. Others may require additional evidence. The use of the word *evidence* is not intended to imply rigorous proof. As mentioned before, a distinction as fundamental as the general/domain distinction is likely not provable. But if one is willing to consider it a possibility, and if it is a valid distinction, then one should be able to find considerable supporting evidence.

3.7.2 *Asymmetry as evidence*

Words and terms use the same alphabet, which obscures any obvious surface-level difference when considering an LTU in isolation. But it occurred to me that contrastive analysis might yield further evidence, even at the LTU level, in addition to studies of longer segments of texts. In 1989, at the invitation of Professor Jean-Marie Zemb of the Collège de France, I embarked on a study of cross-language asymmetry of words and terms.[11] Following are some of the results of that study.

A symmetrical relationship is one that can be reversed without making any false claims. So two LTUs (one in language A and the other in language B) will be said to be perfectly symmetrical if each LTU is equivalent to the other and only to the other. For example, within the domain of solar energy, the English LTU 'heat loss' and the French LTU *déperdition de chaleur* are symmetrical. There are actually international standards which set up symmetrical LTUs in certain well-defined domains. In mathematical statistics, International Standard number 3534 specifies that 'bivariate distribution' is equivalent to the French term *loi de la probabilité à deux variables* and that 'standardized variate' is equivalent to the French term *variable aléatoire réduite*. The cross-language link between symmetrical terms looks like a ping-pong ball bouncing rhythmically back and forth between two skilled players, each cooperating in making it possible for the other to stand still and hit the ball every time.

Our methodological assumption will be that a pair of symmetrical LTUs is linked to symmetrical nodes, or even to the same node, in one semantic network. Here 'semantic network' is used loosely to refer to the concepts associated with a set of LTUs. It is assumed that concepts are related in some way and that those relations form a network, with each concept being a node. When we say that two LTUs are symmetrical, we really mean that they are linked to the same concept. The mention of semantic network should not be interpreted as adherence to any particular school of semantics, especially since I hope to convince the reader that no formal semantic system could possibly encompass the entire network of a human language. But for the purpose of discussion, I will begin as if English and other languages (with most examples from French) each had a well-defined semantic network and that an LTU in either language has a corresponding symmetrical LTU in the other, until proven otherwise.

Pure one-to-one symmetry of technical terms becomes boring very quickly, so I will concentrate on examples of apparent asymmetry of semantic networks, as evidenced by LTUs which do not have a one-to-one correspondence between languages.[12] If terms are symmetrical, then asymmetry may be evidence of LTUs that are not terms and therefore of a general/domain distinction.

3.7.3 Asymmetry of homographs

One easy-to-recognize type of asymmetry occurs when an LTU is a homograph, a homograph being a word that is spelled the same as another but differs in origin or meaning (rather than just in grammatical category as homograph is used in machine translation). When an LTU has two very distinct, possibly unrelated senses, there will almost always be two or more equivalents in another language. For example, the English LTU 'bank' has two very different equivalents in French, *banque* (financial institution) and *rive* (mounded dirt at the edge of a river).

The demonstration of asymmetry consists of the following steps:

(1) French LTU *banque* is equivalent to English LTU 'bank'.

(2) English LTU 'bank' is equivalent to French LTU *rive*.

(3) Symmetry would imply that the French LTUs *banque* and *rive* are equivalent.

Since the conclusion is clearly false, we have an example of asymmetry. A mathematician may describe this state of affairs by noting that the equivalence relation between languages is not transitive. But we will use the term *asymmetry* to emphasize the LTUs rather than the relation.

This asymmetry of homographs is easily repaired, that is, made symmetrical. Simply number the homographs $bank_1$ (financial) and $bank_2$ (river) as is commonly done in general dictionaries. Then the demonstration of asymmetry has been countermanded, since *banque* is equivalent to $bank_1$ but $bank_1$ is not equivalent to *rive*. We now have two symmetrical pairs, and so far we have no evidence from our first glance at asymmetry of a basic difference between general-language and domain-specific LTUs.

In passing, we note that homographs are not always entirely unrelated. An examination of the etymology of the two senses of 'bank' mentioned above reveals that they both derive from "raised shelf or ridge of ground" (*Oxford English Dictionary*, 1989, pp. 930-931) The river sense is literally a mound of dirt. The financial sense came from a money-changer's table or shelf, which could originally have been placed on a mound of dirt.

3.7.4 Asymmetry of evolving word senses

We will give one example of the asymmetry of word senses caused by cultural change. In recent years, more and more men and women have begun to wear a pouch attached around the waist with a belt. Originally, such a pouch was usually worn in the back. Somehow, it became known as a 'fanny pack' in the United States and a 'bum-bag' in England, probably because of cultural differences between 'bum' and 'fanny' (both referring to one's anatomy). 'Fanny' is highly offensive in England and refers to a different part of the anatomy for an American and for a British subject. These pouches, which have been worn by French men longer than they have been worn by British or American men and women, are usually worn on the side or in front in France, rather than in the back. This practice is catching on in the United States, where the pouches are now often worn by both men and women in front or to one side. The French LTU for such a pouch, *banane* (literally, 'banana'), is not predictable from the English LTUs, although it is certainly motivated by the shape of the object (somewhat like a very fat banana).

Now here is the difficulty. When Americans first started wearing fanny packs on their side, they were suddenly no longer truly *fanny* packs. But some people continue to call them 'fanny packs'. Their newness creates a tension. Sometimes people do not know what to make of a pouch worn on the side and they will call it anything from an overgrown coin purse to a tiny briefcase. 'Pouch' and *banane* are not symmetrical since 'pouch' is too broad, and 'fanny pack' and *banane* are not fully equivalent. Given the current high level of international travel and the spreading use of such pouches, within a few years we may see a new LTU in English, perhaps *waist pouch*, more specific than pouch and equivalent to *banane* in that it does not specify where the pouch is to be worn (front, back, or side). This will resolve the temporary asymmetry.

Temporary asymmetry caused by cultural change is not in itself evidence of a basic difference between words and terms, but it does raise the question of culture and how culture obtains a certain uniformity across a group of people and whether there is any pre-assigned range of options that a culture can take on in its concepts and practices.

3.7.5 *Asymmetry of holes*

An interesting type of asymmetry is observed in cases in which an LTU in one language has no corresponding LTU in the other language being considered—in other words, a hole. For example, take the English LTU 'nut'. If we ignore the homonym of 'nut' which means a device for attaching a bolt and instead focus on nut as a family of edibles including peanuts, cashews, and almonds, we may be surprised to discover that there is no corresponding LTU in French.[13] For each specific kind of nut, there is an apparently symmetrical LTU (*cacahuète* for 'peanut', *cajou* for 'cashew', *noix* for 'walnut'). However, there seems to be no generic French LTU corresponding to the English LTU 'nut'. If one insists, there is a scientific term in French, *fruit à écale* (literally, 'fruit with a shell'). But this technical term is not used in everyday conversation. The French LTU *noix* may also suggest a more general center or kernel, since it is used in *noix de coco* (French for 'coconut'), but it is unlike the English word 'nut' in that it is directly associated with a particular kind of nut in general language.

I recently encountered a practical demonstration of the difficulties presented to translators by the hole in French relative to the English nut. I was on a flight across the Atlantic, and before the meal was served, I was presented with a printed description of the meal. The English description of the first appetizer was

"An assortment of warm roasted nuts to accompany your preferred cocktail or beverage".

The French version read:

Amandes diverses grillées, servies chaudes, pour accompagner le cocktail ou la boisson de votre choix (literally, "Almonds, various kinds, grilled, served hot, to accompany the cocktail or the beverage of your choice").

Leaving aside the logical problem in the English of whether a cocktail is a beverage, that is, why the description was not "the cocktail or *other* beverage of your choice", we will consider the nutty problem. After looking at both descriptions, I began to wonder just what I would receive. I suspected that I would receive several kinds of nuts, not just almonds, and that the French translation was just plain wrong. Then again, what if the French description were accurate? I would receive several kinds of almonds. Being an almond lover, I found that a pleasant thought. Soon the flight attendant brought my reality check in the form of a dish of warm roasted cashews, almonds, pistachios, and pecans. I realized that the text presented to the translator did not contain sufficient information to produce an accurate translation. Consultation with the chef would have been in order.

Another example of a hole is the lack of a simple French equivalent for the English LTU 'chicken'. In English, there are female chickens (hens) and male chickens (roosters). Granted, in English, chickens are assumed to be hens by default, but we say 'chicken coop' when a rooster is present, not 'chicken and rooster coop'. The French LTU *poule* almost works for 'chicken', except that it definitely excludes a rooster. Thus we might define homographs for male chicken and female chicken. However, it is not as simple as that. We still lack a symmetrical LTU for 'chicken'. In French, once the bird is dead and prepared for cooking, both a rooster and a hen can be called *poulet*. However, this French LTU is not generally used for the animal while it is still running around the barnyard. So there is a hole in French relative to English chickens.

Other examples of holes abound. Some on which we will not elaborate are the asymmetry between the English LTU 'potato' and corresponding LTUs in French and Japanese (for example, the Japanese word *imo* is a class that includes more than potatoes and does not correspond to any English LTU). There appears to be a hole in French and some other languages relative to the English concept 'pet', for a domesticated animal. Other holes are closely tied to culture, as is the pouch example above. For another example, French bread and American bread are not at all interchangeable without complaint.

The study of asymmetry of holes is interesting, but it is not evidence of a basic asymmetry between semantic networks. So long as there is symmetry at a more specific level, we can posit nodes in a semantic network that are not associated with any LTU (such as the non-LTU node for 'nut' in French) but which do not block communication since one can always use one or more specific LTUs to replace a more generic LTU in a given situation.

3.7.6 *Asymmetry of subdivisions*

When you take apart an object with well-defined pieces, such as an alarm clock, people seldom disagree on how many pieces there are. However, when you butcher a steer, there are several methods of dividing up the meat, depending on what country you are in. Multiple methods produce an asymmetry of subdivisions.

Another asymmetry of subdivisions exists between English and Japanese in the ways to say 'thank you'. The Japanese distinctions are hard for an American to grasp, but they involve such factors as whether the person being thanked was obligated to do what was done, how much effort was put forth, and whether the 'thank you' is in response to a compliment. Even between English and French there is a strong asymmetry concerning 'thank you'. When an American receives a compliment, a normal response is 'thank you'. But a French speaker would never say *merci* in response to a compliment.[14]

These asymmetries of subdivision are complex, but they are not the most intractable. At least there is a well-defined cow to be subdivided and at least there may be a well-defined list of possible Japanese equivalents to 'thank you'. But consider the case of honesty in English and its closest equivalent in French. For a beginning French student, *honnêteté* is a simple cognate of 'honesty'. Later, however, subtle differences are noticed. In modern English, the emphasis of honesty is on telling the truth, but in French, *honnêteté* goes beyond telling the truth and often includes appropriateness. If someone asks a high price for their used car, then it could be outrageous but you would probably not call the price dishonest, while in French it would not be a price that is *honnête*. In the definition of *honnête* in a standard French monolingual dictionary,[15] there is mention of *loyauté* (usual translation: 'loyalty'), which is not usually considered part of the meaning of honesty.

In a discussion of translation mismatches (Kay et al. 1994:22-24), we find a metaphor of a semantic grid. According to this account, each language places a grid on reality and has a name for whatever falls within a given square of the grid. An example is given of the fact that there are two translations of 'fish' in Spanish, *pez* for a live fish swimming around and *pescado* for a dead fish intended to be eaten. There is an interesting comment in the discussion:

> The area covered by the English word "fish" covers two sections of the Spanish grid, one corresponding to the word "pez" and the other to the word "pescado".

The issue is whether a given word in one language will completely fill one or more sections of the grid of another language or whether there are partially filled sections, no matter how fine you make the sections. In other words, are languages commensurate or incommensurate? The French word *honnêté* seems to be broader than honesty. But does it fill the section of the English grid designated by honesty and some entire other section or just a part of another section? In French, *honnêté* is related to acceptability and to loyalty but does not completely cover those sections. If not, then this may be evidence that there is no one universal grid system for general language.

3.7.7 Dynamic asymmetry

Another difficult case of asymmetry of subdivision is encountered in the French LTU *geste*. No simple English LTU corresponds to *geste*. The English LTU 'gesture' would only be appropriate in some situations. In the French expression *faire un geste de la tête*, *geste* does not match with 'gesture', since the whole expression means to shake one's head. There is no rigid list of possible ways to use *geste*, and even a partial list brings in English equivalents that go beyond *geste* on the way back to French. For example, *geste* introduces 'shake' in English, but 'shake' has equivalents in French that are not equivalent to *geste*.

Now with *geste* (and possibly with 'honesty') we encounter a fundamentally different kind of asymmetry. There is no official list of all the possible ways to use *geste*. The moment one thinks such a list has been completed, another usage will pop up in a conversation, a novel, an editorial or some other piece of general language.[16]

Another example of dynamic asymmetry is the English LTU 'run' and its French equivalents. A general French equivalent of 'run' is *courir*, but this does not always work. In French, you do not use *courir* when you run for political office. And you do not use *courir* when you run a machine. There are hundreds of documented expressions in which 'run' is equivalent to many LTUs other than *courir*. If there were a fixed number, however large, everything would be all right. The problem is that one cannot foresee all the situations in which 'run' will be used. And the next new situation may result in a creative translation equivalent different from any encountered so far or an unpredictable (but motivated) choice among existing options.

Examples of this *dynamic* asymmetry among words of general language are abundant. Of course, that which was at first dynamic becomes static when it is repeated. Technical terms are sometimes new words created for the occasion, such as 'laser' (which probably originated as an acronym for "light amplification by stimulated emission of radiation"), and are other times existing words which take on new meanings (such as 'mouse' when used to refer to a pointing device for controlling a computer). The two meanings of *mouse* are thus two separate LTUs, one a word and the other a term. Most often, combinations of existing words take on a new meaning as a unit, forming a multiword technical term such as 'disk drive'. Certainly, a connection exists between the two lexical units 'disk' and 'drive' of general vocabulary and the terminological unit 'disk drive'. The 'disk drive' is a device that 'drives' or 'controls' a 'disk', which is covered with some material (usually magnetic or optical) for storing digital information. The point is that when 'disk drive' was first used it was a dynamic unit of general vocabulary with a motivated but not totally predictable meaning. Then it made a transition from *specialized general vocabulary* (an intentional oxymoron to emphasize the unstable nature of this stage in the life of a term) to the domain of computer technology.

For a time, after the creation of a new technical term, there is a strong asymmetry (namely a hole) compared to other languages spoken by those who share the same domain of technology. A new term is created within general language and passed to a domain; then, equivalent technical terms are formed in other languages and passed to the same domain. In the interim, the technical term from one language may be used temporarily in another. For example, the English term 'software' was used in French; then the French term *logiciel* was created. Now the two terms coexist and compete.

When new meanings are formed and survive in a domain, there is a tendency toward symmetry between languages. It takes a certain energy for a concept to remain in use. If it has enough energy, a cluster of symmetrical terms appear. If it does not have enough energy, then it will disappear. But a term does not take on new meanings dynamically from within a domain. This would be antithetical to the goal of clear communication on specialized topics. People want terms to be predictable.

On the other hand, words of general vocabulary are more like wild horses. They do not want to remain stable in their meaning. At some point, the English lexical unit 'run' took on dynamic meanings when it was first used in each of the following situations: "money ran through his fingers", "the river ran dry", "the colors ran riot", "the play ran long", and "the colors in my shirt ran". At each of those points, the French equivalent for a dynamic meaning was *not* predictable. Each may now have become predictable through repeated use, but that does not change the fact that a new use of 'run' may pop up at any time, and there is no way to reliably predict how that new use will be expressed in another language.

The words 'geste' and 'run' are not rare examples. One could go on indefinitely pointing out fundamental asymmetries between any pair of languages that are not close enough to be borderline dialects.

3.7.8 Summary of observations concerning asymmetry

We have now observed, using studies of relative asymmetry, a crucial difference between general LTUs and domain-specific LTUs. In general language, we are able to produce dynamic meanings as needed for a particular situation, however fleeting, without creating new words. Domain networks are more stable. When a new domain concept appears and a new term is needed, it is created, through the dynamic processes of general language, as a new word or a combination of existing words. If the new concept survives, it forms a new node in the domain network, and terms from various languages spoken by those who share the domain point to the node.

Within a domain of knowledge, terms are not used with a new sense merely for the purposes of a particular sentence. They have relatively stable meanings because that is the way people want them to be. This makes it possible to treat a domain as if it were the whole universe by building a wall around it so that nothing else is visible. Within a domain of knowledge created by and shared by people of various language communities, concepts can be treated as if they were language independent, and terms can be viewed as being unambiguous or at worst superficially ambiguous. This stability allows our current generation of formal computer systems to process domain-specific texts with some degree of success. However, when a text contains dynamic lexical units of general language from outside the wall, what happens to the computer systems designed to process language? If computer systems that work on texts which are composed mostly of domain-specific terms tend to break down when applied to texts that contain more and more units of dynamic general language, then we will have found additional support for a general/domain distinction.

3.7.9 *Evidence from NLP*

When it comes to computer processing, human language is often called natural language, even if it is stilted and unnatural from a literary point of view. In natural language processing (NLP), the term for computer processing of human language, natural language is contrasted with **formal language**. A formal language is an artificial language which conforms to rules laid out in a formal grammar. A computer programming language is an example of a formal language. Another example would be the query language used to access information in a computer database. Usually, a domain-specific text would be said to be written in natural language, but if the general/domain distinction is as important as I have proposed, then domain-specific texts may be more closely related to formal languages than to general human language. And NLP techniques that are based on the properties of domain-specific text may break down when applied to general-language texts. We have already seen (in chapter 2) that this is the case for machine translation, in which there is a sharp distinction between the levels of success in processing general-language texts versus domain-specific texts. Let us further test this prediction by examining briefly some other areas of NLP.

Artificial Intelligence (AI) has dealt with more than just machine translation. In fact, machine translation has for many AI researchers been uninteresting or only a sideline. Some earlier work dealt with game playing, such as chess. It is not surprising that computers have seen substantial success in chess, since it is a prime example of a domain with a fixed cast of players and rigid rules. However, human chess players still seem to use different strategies than computers. In the 1960s, during the same period that Bar-Hillel, who worked at MIT, was arguing against the possibility of human-level machine translation, another MIT researcher, Marvin Minsky, was making strong claims about what progress would surely be made in AI during the coming twenty years (that is, by the 1980s). Minsky repeatedly claimed that by the 1980s, computers (perhaps special-purpose computers) would be capable of every human intellectual activity. Computers, which are based on chips often made from silicon, are sometimes called silicon machines, and Minsky derisively called humans *meat machines*. He claimed that the main difference between computers (silicon machines) and humans (meat machines) is that computers would soon perform every intellectual activity faster and better (Dreyfus 1992). In the past thirty years (allowing an extra ten years for miscalculations in Minsky's estimates), we have seen some spectacular successes in computer processing of language, but not exactly the ones predicted.

3.7.10 Speech processing

Computer processing of speech has seen much progress in the past thirty years. It is now relatively straightforward to build systems that can recognize thousands of words when spoken in isolation by the same person who supplied the input to train the system. But no one has been able to build a large-vocabulary system capable of recognizing continuous speech consisting of general vocabulary which can adapt to a new speaker in a few seconds, the way a human can. I am not claiming that highly accurate speaker-independent continuous speech recognition is impossible, just that it is an entirely different problem from speaker-dependent isolated-word speech recognition within a particular domain. It would be interesting to explore why the two types of speech recognition are so different for machines but not for humans, but we will not pursue that topic here.

3.7.11 Microworlds

In AI, there is a well-known distinction between large-scale, general-purpose systems and systems that operate only on a particular microworld. A microworld is closely related to an extremely narrow domain. Some well-known microworlds are task oriented. For example, there is the microworld of ‘replacing a washer in a standard kitchen faucet’. A fruitful microworld in the classic AI literature is the ‘restaurant’ microworld, in which all that is of interest is the process of ordering a meal, receiving it, and paying for it. One of the first microworlds was the world of SHRDLU, a robot arm at MIT that lived, so to speak, in a microworld consisting of several blocks of various shapes and colors on a flat surface, all within reach of the arm. A human at the keyboard could tell the arm (in plain English) to put a square block on a pointed block and get answers like “I can’t do that—it would fall off”. This early AI system caused considerable excitement because it gave the impression that the computer really understood what you were asking it, and it gave many people, including me, hope that computers would eventually be able to deal with all of natural language in an intelligent way.

This microworld is of particular interest because of the human story that goes with it. Terry Winograd, the well-known AI researcher who programmed SHRDLU, encountered the same frustration as many other AI researchers when he tried to extend the technology beyond the microworld level (Winograd 1987:109). It seemed to become a different kind of problem, not just a bigger one.

Eventually, during the 1980s, Winograd's view of language changed radically, as did mine, for much the same reasons, although we were not in personal contact. He left the field of AI and has since explored the ideas of Heidegger and other twentieth-century philosophers as they apply to NLP, challenging the philosophical basis of AI.

Over the past thirty years, what types of computer software that deal with language in any way have been the most successful? Clearly, it has been word processing software and indexing software.

Word processing software has practically destroyed the market for the classic typewriter, manual or electric. Why? Because a human writer and a computer word processor make such a good team. With word processing software, the human can easily do what a human cannot do with a classic typewriter: correct mistakes, move text, and reformat without retyping the words of the text that do not change in the process.

Indexing software takes many forms. One particularly impressive form is the kind of database search that can be done at many libraries. Hundreds of periodicals are indexed by key words, such as names of individuals. Note that this indexing is done by computer, not by hundreds of clerics laboriously creating an index of all the words used in a publication and then merging many indexes. This automatic indexing allows a human to ask for all the articles that have appeared since 1985 that mention Marvin Minsky. They can be retrieved in seconds. A highly intelligent human placed in front of a stack of periodicals would take days, months, or even years to perform the same task, if indeed the task were accomplished before insanity or at least carelessness set in.

Now at first glance, it would appear that these applications of computers (word processing and indexing) apply to general language, unlike current techniques in machine translation. However, a second glance reveals that they actually apply only to an extraordinarily narrow domain, the domain of characters (i.e., letters), font attributes, punctuation, and format codes. Note that you cannot ask your word processor to delete all words that suggest sadness. But you can ask it to change all occurrences of *disk* to *diskette*. This will be fine unless you only want it to change occurrences of *disk* that refer to computer disks and leave untouched those occurrences that refer to a disk in the spine. In the domain of word processing, the software does not really process words at all, but rather *sequences of characters surrounded by punctuation or spaces*. Likewise, standard techniques of indexing do not deal with content but with *strings of characters*. Sometimes a thesaurus is used to find an article that deals with a certain topic, but here the thesaurus is used to suggest additional words to search for, based on associations that some human has encoded in the thesaurus. Indexing software does not actually deal with the meaning of words any more than does word processing, but it does something that a human cannot do. It quickly finds specific sequences of letters surrounded by punctuation in a large corpus of text. In effect, the success of word processing and indexing comes *from limiting the computer task to a well-defined, extremely narrow domain*.

3.7.12 User interfaces

Another area of language contact between humans and computers is the user interface for software. Over the past thirty years, two very different attempts have been made to replace the traditional command-line interface of Unix, DOS, VM/CMS, and other operating systems with a more intuitive interface. One attempt is succeeding dramatically, while the other has yet to become a widespread commercial reality.

The one which is succeeding is called a GUI (Graphical User Interface). It began with the STAR™ system, which was developed at Xerox Corporation's Palo Alto research center. The user interface from the STAR was seen by Steve Jobs of Apple Computer, and the idea was used by Apple Computer to develop the Macintosh™ computer. Apple and Microsoft made an arrangement for a similar interface to be used in Windows™. Now most personal computers come with either the Macintosh or the Windows GUI, and these two user interfaces are becoming more similar to each other.[17]

The one that has not seen nearly so much success is the natural language interface, in which the user communicates with the computer in natural language. In some cases, the user types commands to a computer program in English. But several problems have not been overcome. One problem is restricting the input. Sometimes the structure of a particular domain is built into the computer system. An example of a built-in domain is adventure games, in which all commands must apply to the microworld of the game, but when there is no well-defined universe of discourse, the human has difficulty restricting commands to what the computer can process accurately. The GUI is actually a very narrow domain in which all that exists are the icons and menus and the **pointing device** (typically a mouse). The user shifts into domain-specific mode and temporarily lives in the GUI domain. When no well-defined domain exists and the user is invited to type commands in English (or Hungarian or any other natural language), the commands may become dynamic general language, and then the human-computer interface fails to function effectively. A few years ago, the Japanese Fifth Generation Computer project included as a major goal the development of a universal natural language user interface. That goal was quietly dropped, confirming the substantial difference between general and domain networks.

3.8 Summary of chapter to this point

We began this chapter by noting my deep involvement in a machine translation project in the 1970s. Using human-computer interaction, the system succeeded in producing syntactic analyses of sentences of general text. However, the system failed to produce acceptable words in the output. During the 1980s, I worked on tools for human translators, as opposed to machine translation, and was struck with the insight that there is a much greater difference between units of general vocabulary (clay) and domain-specific terms (stones) than I had previously suspected. This distinction, if valid, could explain why our project failed to produce acceptable output despite syntactic success, while some other machine-translation projects did produce acceptable output. The explanation is that we attempted to translate general-language texts, while successful projects focused on highly restricted domain-specific texts. Standard techniques that work on domain-specific texts do not apply to general-language texts, perhaps because the semantic network associated with general language is dynamic, while the semantic network associated with a narrow domain is intentionally frozen. I have given evidence for the general/domain distinction from cross-language studies of asymmetry and from the history of natural language processing.

We have now reached a turning point in this chapter. We hope that by this time you are convinced that the general/domain distinction is fundamental or at least that you are willing to use the distinction as a working hypothesis.

The rest of the chapter will build on the general/domain distinction. We will consider possible implications for the status of mainstream linguistics. In the next chapter, we will explore some philosophical issues that have been unresolved for a long time, issues that bear on the distinction and explain it.

In the course of our explanations we will see not only that it is futile to look for the universal set of sememes, but that there are better questions to explore. For example, we will consider the grounding of language. To ground language is to provide a basis outside of language for meaning in language. A domain is grounded in general language, but how is general language grounded? We will look for a grounding of general language that makes language and communication possible without eliminating fundamental ambiguity.

3.9 Mainstream linguistics and the general/domain distinction

Mainstream linguistics in America is primarily concerned with syntax. Semantics is viewed as a process of interpretation which requires a complete syntactic diagram of a sentence as a starting point. Unquestionably, whether one likes it or not, Noam Chomsky, Professor of Linguistics at MIT, is the most influential figure in mainstream linguistics. Chomsky began publishing in the late 1950s, at the height of influence of American Structuralism, which was based on modern synchronic linguistics as begun by Saussure at the turn of the century. Chomsky quickly came to dominate linguistics with his approach. Chomsky's approach and related approaches, such as Lexical Functional Grammar (LFG) and Head-driven Phrase Structure Grammar (HPSG) are collectively known as Generative Grammar (**GG**). Although machine translation systems have not always been based explicitly on the details of American Structuralism and Generative Grammar, the techniques used in typical machine translation systems are based on assumptions about the nature of language that are implicit in mainstream linguistics, as currently represented by GG. It is generally agreed that these techniques apply only to text that approximates controlled language within a domain. The first place to look to discover the source of this restriction would be the assumptions of mainstream linguistics.

3.9.1 Isolated sentences and autonomous syntax

An obvious question to ask is whether linguists of a GG persuasion study general language or domain-specific language. An easy answer is that generative grammarians must be studying general language because they do not take their sample sentences from any one technical domain, such as horticulture or accounting. But why would the techniques based on the assumptions of Generative Grammar work so much better for domain-specific texts if Generative Grammar is oriented toward general language? We should remind ourselves that a domain-specific network is not necessarily high-tech or from the sciences, even though it usually is. The language used to command Winograd's block-world robot was not technical but it was certainly domain-specific. Two aspects of GG suggest that it is dealing with a domain: (1) the restriction to sentences in isolation and (2) the principle of autonomous syntax. In light of the history of GG, we will consider the significance of these two aspects of GG to the general/domain question. After presenting our case that GG deals with a domain, we will explore how ambiguity relates to the general/domain distinction.

Generative Grammar has gone through a substantial evolution since Chomsky published *Syntactic Structures* in 1957. At that time, Generative Grammar was called Transformational Grammar because it had an important component called transformations. Chomsky combined two existing ideas, phrase structure rules and transformations, in a novel way.

Phrase structure rules were borrowed from a branch of mathematics dealing with automata and formal languages. A formal language is a purely artificial language. It has a formal grammar which defines it as a set of sentences using a system of rewrite rules. The phrase structure rules we looked at in chapter 2 are one type of rewrite rules. But we should be careful here. The word *sentence* is used in a special sense to mean a sequence of strings of characters generated by the formal grammar, whether or not the sequence has anything to do with human language. Chomsky was a good mathematician and made a substantial contribution to formal language theory. For example, he defined the Chomsky Hierarchy of different types of formal languages from a finite state grammar (the least powerful) to a context-free grammar (what we have also called a phrase structure grammar) to a context-sensitive grammar (which is totally *insensitive* to context in the sense of situation) to an unrestricted grammar (which can generate any formal language that can be generated algorithmically). Associated with any formal language is an imaginary machine, called an *automaton*, that can tell whether or not a sequence of characters is an element of the language.

Formal language theory has proven very useful in computer science, and computer science majors are usually required to take a course in formal language theory. In particular, most computer programming languages are defined as formal languages, and formal language theory can be useful in developing compilers for programming languages. An important fact to keep in mind is that formal languages are completely self-contained. That is, once a formal grammar has been written by a human and implemented on a computer, it can generate a formal language without any human involvement whatsoever. And the corresponding automaton can tell you whether or not a string of characters is a sentence of the formal language without knowing what sentence came before and what sentence will come next, since each sentence stands completely on its own.

In addition to borrowing phrase structure rules from formal language theory, Chomsky borrowed transformations from his mentor, Zellig Harris, who noted that certain grammatical constructions can be paired, such as active with passive, declarative with interrogative, and affirmative with negative. Any normal speaker of a language can easily transform an interrogative sentence into its declarative counterpart, and some (now outdated) approaches to language learning emphasize such exercises. Harris went further to devise a notation that describes how to go back and forth between a pair of related sentences. What Chomsky did was to combine a phrase structure grammar with a set of transformational rules. His objective was to develop a mathematical notation that would generate a natural language with the minimum possible *power*. Now one might ask what power means in this context and why it should be minimized. For Chomsky, power was defined as the point along his hierarchy of finite-state, context-free, context-sensitive, and unrestricted grammars, with unrestricted having the most power and finite-state having the least. His objective in using the least possible power was to home in on what constitutes a possible human language. His starting assumption was that not all formal languages were possible human languages, and his goal was to define what it means to be a human language. His methodology was to use the least power possible in defining a human language in the hope that the constraints that can be placed on formal grammars while still allowing them to generate all possible human languages will provide important insights into the nature of human language. Note that there is an interesting underlying assumption in Chomsky's thinking: he assumes that any human language can certainly be generated by an unrestricted grammar. That seems like a tautology until you remember that it means that a human language is a special case of a formal language! Suddenly it seems that Chomsky may not be describing natural language at all. To Chomsky the assumption that any human language can be generated by a formal grammar does not seem strange, since it had been proven that any set of sentences that can be generated by an algorithm can be generated by an unrestricted grammar; and surely, from Chomsky's perspective, a human language can be viewed as an infinite set of sentences. With that argument, Chomsky seems to have regained the upper hand, until you remember that the sentences of a formal language must stand on their own. And that brings us back to the first key aspect of Generative Grammar: its restriction to sentences in isolation. Can it be decided whether or not a sentence is acceptable when it is considered in isolation?

As Generative Grammar, both Chomsky's approach and its many non-Chomskyan branches, has evolved from its first version in the 1950s, called Transformational Grammar, to the arrogant version of the 1960s, called The Standard Theory of Syntax, to the Extended Standard Theory of the 1970s, to Government and Binding in the 1980s, to Principles and Parameters (and the Minimalist approach) in the 1990s, it has never wavered in its insistence that sentences should be dealt with in isolation. A non-Chomskyan branch of Generative Grammar can eliminate *transformations* (a prominent element of earlier versions of Chomsky's work) and still be forgiven, but if it strays from the principle of treating isolated sentences as basic, it is banished from the GG family. A grammar is considered adequate if it assigns to each proposed isolated sentence the same score that is assigned by a human native speaker to whom the same sentences are presented. Now the scoring system is not very fine grained: the only allowable scores are acceptable or unacceptable. Unacceptable sentences are marked with an asterisk. From the very beginning of Generative Grammar, there has been a fuzziness about whether the asterisk means *unacceptable* or *ungrammatical*. So long as there are no sentences which are in conflict (grammatical but not acceptable or acceptable but not grammatical) then the fuzziness does not matter. However, sometimes a sentence is acceptable only in a certain situation. For example, consider the following sentence from a standard GG textbook (Radford 1988:134):

*The handle might come suddenly.

In isolation, this sentence does seem strange. Actually, it was given in the text in contrast with the sentence "The handle might come off" and was intended to show that an adverb cannot be substituted for a particle, thereby providing a context for the sentence, in violation of the principle of isolated sentences. Here is a possible context for the sentence which makes it acceptable. You are in a factory, assembling suitcases from parts that appear on a conveyer belt. Your trainer points out that although the big parts have sufficient space between them on the belt for you to react, the handle might come suddenly, and you will not have enough time to attach it and be ready for the next part unless you are alert and efficient.[18] The problem is that what I have just done is taboo in Generative Grammar. One is never allowed to explain the situation in which a sentence was encountered that made it acceptable. Sentences can only be treated in isolation, but this seems unnatural to beginning students of syntax.

Anyone who has taught Generative Grammar has been bombarded repeatedly with questions from students who disagree with one asterisk or another on example sentences in the textbook. The instructor must explain that Generative Grammar does not deal with any unusual readings. *It deals only with the reading that the sentence is taken to have in isolation, without any particular context*.

James McCawley rightly points out (personal communication) that there are at least two ways to speak of a sentence-like object as acceptable or unacceptable. One way is to treat the object in isolation, and another way is to treat the object relative to a meaning and information in context. However, if a sentence is *not* treated in isolation, syntax is no longer autonomous (of meaning).

It would be possible to develop a linguistics in which sentences are treated relative to a meaning. Obviously, such a linguistics would not be a Chomskyan linguistics and would require a total formalization of meaning in order to function as a machine.

The requirement of treating sentences in isolation points strongly toward domain-specific text rather than general text. In other words, Generative Grammar may not even be intended for use with general language! In an interesting novel (as opposed to pulp fiction, which could probably be computer-generated with current technology using minor variations on fixed plots), a sentence at the end of a chapter may require details from the beginning of the chapter or even previous chapters in order to be understood. *Contextual dependence is a hallmark of general language*. No piece of information on any topic can be ruled out in advance as irrelevant to the interpretation of a general-language text until after the text has been read. An editorial about Central Europe may assume an understanding of how clothes were washed before electric washers became available. Before reading a piece of general text, the potentially relevant information is essentially unrestricted—any detail about anything in the history of the world could be relevant. Only after the reader has interpreted the piece can the relevant bits of information be identified.

In contrast, *the desirability of sentences being understandable in isolation is a hallmark of domain-specific text*. An instruction manual that tells a technician how to repair a machine would not be highly prized if a crucial sentence could only be understood in the context of an extended metaphor developed in previous chapters. What *would* be highly prized would be a manual in which one could turn to any section and follow the instructions without remembering what came before. Obvious exceptions would be that one should not enter a step-by-step sequence in the middle, but it would still be desirable to be able to interrupt a step-by-step process, leaving the machine in a state that corresponds to instruction 175, and resuming with instruction 176 after lunch.

3.9.2 Generative Grammar's domain

Therefore, Generative Grammar's restriction to readings in isolation suggests that it treats only domain-specific text. Although this is a logical conclusion, and the logic is backed up by GG's origins in formal language theory, where sentences are also treated in isolation, it may still seem extraordinarily strange that mainstream linguistics would not apply to general language. Wouldn't someone have noticed this enormous oversight? Let me explain an additional insight that helped me come to grips with the claim that GG treats only domain-specific text.

First we must point out that sentences of a domain-specific text are not actually acontextual. Rather, they all have the same context, and that context is the domain itself. A *clean domain* consists of a finite number of fixed core concepts which are tied together into a coherent network of relationships. Once someone has learned all the concepts and their relations, information about the domain can be transmitted very efficiently. Ideally, there is exactly one term per concept. If the domain is shared across experts in several language areas, there may be just one term per language. The goal in a domain network is to allow sentences to be constructed so that they will be understood the same by anyone who is familiar with the domain.

Suppose that generative grammar examples are actually taken from a *domain*, even though they look like sentences of general language. What could that domain be? One day, while reflecting on the general/domain distinction, I suddenly realized that Generative Grammar, in adhering to the principles of isolated sentences and autonomous syntax, has selected the domain of the *utterly boring world*!

Many, perhaps even the majority, of all English sentences are actually excluded from consideration in Generative Grammar. First we eliminate most sentences that pertain to any technical domain. They are not part of the Utterly Boring World (UBW) domain. Then we eliminate all sentences that require any unusual context to be understood; this disqualifies most literature (perhaps all real literature).

A moment's reflection on the sentences used in textbooks and research articles dealing with Generative Grammar reveals that the sentences are often a fairly predictable and uninteresting lot. That is not due to a lack of imagination on the part of the linguist who creates them but is due to the limitations of the sentence-in-isolation approach originated by Chomsky and widely adopted in other approaches.[19]

Even though, in this book, we call the sentences treated by Generative Grammar a domain, that domain is clearly different from a standard technical domain. There is no coherent, well-defined subject matter under consideration, as there is in a technical domain. The UBW domain is instead defined by what Generative Grammar can handle, namely, sentences that can be understood as a syntactic combination of words that have typical meanings. The reason we throw the example sentences of Generative Grammar in with domain languages rather than with general language is that, like domain languages, Generative Grammar allows sentences to be understood without knowing which sentences come before or after. Again, this does not show that generative grammar sentences are acontextual; rather, *they are limited to a uniformly boring context in which nothing truly surprising happens*. The utterly boring world of Generative Grammar may be likened to a soap opera world in which there are endless, predictable variations on who will marry whom, who will divorce whom, and who will cheat on whom.[20]

Further reflection on Generative Grammar as practiced and taught will reveal that there is something missing in generative grammar texts. Even though great emphasis is placed on universals, especially in Chomskyan circles, the term UG (Universal Grammar) often being used to describe the model to highlight the claim that it applies to all languages, and even though examples of syntactic constructions are often given in several languages, I have never seen a section on translation (see also Makkai 1993:15). I suspect that including such a section would raise uncomfortable questions, such as why there is never any mention of the meanings of words other than grammatically based distinctions. Words in the examples in generative grammar texts are assumed to have their *typical* meaning. The devastating effect of this assumption would be highlighted by any attempt to apply UG to the translation of general-language text.

If indeed the restriction to a treatment of sentences in isolation implies boredom and limitations, then why does Generative Grammar retain this restriction? Probably because of the principle of autonomous syntax, mentioned at the beginning of this section as the other domain-oriented aspect of Generative Grammar. Autonomous syntax does not mean syntax unrelated to semantics. Instead, it defines the relation between syntax and semantics. According to autonomous syntax, semantics is interpretive, based on syntax. Thus the meaning of a sentence should be derivable from the syntactic structure of a sentence and from the lexicon. However, the syntactic component must be self-contained, which means that the semantic interpretation module can be removed without disturbing the syntactic module. This implies that the syntactic well-formedness of a sentence cannot depend on its meaning, since its meaning is not available except as an *afterthought* to its syntactic representation. No syntactic rule can refer to semantics, except of course to some part of semantics such as theta roles (abstract cases such as *agent* and *patient*) which is re-baptized as syntax. Semantics plays by different rules. It can and should refer to syntax.[21]

It is clear that the autonomous syntax principle implies the need to treat sentences in isolation. If even one situation-based contextual factor were significant in the decision of whether a sentence should have an asterisk, then that contextual factor would have to be referred to in a syntactic well-formedness rule. Then the syntax component would no longer be autonomous. It would depend on factors outside the uniformity and predictability of the Utterly Boring World. And once a single sentence-external factor from dynamic general language is allowed to influence the assignment or removal of an asterisk, there is no principled basis on which to deny any other factor. The floodgates would open, the single determinative context of the domain would have been disrupted, and sentences could no longer be treated in isolation.

Some may argue that the need to consider context can be delayed until the pragmatics component, after semantic interpretation. They would claim that the semantics component can generate all possible meanings for a sentence without considering context, and that the pragmatics component can then choose the one that is appropriate to the situation. Someone may ask a spouse to close a window by saying, "Honey, it's cold in here and the window is open". To the objection that a request to close the window is the actual meaning of the sentence and that the semantics component should be able to generate it, they would reply that the request is not the meaning of the sentence but an inference based on the meaning of the sentence and that the literal meaning supplied by the semantics component is a sufficient basis from which the pragmatics component can draw the inference that the window-closing request is implicitly being made. However, consider the sentence "Blessed are the young, for they shall inherit the national debt". This statement by Senator Graham can only be understood by recognizing its similarity with a passage in the King James version of the Bible. The scripture in the Beatitudes essentially says, "Blessed are those who are persecuted". Graham is probably suggesting that Americans are persecuting their children by placing on them the burden of a huge national debt. It is not clear how the semantic component can generate any meaning without knowledge far beyond what could be expected to be found in a lexicon. It is not even clear how the syntactic component will handle this sentence without recognizing that it is using King James English grammar. The sentence might even be assigned an asterisk. Yet if the pragmatic component is allowed in just one case to generate a meaning rather than select among alternatives presented by the semantic component, then there would be no well-defined stopping point because more and more aspects of semantic interpretation would be placed in the pragmatic component. This would result in a very different model of language, one in which the semantic component cannot always generate all the possible meanings of a sentence, and one whose pragmatic component could *erase* an asterisk placed on a sentence by the semantic component.

Another class of sentences for which adequate meanings cannot be generated by the **competence** component is illustrated by the sentence "The theory of relativity is blue". The context is an elderly man asking his nephew to get a book from the next room. The man does not remember the title, but refers to the book by topic and color. In context (i.e., knowing that the sentence is intended to identify a book whose title is not known) it is easy to generate a paraphrase such as "The book that concerns the theory of relativity has a blue cover". However, without context, one would have to consider the possibility that every case of incompatibility of attributes could be the identification of a book. If the semantics component approves sentences with incompatible attributes because the pragmatics component *might* discover that the context allows it, then basically everything, including loads of total nonsense, would be approved by the semantics component; and the real burden of semantic interpretation would be turned over to the pragmatics component. On the other hand, if sentences like this one and an infinite variety of others are rejected by the semantics component, then the pragmatics component never gets a chance to consider them in context. Of course, the real problem is that for many sentences there could be any number of other possible interpretations, limited only by context; therefore, the semantics component cannot really deal with meaning without considering context.

The above types of sentences may seem rather unusual. Actually, it is extremely common for a sentence of general language to draw on the context for its interpretation. The previous examples are to show that even theoretically one cannot always put off the use of context until the pragmatic component. In practice, the pragmatic interpretation is what counts, so it does not really help to re-assign work from the semantic component to the pragmatic component. On the other hand, in an informative text that is restricted to a narrow domain, the pragmatics are uniform, and the approach of treating sentences in isolation (well, actually, in the uniform context of the domain) can be workable.

Why has GG been insistent on keeping the principles of autonomous syntax and isolated sentences for so long while the description of many other aspects of language has changed dramatically? Probably because the mixing of syntax and semantics would mean that a GG model would no longer be a self-contained machine which can generate the sentences of a language mechanically, without the presence of a human. Once we leave the Utterly Boring World, there is, as previously discussed, no limit which can be imposed in advance on what might be relevant to the processing of a sentence, and suddenly a mechanical approach of delimited complexity, however large, is no longer sufficient. But the ability to operate as a self-contained machine is a highly important part of the appeal of Generative Grammar.

I am not attempting here to say that GG should or should not drop its insistence on autonomous syntax and the restriction that only sentences in isolation are acceptable objects of study. I am simply suggesting that the principles of autonomous syntax and isolated sentences imply that Generative Grammar, including all of Chomsky's versions and all other branches of Generative Grammar that share these two principles, is actually dealing with a non-technical domain-specific language rather than with general language. As we have already pointed out, this domain language of the Utterly Boring World is different from other domain languages in one respect—the language does not relate to a predefined task or area of knowledge; it grows as needed to define the set of isolated sentences to which Generative Grammar applies.

At this point we hope you are at least willing to explore some consequences of the hypothesis that GG deals with a type of domain rather than with dynamic general language. We will now consider some consequences of this hypothesis for the treatment of ambiguity in Generative Grammar.

3.9.3 Superficial or fundamental ambiguity?

We have discussed ambiguity throughout this book and distinguished two types of ambiguity earlier in this chapter: superficial and fundamental.

Superficial ambiguity, be it a distinction between broad grammatical categories in homographs or more refined cases of polysemy within a category, is the association of one symbol with two or more concepts (sometimes called categories in philosophy, but not to be confused with grammatical categories), such as the symbol 'mouse', which is associated with both a rodent and its metaphorical electronic cousin. In superficial ambiguity, one can make a finite (and in practice very short) list of word senses, each representing a *well-defined* meaning. Thus, a superficially ambiguous symbol can be considered to be the name of a mathematical set of two or more well-defined concepts, and an unambiguous symbol would obviously be the name of a set consisting of just one concept. Superficial ambiguity is simply ambiguity as we normally think of it.

Fundamental ambiguity, the association of one symbol with a dynamically extensible set of concepts, involves the formation of fundamentally new concepts, not just mechanical combinations of existing concepts. New concepts and variations of existing concepts can be formed dynamically by viewing a situation in a novel way, often with the help of metaphor. Martin Kay and his colleagues (Kay et al. 1994:11) put it well. They say that language is *situated* and that words take on shades of meaning according to the situation. There is no limit to the ways the world can be viewed. However, in a system *without* fundamental ambiguity, there could only be one correct basis for viewing the world. This basis for meaning would somehow be *available* to everyone. Since superficial ambiguity could be eliminated using homograph numbers, we could speak of language in such a world as being potentially *unambiguous*, in that it would be lacking in fundamental ambiguity, and the use of homograph numbers could eliminate word-sense ambiguity. If, however, there is no determinate list of word senses and no single basis for deriving them, we do have fundamental ambiguity. Potentially, one person's view of the world could be different from and incompatible with that of another person: and there is no universal basic set of concepts that corresponds to reality to the exclusion of all others. Even if there is one view of the world that is in some sense the best one, we do not need access to that view in order to learn a language, distinguish between true and false statements in that language, nor engage in meaningful dialogue with others.

Which type of ambiguity is treated in Generative Grammar? Although details differ, a crucial assumption underlies all discussions of the semantic component: meaning is derived by bottom-up composition. That is, a syntactic representation of a sentence is processed from the bottom nodes (to which the words—called lexical items, although they should perhaps be called terms—are attached) up to the top of the syntactic tree. Each word attached to a terminal node displays only superficial ambiguity, since each semantic interpretation involves choosing one of the concepts associated with each symbol and combining the basic concepts into a complex concept that represents one meaning of the sentence. These basic concepts are stored in the lexicon as word senses. It is extremely important to note that the semantic interpretation component also treats sentences in isolation, as does the syntactic component. Thus the syntactic component treats the symbols (LTUs) and their syntactic relations, while the semantic component treats the concepts associated with the symbols and combines them into semantic structures. Each semantic structure is assumed to be unambiguous, since it consists of well-defined concepts combined in well-defined ways. Only in the pragmatic component, in which context and situation are finally allowed to be considered, is one of the semantic structures selected as the correct meaning of a sentence in context. Generative Grammar has no room for fundamental ambiguity unless the pragmatic component is allowed to introduce new meanings rather than just select among possible meanings proposed by the semantic component. But in that case, the pragmatic component becomes a magic box which has the power to create meaning but whose operation we do not understand. Such a stance would seriously weaken the claim of Generative Grammar to be an explicit and self-contained model of human language, and we will not pursue it here.

Thus, Generative Grammar uses superficial ambiguity to fulfill its overall purpose of defining a mathematical device (the total grammar, including the syntactic and semantic components) which associates each surface sentence (a simple sequence of characters) with one or more syntactic structures and associates each syntactic structure with one or more semantic structures. In other words, a generative grammar defines the relationship between sound (surface sentences) and meaning (semantic structures). Defining the relationship between sound and meaning, which many would say constitutes knowledge of language, is a classic goal of linguistic theory. Another is explaining how this knowledge is acquired. Astonishingly, however, in Chomskyan linguistics the actual use of language to communicate is considered separable from knowledge and acquisition (Chomsky 1986:3) and outside the realm of linguistics as Chomsky views it. The reason Chomsky finds it natural to separate meaning from communication is that for him, meaning is a purely mathematical object that exists independently of humans. For many others, meaning does not exist outside of the human mind and outside of a communicative situation. One cannot remain neutral on this issue once it is contemplated. Within GG, many believe that language is for communication, but that view is not essential to any approach that is based on autonomous syntax.

Generative Grammar does not allow for fundamental ambiguity. Fundamental ambiguity would be inimical to the principles of autonomous syntax and isolated sentences, since it would make it impossible to store in the lexicon, in advance, all the information necessary for computing all possible meanings of a sentence. Fundamental ambiguity may go beyond Bar-Hillel's concerns. Bar-Hillel said it would be too difficult to store encyclopedic knowledge in a computer. If fundamental ambiguity exists, then no formal representation can capture all knowledge from all possible points of view, past, present, and future. Perhaps Bar-Hillel did think it through along these lines. Chomsky denies that there is fundamental ambiguity, although perhaps not consciously; he believes that all ambiguity is superficial. He is not at all alone in believing this way, nor should he be credited with or blamed for this view. He is simply working within a very well-received framework that has been pursued for centuries. This framework is part of what is sometimes called *objectivism*. It assumes that all meaning can be built up by a process of composition from a pre-defined list of basic concepts. Generative Grammar did not originate the process of composition but rather adopted it uncritically.

Mathematics is a prime example of the bottom-up methodology. (It is not irrelevant that, as previously mentioned, when I began working in machine translation, I was finishing a degree in mathematics.) A formal mathematical proof is based on an explicit list of *undefined* basic terms (else they would not be basic symbols) such as *point, line*, or *set*; a cluster of *unprovable* axioms (else they would be theorems, not axioms); and *undemonstrable* basic rules of proof (else they would not be basic rules). From this self-contained system, any mathematician anywhere in the world, regardless of situation, can verify the proof, so long as he or she has understood the system. An intriguing unanswered question is whether the terms, axioms, and rules of mathematics are an arbitrary human creation or whether they are built into the structure of the universe.

My experience in machine translation tells me that language does not always behave as neatly as mathematics. So perhaps now we have a basis for an explanation of the nature of the difference between dynamic general language and a very narrow and well-defined domain-specific language. Such domain-specific language is a special, highly limited case of general language that *can be treated as if there were no fundamental ambiguity!*[22] In other words, it is a highly limited kind of language that can be treated as if it were something that language, in general, is not. That would explain why there is a continual back-and-forth play between general language and technical terms, yet also explain why techniques that apply to domain-specific language cannot necessarily be extended to general language: general language violates the assumptions about compositional superficial ambiguity on which the techniques are based.

3.9.4 Closed or open infinity?

Another perspective on the general/domain distinction is to propose a distinction between a closed infinity and an open infinity. A closed infinity would be something like the infinite set of positive integers (1, 2, 3, 4, 5, and so on). It is closed because there are no surprises. It is completely predictable. Give me any integer, even one that I have never seen before, and I can immediately generate it mechanically as a completely predictable member of the closed infinity of integers. The *creativity* of Generative Grammar is based on a closed infinity, since it is entirely dependent on the mathematical operation of recursion. The set of phrase markers generated by recursive embedding is entirely predictable. An open infinity is one in which there *are* surprises. An example would be the infinity of plots that can be found in a theoretical novel which has no limits to its length. From the point of view of a novel as a sequence of approximately one million characters (characters such as the letters A, B, C, rather than people), one can predict all possible novels mechanically by permuting all possible sequences of characters. But this falls far short of the mark, since the vast majority of the sequences would not be a valid text at all. A mechanical procedure would only be interesting if it could also determine whether a particular sequence of characters is or is not a novel, or better yet, a good novel. We all know that a novel can be a truly creative work of art or a variation of a well-known plot. The next truly creative novel will be recognized as adding a member to a set of distinct plots, but we cannot, before the writing of that next novel, predict, in any meaningful way, exactly what it will be like. Of course, domains are not completely static, but they draw on general-language principles for changes in their inventory of terms and then are treated as static until they break down, whereas general language should not be static and is not considered *broken* in the case of dynamic metaphor.

A domain language implies a closed infinity of texts, while general language implies an open infinity of texts. Chomsky places himself in the closed infinity camp when he states that "the language faculty is a computational system that is rich and narrowly constrained in structure and rigid in its essential operations" (1986:43). Yet he acknowledges that there is more to language than rigid cause and effect. Later in *Knowledge of Language*, Chomsky writes, "We cannot predict what people will say. Our behavior is not 'caused' by our knowledge, or by the rules and principles that constitute it. In fact, we do not know how our behavior is caused, or whether it is proper to think of it as caused at all, but that is another matter entirely" (1986:260). Presumably, assuming that his two statements are not contradictory, he is saying that we cannot predict what a person will say next, but whatever it is, it will conform strictly to the closed infinity of possibilities offered by the computational system which we call language. There is a tension that stems from an attempt to decide whether all language is a closed or an open infinity. This tension can be resolved by the general/domain distinction. For some purposes, such as technical communication within a domain, it is useful for language to be closed. But we would not want general language to be closed. It is unproductive to try to decide whether all of language is one way or the other, and it is unrealistic to expect a "narrowly constrained" and "rigid" system to explain general language.

3.10 Linguistics and machine translation

At the beginning of the previous section, I claimed that Generative Grammar and machine translation share assumptions about the nature of language. The major assumptions they share are that all language acts like domain-specific language and that a text can be viewed primarily as a sequence of sentences, each to be treated in isolation. In practice this means that they both use bottom-up techniques of semantic composition for sentences in isolation; this restricts their application to domain-specific text or highly uncreative general language. It is far from clear that this limitation would be easy to repair. Indeed, the arguments I have given from considerations drawn from translation theory and practice, together with observations about what generative grammarians do, indicate that it is highly doubtful that their current techniques can be extended to apply to dynamic general language. Entirely new techniques may be needed, and with them, entirely new assumptions, so thoroughly different from current ones as to make their current shape and their future shape appear nearly unrelated.

Statistical approaches based on large parallel corpora are clearly not the answer. If anything, they are even more restricted than grammar-based approaches or domain-specific AI approaches. Using statistics, there is no creativity at all. Pieces of existing sentences are simply regurgitated. After an initial period of enthusiasm for the statistical approach, even its proponents admit that the accuracy of the results is fairly low and is unlikely to improve without additional techniques.

My startling claim that no current techniques will ever be extended to handle dynamic general language is based on observation of language from the point of view of one who has worked intensively with translation, both human and machine. The basis for this claim is translation, but its implication is much broader.

If the hypothesis developed so far in this book is correct, that is, if Generative Grammar describes the UBW (Utterly Boring World) domain rather than describing dynamic general language, and if one is interested in dynamic general language, then an alternative approach to language is needed. Autonomous syntax and isolated sentences are so fundamental to Generative Grammar that it is difficult to imagine how GG would look without these principles, so we will look outside Generative Grammar to work by Lakoff and, in the next chapter, by others.[23] Generative Grammar has effectively confined itself within a wall by insisting on these principles. If someone feels that there is no need to look outside the wall of GG and its basic assumptions for an adequate account of dynamic general language, and if that person claims that general language is fully computable, then the burden of proof is on that person to explain how to design a machine translation system so that it provides fully automatic high-quality translation of unrestricted text, or at least to explain why so much effort to do so with approaches based on the assumptions of Generative Grammar has failed to achieve this goal.

Roy Harris (1990) suggests that Generative Grammar and most other approaches to language share the basic assumption that the systematicity of language is internal. These approaches he groups under the heading *segregationist*. The emerging alternative view places external social practices at the heart of language. This view he calls *integrationist*. Montague Grammar is squarely in the segregationist camp. Systemic linguistics has in some ways crossed the line into integrationist approaches. The problem for machine translation is that once one firmly crosses the line to become integrationist, the approach can no longer be programmed to run on its own. This is because there is currently no way to program into a computer context and situation outside of domains. Some have even tried programming multiple domains, but this still falls short of a computable approach to general language and keeps machine translation from treating general language.

George Lakoff, who came from within Generative Grammar as a proponent of Generative Semantics, challenged the autonomous syntax and isolated sentence principles long ago. We will look at his recent work in cognitive linguistics as an approach to language that may help us deal with dynamic general language, though not in a fully computable manner as Chomsky would expect. This will in turn lead us, in the next chapter, into a consideration of the nature of categories (that is, conceptual categories, or concepts), how they are grounded (that is, what they are based on), and whether they exhibit 'fundamental ambiguity'.

3.11 George Lakoff

In his book *Women, Fire, and Dangerous Things* (1987), George Lakoff describes two contrasting approaches to language: objectivism and experientialism. Objectivism is the name Lakoff gives to a traditional view with ancient roots. In its modern form, objectivism assumes that

> rational thought consists in the manipulation of abstract symbols and that these symbols get their meaning via a correspondence with the world, objectively construed, that is, independent of any organism. (Lakoff 1987:xii)

The *organism* referred to is the human organism. The abstract symbols may be sequences of characters (which are often called words).

Lakoff then lists more specific aspects of the objectivist view (pp. xii-xiii and throughout the book), including the following:

(a) Thought is the mechanical manipulation of abstract symbols.

(b) The mind is an abstract machine, manipulating symbols in the way a computer does.

(c) Symbols get their meaning via correspondences to things in the real world. There is only one correct correspondence, the one that corresponds to the structure of the real world. In terms of the discussion in this chapter, superficial ambiguity of symbols is allowed, but no fundamental ambiguity, since there is just one definitive set of things that symbols can correspond to.

(d) Thought is abstract and does not require a human body (a computer will do as well). Thought is independent of any limitations of the human body, the human perceptual system, and the human nervous system.

(e) Machines that do no more than mechanically manipulate symbols that correspond to things in the world are capable of meaningful thought and reason.

(f) Thought is atomistic, in that it can be completely broken down into simple building blocks which are combined into complexes and manipulated by rules.

(g) Thought is logical in the narrow technical sense used by philosophical logicians; that is, it can be modeled accurately by systems of the sort used in mathematical logic.

Lakoff points out that not all of these assumptions are held by every objectivist, but most hold many of them.

Central to such views is the notion of category. On the objectivist view, a category is a mathematical set, and something is either a full-fledged member of the category or not a member at all. Things are in the same category if and only if they have certain properties in common. All conceptual categories must be symbols or symbolic structures which can designate categories in the real world, or in some possible world. And the world must come already divided up into nice, clean categories whose members all share certain properties.

Lakoff's alternative to objectivism he calls experientialism (pp. xvi-xvii and throughout the book). On the experiential view, thought is embodied. Meaningful thought and reason are directly tied to the nature of the organism doing the thinking, including the nature of its body, its interaction with its environment, and its social character. In experientialism, each of the aspects of objectivism listed above finds a contrasting aspect as follows:

(a) Thought is not just a mechanical manipulation of abstract symbols. It uses **cognitive models** that are meaningful.

(b) Our minds do not manipulate symbols the same way a computer does. General cognitive mechanisms for recognizing the similarity of mental images and for using metaphor are essential to language.

(c) Thought is imaginative and goes beyond correspondence to things in the real world. There is not just one correct view of the world.

(d) Thought is embodied. It is influenced by the nature of the human body.

(e) Thought is more than the mechanical manipulation of symbols. For example, it has *gestalt* properties, that is, properties of the whole that are not straightforward combinations of properties of the parts.

(f) Thought is not atomistic. We can start with fairly complex concepts and then become more specific or more general; we do not have to build up from the bottom, starting with atomistic concepts.

(g) Mathematical logic is insufficient to model human thought.

Lakoff's view of categories is much richer than the view of categories as mathematical sets. He reviews a large body of experimental research on human conceptual categories. It is well established that they display **prototype effects**; that is, some members of the category are privileged as better members of the category than others. Lakoff calls human categories **cognitive models**. Some are scalar (such as 'tall man' on a scale of inches). Some are metonymic and metaphorical. Some are radial; that is, they involve several models around a center. The various models are motivated by the center but are not entirely predictable. Each of these types of category accounts for some prototype effects. In classical categories, all members have an equal status; therefore, prototype effects are not adequately accounted for in classical categories.

Lakoff argues convincingly that metaphor is not a *sideline* of language but rather a *pervasive* aspect; this goes a long way toward explaining dynamic creation of meanings in general language.

The reader is encouraged to refer to Lakoff's 1987 book for a much more detailed explanation of arguments against objectivism and for experientialism (which is the basis for Lakoff's cognitive linguistics) and for an interesting account of metaphor, in which dynamic meaning is unpredictable yet motivated. The phrase "unpredictable yet motivated" is very important. From an objectivist point of view, the only alternative to predictability is randomness, complete disorder. However, from an experiential point of view, a phenomenon may not be predictable in advance, but may still be highly constrained in that it must be possible to see its motivation after the fact. We have seen that the translation of a new usage of a lexical unit in general language is not predictable by some mechanical procedure, but when an acceptable translation is found, it can always be analyzed after the fact as being motivated by previous meanings. We may not know how a particular language will translate 'run' in the sentence "When he washed his new shirt, the colors ran", but we know that once we see the translation it will make sense, and we will see the motivation for it.

3.12 The wall between Lakoff and objectivist approaches

The connection between Lakoff's work and the general/domain distinction is fairly obvious. Experientialism seems to be concerned with dynamic general language rather than with domain-specific language. Objectivism seems to be the intellectual framework for a domain-specific treatment of language, such as Generative Grammar or other segregationist approaches, which we can now call objectivist approaches. In a later book, Lakoff and Turner (1989) apply their approach to the analysis of poetry, especially poetic metaphor. There is no attempt to require that sentences be treated in isolation, and no attempt to keep syntax autonomous, since these two principles—central to Generative Grammar and consistent with objectivism—are not consistent with the experiential view. Generative Grammar and machine translation both shy away from poetry (some would say it is outside their *domain*); experientialism is drawn to it. Clearly, the wall between Lakoff and objectivism is the same general/domain distinction we have been discussing all through this chapter.

If Lakoff's approach can provide an insightful analysis of poetry, while Generative Grammar cannot, then why has there not been a wholesale exodus from Generative Grammar? One real but cynical answer would be that too many tenured professors of linguistics are not at the stage in their career where a major change in paradigm is likely. But what about the new generation of linguists? Are they ready to embrace experientialism? I think that many are not ready to make the paradigm shift because they are not willing to give up computability. Unsurprisingly, Lakoff's approach cannot be programmed using domain-specific techniques, and no other techniques are currently available for processing natural language on a computer. Lakoff's approach can only be applied using the insight of a human linguist. Therefore it is not computable; that is, it is not a self-contained algorithmic process that can be converted to a computer program that runs without human interaction beyond initial input.

To my knowledge, no fully integrationist approach is computable and therefore all such approaches are disqualified from forming the basis for machine translation. Why are we so fascinated by computable approaches to language that eliminate the human element? In the next chapter, we will review the history of this fascination with language as a machine from the point of view of philosophy. Within linguistics, at the time of the Chomskyan revolution, the American Structuralists were striving for a mechanical approach to linguistics which would allow them to feed a corpus of transcriptions of speech of an unknown language into a computer and have the computer do their work for them by identifying the phonemes and morphemes of the language. Unfortunately, they bit off more than they could chew. Chomsky came along and said that it is allowable to use human insight in setting up the rules of a grammar so long as it could run on its own once set up. He was smart in that he provided job security so long as they tinkered with the grammar of a language, making at least apparent progress, while at the same time satisfying the yearning for an objectivist model of language that does something without human intervention.

I propose that it would be problematical to be forced to choose between Chomsky and Lakoff, between computable domain-specific approaches and non-computable general-language approaches, between segregationist and integrationist approaches. Both are needed. Integrationist approaches are needed when humans analyze language and discuss general language with other humans. Domain-specific approaches are needed when humans want computers to process language for them. Even if we disagree on its assumptions, we can salvage objectivism by using it as a framework for analyzing domain-specific text. As mentioned before, a domain-specific sublanguage or controlled language is a restricted form of language which can be treated like something it is not. It is not a description of the one way the world objectively exists, but by using human intelligence and dynamic general language to build a wall around some set of ideas that are internally consistent, the ideas inside that wall can take on a life given to it by the humans who create and maintain the wall; in other words, the domain can be treated as if it were the real world, the whole universe, so long as one is careful to stay within the wall around the domain.

That is to say, general language provides the metalanguage and, effectively, the metaphysics of domain languages, especially controlled languages; and objectivism can provide a model for treating domain language. In a domain language, it is desirable to define the concepts so that the meaning of a sentence can be obtained through a bottom-up combination of its terminological units. It is essential to point out that relatively few texts, even domain-specific texts, faithfully conform to a purely bottom-up notion of meaning. Most LSP texts are a mixture of general language and domain-specific terminology. We are discussing the extremes without claiming that most texts are at the extremes. In some cases, domain-specific texts can be highly controlled. Any exceptions to bottom-up processing are simply removed from the domain language until the domain language is consistent with the framework of objectivism. We do not have this luxury when working with general language in context. For the purposes of information retrieval, it is very useful to require that any mention of a concept use a consistent technical term. Dynamic metaphor is not allowed, even though many of the technical terms were first created using metaphor then standardized or frozen. The standard paradigm for machine translation (analysis, transfer, and synthesis) can apply because the language is adjusted artificially until it does apply. Everyone is happy except the person who wants to use a computer to process language and is not willing to conform to the requirements of a controlled language.

Chomsky's approach applies only to certain extreme examples of domain-specific languages and is not extendable to dynamic general language. Lakoff's approach seems to apply to general language, but it may be more powerful than is necessary for working with a sufficiently controlled domain-specific language. Such a dual-method approach is not uncommon. In engineering, one can usually use Newtonian physics and ignore relativistic effects. However, if one is designing a particle accelerator in which the particles travel at ninety-nine percent of the speed of light, one can no longer ignore Einsteinian physics. If one is designing a normal light bulb, quantum effects can be ignored, but when one deals with individual photons, quantum mechanics must be taken into account. Yet one does not want to use the more complex relativistic or quantum mechanics if they are not needed. These examples are perhaps not good, because domain-specific language is an extreme case which dictates less complex tools rather than more complex ones. A better example might be the computation of the speed at which an object falls. If one can restrict the situation to eliminate friction by creating a vacuum, then the computations are greatly simplified. Likewise, restricting language to a narrow domain greatly simplifies computation by allowing the domain to be treated according to objectivism.

Now we are in a position to comment further on why it is not realistic to try to create a list of universal sememes and to map words of general vocabulary onto and out of them. Although there is every reason to believe that the universal sememe approach can be used within a domain of knowledge shared by speakers of various languages (one simply adjusts the concepts until the approach works), there is no reason to assume that it is possible to list all the senses of a lexical unit that represents a general-language category, since new ones can be created as desired. And there is no reason to assume that each language has the same general semantic network as every other language—that is, unless we all have the same innate ideas. This possibility raises the question of what the positions of Chomsky, Lakoff, and others are on the origin of our concepts.

Chomsky's position on the acquisition of syntax is well known. He claims that there is an innate language faculty in which *switches* are set while one is still a small child, based on meager linguistic data. The faculty then becomes the core syntactic component of one language or another.

Chomsky has written less that discloses his position on the acquisition of concepts. However, he does state that a generative grammar of a particular language is "a theory that is concerned with the form and meaning of expressions of this language" (1986:3). He has claimed repeatedly that language acquisition depends on an innate language faculty. Since he does *not* qualify language acquisition to be solely the acquisition of syntax, even though in practice he deals primarily with syntactic rules, we will assume that the possible concepts, as well as the possible syntactic rules, are, for Chomsky, somehow determined by the language faculty. What is more important is that they are devoid of fundamental ambiguity. This is consistent with an interview (Horning 1991) in which Chomsky talks about the concept *climb*: "Every child learns it perfectly right away. Now that can only mean one thing. Namely, human nature gives us the concept *climb* for free." The interviewer notes that Chomsky goes on to submit that the same is probably true for "most concepts embodied in words". Chomsky clarifies his disbelief in fundamental ambiguity when he asserts, "This is the way we learn language. We simply learn the label that goes with the preexisting concept". Strictly speaking, the claim we are making here—that there *is* fundamental ambiguity—is not incompatible with the idea of an innate cognitive capacity of some kind. It is incompatible with the idea that all concepts for all people are built from one universal set of primitive concepts.

Lakoff's position on the acquisition of concepts is that concepts are not directly determined by the nature of reality. Rather, they are tied to the nature of our physical bodies, our interaction with the environment, and our social character. He seems to imply that there is not just one set of possible concepts (1987:261).

I invite you to explore your own position and that of others on the pivotal issue of the acquisition of concepts.

As discussed above, the origin of domain-specific concepts has been resolved. They originate within general language by the dynamic process of creating new LTUs. These LTUs become stable and form terms which can be processed in a straightforward way within a domain, using a well-developed tradition of bottom-up composition, because that is the intent of their creation.

I have suggested that a well-defined, coherent domain-specific language can be usefully treated according to the methods of objectivism, but that language in general requires a more dynamic approach, perhaps along the lines of experientialism. What is not yet resolved is how we acquire the categories of our *general-language* network that allow us to communicate and to create domain-specific networks. In the next section we will consider some philosophical traditions that bear on the nature of language and ultimately on the question of the relation between our concepts and the real world, and we will present the beginnings of a new approach to how we acquire concepts in general language.

4 Possibilities

4.1 The tradition of bottom-up processing from primitives

We have seen that when we create a narrow, well thought-out domain we build a wall around it so that from inside the domain the universe appears to be orderly and computable. Concepts are given to us by the creators of the domain, and most of those concepts are unambiguously linked to terms in various languages. At worst, only superficial ambiguity is encountered in texts restricted to the domain and even superficial ambiguity is easily eliminated unless two uses of the same term both have a strong history of use within the domain. Meaning can be built up mechanically from the basic concepts of the domain, and texts can be translated and otherwise processed using computers. In other words, objectivism (as described in the previous chapter) reigns. The origin of the concepts of a domain is not an issue. They are created using general language and maintained inside the wall of a domain by humans who are influential in the domain. But what about concepts outside any wall—the concepts of dynamic general language? Where do they come from? How do we acquire them? In sum, domains are created by humans who already possess general language; but how is general language possible? These questions are the concerns of this chapter.

We will begin by examining the possibility that general language is adequately accounted for by the tradition of bottom-up processing from primitives, that is, the view that general language works as follows:

(a) There is no fundamental ambiguity; that is, there is one and only one set of primitive concepts, and they are somehow available to us as atomic building blocks. Some words are linked directly to atomic concepts.

(b) Meaning is generated from the bottom up by combining the atomistic concepts mentioned in (a) into more complex concepts in accordance with certain rules. Sentences and some complex words are linked to these complex concepts.

We have already concluded in the previous chapter that there *is* fundamental ambiguity in general language, so we have rejected (a). And (b) is based on (a), so we have already rejected this tradition as a possible explanation of language outside of walls. Nevertheless, in this section we[24] will re-examine assumptions (a) and (b) because of their importance within Western philosophy; this will include examining views on the origin and acquisition of atomistic concepts. This will lead us to the issue of grounding versus arbitrariness.

Assumption (b) has a long tradition. Its proponents include just about everyone who has taken mathematics as a model for intellectual work and for the operation of the intellect itself. This tradition includes Galileo, Descartes, Hobbes, Newton, and Hume. For some, it is only a methodology of intellectual analysis, to be employed when one wants to understand and explain accurately and thoroughly. Newton seems to be a clear example of the methodological branch. Perhaps this branch would be amenable to the general/domain distinction we have developed in this book and would agree that the methodology is useful within a domain but would not claim that it provides a complete explanation of human language. For others, it is an epistemological model of meaning acquisition that applies to all language. Hume and Chomsky are examples of the epistemological branch.

Assumption (a) places limitations on the range of answers we can give to the question of how it is that language can be meaningful, that is, how it is that we can acquire concepts and deploy them in our perceptual experience and in our thinking. How does it come about that reality provides us with a basis for acquiring concepts and rules that we use in forming sentences and linking sentences together in discourse in order to communicate and reason?

4.1.1 Concepts and rules as given

One type of answer to questions about the nature and acquisition of both concepts and rules is that they are **given**. In philosophy, this means that they are somehow provided to us or instilled in us independently of our use of language. We will emphasize the acquisition and application of *concepts*, treating the acquisition and application of *rules* only lightly.

One idea of the way concepts might be given is this: they are acquired in the first place by direct experience with things in the world and later applied in the same way. That is, we hear words spoken by those around us, and, by paying attention to situations in which those words are used, we discover what objects, properties, or circumstances the words apply to. On this view, a concept is merely a mediation between a word and a directly experienced thing. When we master a connection, that is, a hook-up, we have mastered the relevant concept and we can thereafter use the word accurately ourselves.

Is there anything wrong with this common-sense picture? Yes, and it has frequently been pointed out by philosophers. We cannot identify a thing prior to having some kind of concept to apply to it. To identify an object as being a book, we need to already have the concept of a book. Once we have some concept of what a book is and once we have identified a book, we can refine our concept to distinguish hardcover and paperback books (that is, if we have concepts to distinguish those two kinds of cover). Or we can discover that the object we thought was a book is really a container to hide a bottle of whiskey. But we cannot identify anything at all if we have no starting concepts. At least in the case of atomistic concepts, we encounter the dilemma of having to acquire a concept and apply it in order to acquire it. Applying the concept acontextually, asocially, once it is somehow obtained, is, as we shall see, equally problematic. So this account of how concepts are given invokes either (a) the necessity of acquiring and applying concepts prior to acquiring them, or else (b) the necessity of making identifications of objects *without* applying concepts to them. Neither of these alternatives make any sense at all. For when we try to correlate language with the world, the world we encounter is one we are already describing using language. In some quarters this has been called *the problem of the given*; in others, it is the insight that we cannot escape the circle of language. Philosophers may not agree on how to solve the problem of the given, but they agree that it is a serious problem.

Plato's intuitions about this problem lie behind his doctrine that says we must have encountered, prior to our mortal cognitive experience, exemplars of at least the key concepts that we use in organizing our experience. Although we may not be able to decide whether Plato views our pre-mortal experience as myth or fact, we can be sure of his belief that it is by the **eye of the soul**, a faculty of direct intellectual intuition presumably operative in that existence, that we apprehend the pure forms or ideas of triangularity, circularity, justice, and so forth, in a manner that does not presuppose that we have these forms in mind already. Possessing familiarity with the forms—in our modern parlance we would say possessing the concepts—we can in this life recognize and categorize the various particular things we encounter, none of which is a perfect exemplar of the categorizing idea we employ. Plato's strategy of providing for a *pre-provisioning* of our concepts is just one attempt at avoiding the circularity present in supposing that we acquire *all* our concepts and/or rules using concepts and rules, but of course it just pushes back the problem of the given to some other realm of existence.

Another attempt to solve the problem of the given is the doctrine of innate ideas. Many philosophers, most notably Descartes and Leibniz, believe that at least some concepts and/or rules are innate; nowadays, we say, 'built-in' or 'hard-wired'. Descartes holds that at least one concept, and probably not more than one, is innate, namely, the idea of God. He also believes in a built-in capacity (also called a faculty) for rationally evaluating one's own judgments or beliefs, which are for the most part arrived at through empirical experience. By means of this faculty, which he calls the 'light of nature', the individual can tell whether a proposition is necessarily true, that is, whether it cannot possibly be false.

Descartes' 'light of nature' seems more an ability (one that works in a rule-following way) than a concept. When we review the history of philosophy, it appears that what has generally been thought of as innate ideas are either rules governing the operations of the mind or a faculty that operates according to such rules. Even Kant's 'pure categories' are not concepts or categories in any ordinary sense, but rather principles or rules, such as the principle of causality. As they have usually been conceived historically, innate ideas lack content. Chomsky on the other hand has claimed for human beings innate ideas in both the faculty and the content senses, which makes him a bit of an oddity in the tradition of which he claims to be a part. It is difficult to evaluate the position of other linguists on this issue since they have not generally written about it. Indeed, most people have probably never really addressed the problem of the given at all. For them, concepts are just *there*.

Concerning innate rules, Chomsky has proposed that people are born with a genetically determined language faculty, which includes a set of possible rules of grammar for which we unconsciously choose options as a child learning a language, based on the sentences we hear. As Chomsky has insisted, the idea of some kind of innate faculty is in itself innocuous. Surely children possess innate capacities, and just as surely, there is some physiological realization of these capacities that supports, among other things, our linguistic behavior. These claims are no more objectionable than the idea of physiological support for vision, including an eyeball and nerves that go from the retina to the brain and the idea that the brain is somehow predisposed to support sight. Our mouth, throat, and brain are certainly predisposed to support speech. But this claim of some innate capacity is not the issue raised by the problem of the given and neither is it the substance of Chomsky's claim about language acquisition, namely the claim that the innate faculty can generate language internally, needing only minimal data from outside to decide how to set each of various switches to one of the settings among the options allowed by the language faculty.

4.1.2 Our intellectual heritage

Let us survey enough of our communal Western intellectual heritage to appreciate the position of Chomsky and others with regard to the subject of innate concepts. Most present-day intellectuals work in a broad tradition that owes much to Gottlob Frege and to the *early* work of Ludwig Wittgenstein, the author of the *Tractatus Logico-Philosophicus* (often referred to as the Tractatus). As Gordon Baker and Peter Hacker have pointed out (Baker and Hacker 1984), this tradition radically separates the *sense* of a sentence from its *force*. An interrogative sentence is seen as having the sense of a declarative sentence plus the force of a question. For example, "Does John own a dog?" has the sense of "John owns a dog" plus the force of a question: "Is it the case that John owns a dog?" In Generative Grammar, this distinction has become the supposedly clean separation of *semantics* from *pragmatics*, and surely it influenced Chomsky's early decision to use the declarative form of a sentence as its **deep structure** and to use a transformation to form an interrogative. Let us briefly trace this heritage, starting with Descartes, along the lines described by Baker and Hacker.

Broadly speaking, modern philosophy starts with Bacon in England (1561-1626) and Descartes on the European continent (1596-1650) with the coming of the seventeenth century. There was tremendous excitement over the progress of the physical sciences, starting with Kepler and Galileo and culminating with Newton. Nature had finally become intelligible to human reason and appeared to be subject to mathematical laws. But there was now a gulf between appearance and reality. The world appeared to humans in terms of noise, odors, warmth, and other sensations, but reality was now viewed as millions of invisible particles in motion. During the seventeenth and eighteenth centuries, language had little claim on philosophical attention, because ideas were typically assumed to be language-independent. Thought has no need for language and goes along quite well without it. However, when it is time to communicate ideas to another person, language is needed as a vehicle. Ideas are then encoded into language, transmitted to another person by speech or writing, and then decoded back into language-independent ideas. According to this view, words correspond to ideas. Words which can be defined in terms of other words correspond to complex ideas, and a word which cannot be defined in terms of other words corresponds directly to a basic idea. This is essentially assumption (a) from the beginning of this chapter. This assumption actually did not begin in the seventeenth century; Augustine was essentially in agreement with it. In chapter 1, Augustine's adherence to this view of language was mentioned in connection with Robinson's approach to translation theory.

Assumption (b), however, would have to wait until the latest blossoming of *formal* logic, starting in the nineteenth century. Logic was viewed by Descartes as a tool to help people think correctly, not as an aspect of natural language. Early formal logic based on syllogisms, which was later to be extended and become very important in both philosophy and linguistics, fell into disrepute during the seventeenth century (see Baker and Hacker 1984:26), largely because of Descartes' criticism that it did not guarantee correct results unless one started with correct premises. Today, this criticism seems ridiculous, much like criticizing a calculator because it only gives the correct answer if you enter in accurate starting numbers; but as mentioned above, Descartes believed that humans are endowed with the intellectual ability to identify statements that surely must be true, even those that are not implied by other statements we have already identified as true. He therefore had a relatively low opinion of formal logic, because it only allowed one to draw conclusions that are already implicit in the starting assumptions of the system. Today, no one expects any kind of logic to do more than that.

The most influential textbook on logic from the era, the *Port Royal Logic* (originally published in 1662), took pains to point out what at that time was obvious (in a discussion of whether the meaning of a word is arbitrary):

> It is indeed a thing quite arbitrary whether we join a certain idea to a certain sound [i.e., a word], rather than to another: but the ideas are not arbitrary things, and do not depend on our fancy.... [A man's reasoning] is not an assemblage of names according to a convention which depends entirely on the fancy of men; but a solid and effective judgment on the nature of things. (Introduction)

This quote reflects both a belief in one set of universal, language-independent ideas [sememes] and the infallibility of proper logic in arriving at an understanding of the true nature of things.

The mid-nineteenth century saw a revolution in logic. George Boole, a mathematician, recast syllogistic reasoning in terms of algebraic operations on sets, thanks to a then recent generalization of the notion of algebra in theoretical mathematics. Boolean algebra has an appeal to someone who is mathematically oriented. When I was a child, I played a game called WFF (pronounced 'woof') and Proof, which was a popularization of Boolean algebra. A WFF is a well-formed formula in which letters stand for statements that are combined in various ways to construct proofs. I was so intrigued by Boolean algebra that I learned enough about it to be able to use it to design logic circuits for a special-purpose computer I constructed as a science fair project. Boolean algebra did not include a bottom-up combining of concepts within a sentence, but it did show how propositions could be combined from the bottom up. Nevertheless, Boole did not see his algebra as applicable to the study of language. Rather, he viewed it as the algebra of thought.

Then toward the end of the nineteenth century, Frege (1848-1925) used another then recent advance in mathematics, namely function theory, to further evolve formal logic into what is called *predicate calculus*, which was further developed by Russell and Whitehead in the early twentieth century. For the first time, much more complex proofs could be stated in terms of formal logic. Then Wittgenstein, in his monumental 1921 *Tractatus*, made the jump of applying formal logic to natural language by proposing that the hidden structure of *any* possible language, including human language, is akin to that of a formal, function-theoretic, logical calculus from the Boole-Frege-Russell-Whitehead tradition. It is generally supposed that Wittgenstein's ideas caught on with the so-called logical positivists of the 1920s and 1930s, who took inspiration from his work, but they read it through an epistemological filter which distorted it. Whereas the *Tractatus* itself did not make assumption (a), their interpretation of it did. (As for assumption (b), Wittgenstein's use of truth-tables expressed Boolean concepts in a way that enabled logicians to think very explicitly of the ways primitives can be combined from the bottom up.) Logical positivism went into eclipse about the time Generative Grammar began to attract attention. Philosophers in the 1960s devoted much energy to informal analysis of ordinary language, inspired in large part by Wittgenstein's later work and the sensitive studies of J.L. Austin. But recently linguistics and philosophy have come close together once again with a renewed interest in formal logic. Some prominent contemporary philosophers, such as Dummett and Davidson, feel that the primary task of philosophy is to construct a theory of meaning for natural language.

Developments in linguistics since the beginning of the century, although not at first synchronized, have reinforced developments in philosophy. At the turn of the century, while formal logic was flourishing in philosophy, Saussure made the case for modern synchronic linguistics as opposed to diachronic linguistics (usually called historical linguistics), which had dominated linguistics in the 1800s. By introducing the notion of *langue* (the abstract structure of language) versus *parole* (actual speech), Saussure allowed for language to be viewed as a self-contained sign system with a psychological reality of its own. Within *langue*, Saussure identified the sentence as a primary unit of analysis and, within the sentence, two axes: the paradigmatic (which he actually called the associative axis and which deals with morphological patterns such as the various inflected forms of a verb) and the syntagmatic (which deals with how words are combined to form sentences and was the beginning of modern syntax). Thus was born structuralism. Assumption (a) from the beginning of this chapter continued its long tradition and was built into Structuralism with Saussure's distinction between *signifiant* (the sign, that is, the word itself) and *signifié* (the meaning of the word, the concept) without addressing the problem of the given. After an interlude with behaviorism (American Structuralism from the 1930s to 1950s) during which it was taboo to discuss meaning, Chomsky, in the late 1950s, picked up on Saussure's framework, retaining the synchronic perspective, retaining roughly the *langue* versus *parole* distinction as the competence versus **performance** distinction (although for Chomsky, syntax is clearly in competence while for Saussure it was shared between *langue* and *parole*). As mentioned in chapter 3, Chomsky borrowed the notion of transformations from his mentor, Zellig Harris, and made in linguistics a move somewhat parallel to Wittgenstein's move to bring human language under the purview of philosophy. Wittgenstein posited a hidden, formally representable structure underlying natural language—though he did not suppose that the primitive elements of that structure possess any psychological or even physiological reality. Chomsky posited deep structure underlying **surface structure**, using transformations to relate the two levels, and has stated often that syntax is tied to a physiological reality in the brain. The issue of *psychological* realism has been heavily debated within Generative Grammar. The use of transformations in Generative Grammar has diminished, but the notion of multiple levels or strata has remained, even in non-transformational branches of Generative Grammar such as Lexical Functional Grammar. As Chomsky introduced semantics into Generative Grammar in the 1960s, the revival of formal logic, also in the 1960s, allowed a match made in history, as mainstream linguistics and mainstream philosophy came together, linguistics borrowing predicate calculus from philosophy as its semantic representation and philosophy borrowing deep structure from linguistics as its syntactic representation, each being spared a lot of work in developing the piece missing from their discipline and each agreeing implicitly that between the two, language can be completely analyzed (except for seemingly incidental aspects such as human communication).

Thus by 1970, linguistics and philosophy had agreed on the following rough sketch of a theory of meaning. The objective was to provide a formal explanation of the human capacity to understand the meaning of sentences never heard before. By *formal explanation* was meant a mathematical system which could operate on its own without the human body, not even needing the human brain. This was a radical version of dualism in which meaning is not essentially tied to the body or anything human, in other words, a type of objectivism as described in chapter 3. The method of explaining meaning was to formulate an explicit set of principles which show how to derive the meaning of a sentence from the meanings of constituent words, using the structure of the sentence. The shape of the method was to identify three aspects of language: syntax, which is the science of constructing grammatical sentences; semantics, which is the study of the meaning of sentences using formal logic representations as mechanically derived from their syntactic representation and the lexicon; and pragmatics (an aspect generally ignored on the basis that syntax and semantics should be completed first), which is the study of those features of sentences related to their use by speakers in particular contexts.

It should be clear by now that Chomsky was not as innovative as it might first seem. He did break away from aspects of American Structuralism which seemed to him overly restrictive (such as strict limitation to the taxonomy of an un-elicited corpus and prohibitions on the discussion of meaning and universals) to join in with a long intellectual tradition starting at the time of Descartes or before and culminating in syntax and semantics as separate from humans but compatible with philosophy and computers. All modern linguistics which is computable, not just Generative Grammar, shares this syntax/semantics/pragmatics framework.

Just before this a-human view of language came together in the 1960s, helped along by Wittgenstein's early work, Wittgenstein's last treatise, *Philosophical Investigations*, was published posthumously. In it, Wittgenstein rejected or radically revised much of the *Tractatus*, and developed a more recognizably human analysis of meaning. In this new approach pragmatic considerations are involved in the determination and the understanding of meaning, not just in the deployment of language whose meaning has already been established. Baker and Hacker agree with the later Wittgenstein and propose that the a-human approach be abandoned wholesale—but they also acknowledge that these ideas are so deep-seated that such an abandonment is extremely unlikely any time soon. If the general/domain distinction is valid, then we do not need to and do not even want to abandon this model but can simply recycle it for use with domain-specific controlled languages for the processing of language on computers. If computers are so underprivileged as to be deprived of minds capable of processing human language in its generality, then humans, thanks to the flexibility of their minds, can learn to work with domain-specific language that computers can *understand* in the sense of the mainstream model of meaning. Computer programming languages, such as Pascal, Basic, and C, can be considered as extreme examples of domain-specific languages. Though people may talk to their horses as if they understood all their stories, the rider knows that the horse responds to a domain-specific set of instructions and is quite happy to use this controlled language in order to benefit from the services of a horse. Computers can deal with controlled languages so complex that we can almost pretend that they understand general language, until we ask them a question outside their domain.

4.1.3 Chomsky's solution to the problem of the given

We have seen how Chomsky's approach to language is a product of his intellectual heritage. However, that heritage did not provide a solution to the problem of the given, at least not one that Chomsky was willing to use. There have been thinkers who have argued that God is the source of our ideas. Although Chomsky may be a believer, it was not fashionable in the 1950s to use God as the source of our initial concepts. And until Chomsky got into semantics, the problem of the given was irrelevant to his work. When Chomsky began in the 1950s, he presented a purely mathematical approach to language in which *language* was defined as an unordered infinite set of *sentences*, where each *sentence* was merely a sequence of characters that corresponded, completely devoid of context, to the characters (letters and punctuation) one would produce when typing a meaningful sentence of human language. His goal was to build an abstract finite *machine*, called a formal grammar, which would define or *generate* (hence, generative grammar) exactly the infinite set of sentences of the language. The whole endeavor was merely a game, and anyone who was willing to play by the rules was invited to join in. One of the rules was the acceptance of the assumption that any machine which could randomly spit out *acceptable* sentences, whatever that means, and not spit out *unacceptable* sentences, had somehow captured the essence of human language. Meaning was only a minor consideration at that time, but there was the hope that at some point in the future certain connections could be established between this machine called a grammar and meanings of sentences. Chomsky even hoped early on that his mathematical model would shed some insight on the mind. Later, he added an interpretive semantics component to his model, buying into the linguistic and philosophical tradition we have outlined, and formulated ideas about language acquisition.

By the mid-1960s, Chomsky had discovered Descartes and others of the Cartesian period and felt an affinity between the ideas he had developed (independently, he supposed) and the Cartesian approach. An innate faculty seemed to him necessary for the acquisition of language; reception of the data of early-life experiences could not by itself account for our linguistic performances. It can be instructive to consider why Chomsky considered a child's linguistic experience as insufficient to justify the acquisition of language. Chomsky assumed that learnability theory, as it applies to formal languages, applies to humans. Learnability theory concerns formal methods of deducing the formal grammar that generates a set of isolated sentences presented in random order. If one assumes that a child is learning a formal grammar somewhere in power between context free and unrestricted and that the sentences the child hears are random and isolated, then indeed it is doubtful that a typical child receives enough input to deduce the formal grammar. I also assume that this argument has nothing to do with human children since general language is probably not based on a formal language and the sentences a child hears are certainly not spoken in isolation. But in order to understand Chomsky, we must try on his assumptions and see where they lead. For Chomsky they led to the need for an innate language faculty to explain language acquisition. Physiology provided an immediately available potential content for this formal or abstract notion of an innate language faculty, since this faculty, Chomsky plausibly suggested, may turn out to be in the brain, the operations of which are structured in such a way as to be able, on the basis of the sensory experiences of infancy and childhood, to produce sentences. And computers provide a compelling if simplistic model for how the brain might do this. Discussing the way in which computers might serve as such a model can help us appreciate the plausibility, for many people, of Chomsky's approach, and also suggest the way in which this approach can deal with the problem of the given.

In computers, there is a problem called *bootstrapping*. When you turn on the power to a computer, no program is running. So how do you get a program started? You might say it is simply a matter of running it from the DOS prompt (or the main menu, depending on the kind of operating system you use). But there is a problem here. The operating system is a program, too, a program that runs other programs. And the operating system is not running either. You might suggest that the computer should just load the operating system from disk and run it. But here we have the same problem. We need a program even to read in the operating system from disk. So how do we get things started? Obviously, things do get started—at least they usually do unless your computer needs to be repaired. But it should not be obvious at this point, unless you know a lot about computers, exactly how things get started. (By the way, the term *bootstrapping* suggests the mystery of the operation, since it stands for 'pulling oneself up by one's bootstraps', which is a real trick.) The answer is that there is a simple program built into your computer which runs every time you turn on the power. This program and the circuitry that runs it at *boot* time are *hardwired* (that is, physically built) into your computer. All this *boot* program knows how to do is to read the information from a pre-defined spot on the disk (the *boot sector*) into main memory (RAM) and assume that it is a program. This program is then responsible for reading in the operating system and running it. The operating system in turn allows you to decide what to do next.

The problem of *booting* (short for bootstrapping) a computer can be compared with the problem of acquiring basic linguistic categories (the basic concepts and rules of general language). How do we acquire a new concept? One might be inclined to answer, along the lines of mainstream semantic theory we have outlined, that we acquire a new concept in terms of concepts we already have. This is certainly true for derivative concepts which can be completely defined in terms of other concepts. For example, 'pyromania' might well be explained in terms of the concepts of 'arson' and 'compulsive behavior'. But what if you do not know what 'arson' is? Well, that can be explained in terms of setting a fire with the intent to destroy. How far can this go? Eventually, you get down to basic concepts that can only be defined in terms of other basic concepts or cannot be defined at all. How many basic concepts are there that we need to understand in order to acquire a full-blown adult general-language vocabulary? The *Longman Dictionary of Contemporary English* is one of the few dictionaries that takes this question very seriously.

In it, all definitions are written in terms of a defining vocabulary of about two thousand words. Of course, this does not really account for an adult vocabulary, since it ignores the question of proper nouns. But most proper nouns can be defined by using some general vocabulary to focus one's attention and then by pointing at an object and associating it with the proper noun. So as a working hypothesis, let us say that we need a couple thousand basic concepts to get things started, to *bootstrap* our acquisition of vocabulary. The obvious question then is whether these basic concepts are *hardwired* into our brain, so that we can use them to understand other material we encounter. And if they are not hardwired, how could we acquire them?

Although we did not mention it in the description of booting, a computer has substantial built-in capacity for operating according to rules; this is called an *instruction set*. The instruction set determines the ways in which a computer can *think* (to use the popular metaphor). It would be better to say that the instruction set determines the low-level steps that can be used in an algorithmic procedure called a computer program. Although the number of algorithms that can be implemented on a computer is infinite, it is what we have called a *closed infinity*. Unless the hardware malfunctions, there are no true surprises. We are sometimes surprised by what computers do, but it is usually because we are surprised at their stupidity in blindly following instructions instead of *thinking* about what we really want them to do.

As mentioned in chapter 3 (Horning 1991), Chomsky asserted that our basic concepts and rules must be *hardwired*. Although I have not decided where I stand on the issue of innate syntax, I certainly cannot accept the proposal that concepts are innate. Nevertheless, there is an element of internal consistency in this solution to the problem of the given. By saying that basic concepts are innate, Chomsky does not need to presume that we build them up out of experience, and thus can avoid the contradiction of supposing that we can use language to formulate our concepts before we have language. We are convinced that intuitively or explicitly, Chomsky sensed himself up against the problem of the given and could see no other way around it than to extend the doctrine of innateness of the general-language syntax faculty to include basic concepts. We have already noted, however, that those thinkers who in the tradition espoused the notion of innate ideas did not typically suppose that concepts (as opposed to rules in Descartes and Kant) were among these ideas.

At any rate, by taking this route, Chomsky unwittingly abandons the idea that semantic atoms derive from the basic components of the world. Words cannot be endowed with their meaning by what they refer to, that is, by their referents in the real world; for Chomsky, concepts—at least the basic, atomic ones—pre-exist our experience of the world. Though odd to a philosopher, this doctrine has advantages. It saves language, as conceived by Chomsky, from arbitrariness. Language, including options for syntax and semantics, is genetically determined. This is asking a lot of genetics, but so is the complexity of other aspects of a human being, such as the visual and auditory subsystems. So long as one subscribes to the approach to meaning that we have described as Chomsky's heritage, it is reasonable to assume that language is sufficiently self-contained to be genetically determined, even if this approach does not explain how genetics came up with our concepts in the first place. If Chomsky did not assume that atomic concepts are genetically determined, then he would be in the awkward position of having clearly and repeatedly stated that the language faculty, especially its syntactic aspect, is genetically determined and then having no way for a human to obtain the atomic concepts needed to start using syntax to construct meaningful sentences. He would be confronting the problem of the given.

But though Chomsky achieves something by this move, he does not achieve enough. While we believe it critical to provide a grounding for language—to show why meaning is not arbitrary—we have been looking for an approach to dynamic general language which allows for fundamental ambiguity. However, Chomsky's doctrine of innateness is couched in the framework of objectivism as described by Lakoff in the previous chapter, except that it is not clear whether he believes our genetically determined concepts to be the only possible ones. Nevertheless, he fully subscribes to the two assumptions listed at the beginning of this chapter; thus, *even if Chomsky came up with another solution to the problem of the given, so long as he remains within the framework of objectivism no solution will allow for fundamental ambiguity*, and he cannot deliver what we have been searching for.

So we can say this another way. The plausibility of Chomsky's model as applied to domain-specific language disappears when it is applied to dynamic general language, simply because it does not allow for fundamental ambiguity. Let us repeat: we are not opposed to the notion of grounding; on the contrary, we think reality *must* somehow play a normative (that is, constraining) role in language use. What we are looking for is some approach to grounding that does not require language in its basic concepts and propositions to be limited to superficial ambiguity.

In summary, Chomsky's self-proclaimed connection with Cartesian thought (defined in his 1966 book *Cartesian Linguistics*) places him in the objectivist camp. In that book Chomsky even questions whether anything of significance happened in linguistics since the Cartesian period and before the advent of Generative Grammar. And twenty years later, he reaffirmed that "generative grammar shares with other approaches the belief that certain aspects of the mind/brain can be usefully construed on the computational systems of rules that form and modify representations" (Chomsky 1986). To this approach he has added a claim that concepts are innate. In an exchange between Noam Chomsky and James McCawley (a fellow linguist), Chomsky, when asked how the meaning of words is made available to the language learner, replied that the language faculty must make available some primitive concepts, because he knows of no alternative explanation.[25] Chomsky's views may be internally consistent, but we have argued that they, and other variations on the tradition of bottom-up processing from primitives, are insufficient to explain the richness of general language as we see it, with its fundamental ambiguity. Therefore, in our search for an alternative explanation, we will look at other traditions for answers to our questions about how dynamic general language is possible.

4.2 Concepts as arbitrary

A radical alternative approach to givenness (and one that also has a long tradition) is to assume that concepts are not given at all. They are neither acquired empirically nor built-in. Instead, the meaning of every concept or rule is contextually determined by other concepts and rules. Significations (meanings) do not break through the network of meanings always expressed in terms of signifiers that are expressed in terms of still more signifiers. There is no correlation with a language-independent reality. The meaning of signifiers is always derived *laterally*, along the network of signifieds expressed in terms of signifiers, rather than *down* to some grounding. In literary theory, this approach is often associated with **deconstruction**. Deconstruction is often associated with Derrida, and Derrida claims that this approach is the logical conclusion of structuralism as first proposed by Saussure. Although it is not clear whether Saussure actually took a strong position on the problem of the given, it has been repeatedly pointed out that Saussure's *signifiant/signifié* duo is missing an explicit third member, namely, the object in the real word that the *signifié* refers to. Apparently, Saussure did not feel the need for a third member. The approach of Peirce, on the other hand, includes all three and does not treat concepts as arbitrary. As we have pointed out, the tradition of bottom-up processing does not include a solution to the problem of the given, so it is not surprising that several solutions to the problem of the given have arisen, such as Chomsky's innate concepts and Derrida's arbitrariness.

In philosophy, the Hegelian tradition has taken the position that there is nothing alinguistically given to the mind upon which language can be based. This obviously is a version of that sort of idealism which holds that whatever we can encounter and make use of in knowledge and thought has the form of an idea, and therefore, so far as we are concerned, no idea can be grounded in anything non-ideational. Rorty and other *postmodern* thinkers make the relativistic claim that neither truth nor meaning can be obtained from or connected to a language-independent world because the *world* from which we would obtain them is already linguistically *saturated*. In effect, such thinkers have understood the problem of the given and have given up trying to find a solution, thus claiming nothing to be given. Fundamental ambiguity is no longer an issue, since there is no grounding of language in the real world. Meaning can conceivably be derived from the bottom up, but what is there to tell us which concepts should be at the bottom? In much philosophical postmodernism, all is arbitrary. We, along with others, feel that the radical relativism branch of Postmodernism fails to respond to a deep-seated human intuition that language is somehow grounded, and that this failure may contribute to the belief of some that the movement is losing steam. We will pursue other options.

4.3 The search for an alternative

It seems we are trapped in an intolerable dilemma. The semantic tradition in which Chomsky participates, summarized by the two assumptions we stated at the beginning of this chapter, allows no fundamental ambiguity. Disallowing fundamental ambiguity is a consequence which we have found to be false in the course of work in translation, and which we will later claim to be false on other, ethical grounds. This tradition *does* have the virtue of implying that language is somehow grounded in reality so that it is not completely arbitrary, even if that issue is not always addressed. But the price for eliminating arbitrariness in this way is exorbitant, for it eliminates the possibility of fundamental ambiguity. On the other hand—and this is the other horn of the dilemma—the radical relativism approach in postmodernism can allow for fundamental ambiguity, but it does so by making arbitrariness a basic fact of language. This is intuitively unsatisfying, for we feel there is some kind of connection between our speech and the real world. We would like to have both, that is we would like to have nonarbitrariness—that is, some kind of groundedness—while retaining the freshness of fundamental ambiguity which we believe to have found in language. Fundamentally ambiguous grounding is a tall order, if not an oxymoron. But, as we shall see, it is not a hopeless endeavor. It is more like a classic dilemma, such as the problem of how to send a signed contract, by telephone or by mail, where the mail is too slow and what is communicated by telephone is not written down. Then, suddenly, a third alternative appears, such as the fax, which is as fast as a phone call but is written and can even include a signature. We have rejected radical relativism. What might be our third alternative?

Although it could not be considered a mainstream activity and though the dilemma has not been expressed in the same way as we've expressed it, many have explored the possibility of explaining the nature and acquisition of concepts as nonarbitrary yet fundamentally ambiguous. We have already looked at one such explanation, the one by George Lakoff. Lakoff combines work by many researchers, especially psychologists (including Kay, McDaniel, Brown, Berlin, Ekman, and Rosch), who present evidence for our concepts being related to the size and capacities of our physical body and nervous system without being mathematical sets as specified by objectivism. Lakoff's main result, a non-objectivist approach to various aspects of language, especially metaphor, is a significant contribution. Grice, who is not treated in this study, deserves attention as well.

We would next like to briefly mention two philosophers who have offered a grounding for language that accommodates fundamental ambiguity.

The first is Heidegger, who made several attempts to work out possibilities in this area. The best known is his great work *Being and Time*. In this work, language is the medium of the emergence of the world—the world in which and with which the individual is engaged in all sorts of ways (practical, idle, theoretical, etc). Therefore, the idea that this world might stand independent of the use of language or of the being who uses language, and that certain words that represent this independently-standing reality are consequently endowed with atomic, human-independent meanings—this idea cannot be wedged into Heidegger's account. For him, the grounding of language is our way of being-in-the-world, where our being and our world are not separate. So the world for Heidegger is at the same time grounded, that is, determinate, for any particular language user, and yet not necessarily unambiguous.

The second philosopher is the later Wittgenstein. For him meaning is a kind of use. Words do not essentially stand for things in an objectivist correspondence to the world, but function in a wide variety of linguistic practices which are in turn embedded in larger social practices and forms of social life. To acquire an understanding of these words is just to enter into and participate in these practices successfully. We learn how things are done in our community, in conjunction with other people. To learn to speak a language, then, is to enter into many ongoing social practices of which naming, description, and assertion are only a few of many things that can be done with words.

The views of Lakoff, Heidegger, and the later Wittgenstein have conceptual connections one with another. We bring them up here to show that there are attempts which seem to at least implicitly recognize the dilemma that we have outlined. They are attempts to cut through the dilemma in that they develop theories of meaning which are not reductionistic[26] in the manner of Chomskyan linguistics (that is, they are not based on bottom-up composition from universal semantic atoms), and are not arbitrary in the mode of the radical structuralists.

Our major objective for the previous chapter was to point out that domain-specific language, although describable reductionistically, is created from within general language. Our major objective for this chapter is to increase interest in the following question: How can we further develop an understanding of dynamic general language that accommodates both fundamental ambiguity and nonarbitrariness? Only by answering this question adequately can we account for the possibility of dynamic general language. And because domain-specific language is a special, restricted case of general language that depends on general language and only appears to spring forth autonomously from the reductionist assumptions with which we began this section, we need this answer even to account for domain-specific language. Substantial interest in answering this question would change the course of contemporary linguistics—or at least allow for two parallel paths, one for domain-specific language and one for dynamic general language. In the next section, we will discuss ideas that can be supported by the insights of another philosopher, Emmanuel Levinas. We hope these insights and the broad account we will offer will exemplify the inventiveness and richness that will increasingly come into linguistics as the new question is taken seriously and various new approaches are proposed.

4.4 An introduction to Levinas

We are looking for a grounding of general language that is normative, that does not run afoul of any form of the problem of the given, and that allows for fundamental ambiguity. Drawing on our own lifelong work, fortified by Levinas[27] (a contemporary of both Heidegger and Wittgenstein), we will sketch a novel approach to this quest that neatly accommodates the hard facts of translation experience discussed earlier in this study. At first, it may seem that the approach is not relevant to linguistics, but it will eventually provide new insights into the general/domain distinction. This approach differs radically from a Chomskyan one. Chomsky views linguistic theory as a branch of *individual* psychology (Chomsky 1986). The approach taken here is a *social* one, or rather an *ethical* one: language is possible only in virtue of our relations with other individuals—which we will show to be ethical relations of obligation.[28]

What can be meant by this odd assertion that language is ethically based? First of all, let us recognize that we often view other people as objects that possess properties and that populate an objectivist universe—a universe that can be adequately represented by declarative sentences. But for Levinas, viewing people in this way *totalizes* them—brings them under a single perspective by means of which the person who holds this view reduces them to replaceable role-takers in one vast system. When people are brought under this purview, the cognitive totalizing process is analogous to *political totalitarianism*; its motivation is the "conquest of being by [the mind of] man over the course of history" (Levinas 1987:48). Levinas means by this analogy to express what he considers a profoundly unethical aspect of the quest to gain intellectual command of social reality and by this command to consider others as existing for our intellectual if not our political use. For it is possible to regard others not as objects but rather as subjects or agents, which means regarding them in the way we regard ourselves when we take into consideration our own inward life, our consciousness, with all our hopes and fears and feelings, our freedom. We can acknowledge their **otherness** with respect to ourselves.

It is precisely this otherness that we obliterate, or try to obliterate, when we view other people as objects. Jean-Paul Sartre considers the otherness of others a fundamental threat to our own identity and freedom, since it presents to us a constant freedom we cannot reduce to our systematic control, a freedom that can surprise us, oppose us, confound us. For Sartre, life is a quest to consolidate our personal identity, which for him means that others who are trying to consolidate *their* identity may threaten our project. And indeed, insofar as we consider others threatening, we will seek in the name of damage control to suppress their independence in a totalitarian way. Their otherness can and will constantly disrupt the complacencies of our systematizing, controlling mentality, just because it does not fit—it cannot fit—into any conceptual scheme. The subjectivity of others, that is, their agency or ability to act on their own, always lies outside and beyond any ordering of the world as a system of objects. Thus otherness is inconsistent with the basic tenets of objectivism.

As we shall see, whether we regard people as others or as objects is an ethical question with linguistic consequences, not a linguistic question with ethical consequences.

How does this apply to our discussion of Chomsky? His view, and that of many others, is an objectivist view. Language is a system of sentences. All sentences start out in deep structure as declarative. All words are names of concepts. These words are combined syntactically, thus combining the concepts they are linked to. The world, accordingly, is a system of states of things and of events brought about by, or happening to, such things. Objects and their happenings comprise the whole picture. Not only is this view of linguistic competence a part of individual psychology; the world to which the sentences produced by competent speakers applies is a totalized world. This is fine for a description of how to maintain and repair a machine. We should totalize machines and use them for our benefit. But this objectivist world falls short when other people appear.

In the determination of meaning, the objectivist view only allows for other people in the role of denotata, that is, objects represented. That they might be regarded as regarding the world themselves does not and cannot figure into Chomsky's theory or the tradition on which he draws. It does figure into the view of Levinas. For him, to be a person is to recognize or acknowledge the subjectivity or *otherness* of others. I cannot be a subject or agent, an *interiority* as Levinas would put it, unless there is something *external* to me. For there to be an inside requires that there be an outside. Levinas argues that to conquer the world by systematizing it intellectually is to grasp it with one's mind; quite literally, to comprehend, 'to take it into oneself', to extend the boundaries of oneself over it, to totalize it. This eliminates or profoundly obscures the internality of others by reducing them to the character and status of objects.

The history of philosophy stands witness for Levinas as to his claim that totalizing reduces others to the status of object, because as soon as the world began to be considered by some person as a system of objects falling under categories determined by their properties, the properties migrated to the side of the perceiving agent, in the mode of ideas being experienced, and it became problematic whether they could be said to exist *out there* in the world at all. In the *Meditations*, Descartes devised his several proofs for the existence of God precisely to establish that objects do exist independently of minds, being unable to find any other basis for believing this. Locke, reacting to Descartes, tried to forestall the migration; following Galileo, he distinguished primary or quantifiable properties from secondary or qualitative ones; both exist in the mind, as our ideas, but the primary ones correspond to properties of which the object *out there* is a substrate lying beyond our knowledge, like Kant's 'thing in itself'. Since that object out there is individual and not repeatable, we can obtain no idea of it. Then, by a series of devastating arguments, Berkeley demolished the tenability of the distinction between primary qualities and secondary ones: as far as we can possibly know, both are only ideas, and consequently we are left with no good reason at all for believing in the existence of anything but our own subjectivity (with the possible exception of God's subjectivity, since, with objects gone, there's nothing else that will explain where our ideas come from, assuming that we ourselves do not produce them at will). This subjectivist development was then recycled, with Kant working out a compromised version of objectivity consistent with Berkeley's and Hume's proposition that we know only our own ideas. Out of Hegel's dismantling of Kant's effort, varieties of subjectivism ensued, including Romanticism, Existentialism, Phenomenology, and contemporarily, some Postmodernist positions. But none of these approaches, whether subjectivist or objectivist, makes a consistent accommodation for otherness. Once the world is regarded only as a system of objects, this lapse follows inevitably as a series of logical consequences.

We are not opposing the totalizing of objects when doing so benefits us. The only items that cannot and should not be conquered with the mind and drawn over to the side of the thinking agent, the only items that cannot be reduced to objectitude, are *other* subjectivities. The interiority of other people is the one irreducible exteriority. For Levinas, to be a self at all consists in acknowledging other selves.

Being face to face with others, acknowledging their needs and feelings, places us under obligation to treat them accordingly. The instant we begin to use them for our own purposes, we reduce them to object status; hence, to see them as agents is to be under obligation *not* to see them as objects. Or, to put the point differently, we sense from them the same gentle demand, when we respond to their inwardness, as we want to make upon others, namely, that they recognize our own needs and feelings, a demand not to neglect, not to ignore need, not to allow to suffer or die.

Notice that the fact that we feel an ethical obligation[29] does not imply that we will act accordingly. We may resist it. We may refuse to let others be who they really are. But when we do, we implicitly acknowledge, by our act of refusal, our obligation to the other (in the way that we take account of other persons in order to act dismissively toward them—in order to act as if we weren't taking account of them).[30]

4.5 An approach to how language is possible

With this Levinasian background in mind, we can sketch the broad outlines of a theory of how dynamic general language is possible. Though not Levinas' theory, it does draw upon his basic insights about the conditions of selfhood.

First, let us point out that the obligation or ethical demand of which Levinas speaks is not a matter of moral rules or social *shoulds*, but of an immediate face-to-face relationship that constitutes our very being, prior to our acquisition of moral rules and social *shoulds*. A passage from *The Adventures of Huckleberry Finn* illustrates the difference well:

> Jim said it made him all over trembly and feverish to be so close to freedom. Well, I can tell you it made me all over trembly and feverish, too, to hear him, because I begun to get it through my head that he *was* most free—and who was to blame for it? Why, *me*. I couldn't get that out of my conscience, no how nor no way. It got to troubling me so I couldn't rest.... I tried to make out to myself that *I* warn't to blame, because *I* didn't run Jim off from his rightful owner; but it warn't no use, conscience up and says, every time, "But you knowed he was running for his freedom, and you could 'a' paddled ashore and told somebody". That was so—I couldn't get around that no way.... I got to feeling so mean and so miserable I most wished I was dead. I fidgeted up and down the raft.... I knowed very well I had done wrong, and I saw it warn't no use for me to try to learn to do right; a body that don't get *started* right when he's little ain't got no show—when the pinch comes there ain't nothing to back him up and keep him to his work, so he gets beat. Then I thought a minute, and says to myself, hold on; s'pose you'd 'a' done right and give Jim up, would you felt better than what you do now? No, says I, I'd feel bad—I'd feel just the same way I do now. (Twain 1953:112-113, 116)[31]

The last sentence of the Twain quote reveals a face-to-face relationship underlying and different from social rules. Obligations of the sort we are interested in cannot be reduced to generalizations or rules but flow from one person's reading of another's subjective perspective on the world. This point has significant implications: *neither general linguistic performance nor any other ethical activity can be adequately modeled as rule-following behavior*.

Now we arrive at the linguistic crux of the matter. The influences and constraints of reality that make every form of discourse possible make up a portion of the broad range of moral obligations toward others under which we find ourselves. Speaking involves trying to make oneself intelligible to others; to be meaningful is to strive to be understood. Thus, by speech, we acknowledge the need of the other, whose dialect, social background, emotional state, and so on, guide and constrain not solely our choice of *what* we will mean, but *how* we can mean—the form as well as the content of expression. Even in speaking to oneself, others who are absent or possibly imagined guide and constrain us. With some, we may characteristically employ forms of language that generative grammarians would call degenerate, and with others we may speak in syntactically canonical sentences. And similarly, in trying to understand another person who is speaking, we regard him or her as striving to be intelligible to someone else, possibly to ourselves with our peculiarities. Hence to enter into the circle of discourse means to regard the other's need to understand as normative for us and to regard the other as regarding yet others' needs as normative. Equally, each person in the discourse takes in what others are saying as something intended to be intelligible, that is, to provide intelligible matter for intake. On this approach, the non-arbitrariness of language is grounded not so much in the structure of the world, but by the following necessity: to speak requires seeking to secure successful intake by some other or others, and to understand requires assuming that the speaker has this same sort of purpose.

You may be considering the fact that one can 'talk' with a machine such as a microwave oven. You tell it how to cook your food, and it replies with a beep when done. Surely, this is a form of communication, but it is clearly domain-specific and derivative of general-language ability rather than leading to general language. In the present discussion, we are outside the walls of domains.

The idea here is that understanding another's utterance as meaningful is perceiving or understanding it as that person's act of taking others into account. This idea implies that something more is going on in language than the production of sentences. In Levinasian terms, what is taking place is *a saying* of a *said* rather than just a *said*. The said is abstracted from the saying, after the fact. The tradition of objectivism deals only with the said and ignores the *saying to another* as such, since it emphasizes the individual processes of language and what they produce for their own sake. Once we get out of the trap of objectivism, we can talk about 'meaning-for', the meaning of a piece of language for someone else. This *meaning-for* is central to the possibility of meaning; what an expression might mean for others is normative for our use and determines *meaning-of*.

We are well aware that the objectivist tradition in which Generative Grammar developed supposes the semantic component to be available prior to use in some situation, prior to all considerations of pragmatics, and that the source of its availability is regarded as a secondary issue to be worked out independently of the theory of the conditions of sentence production. Chomsky currently views the source of the concepts of the semantic component to be genetic, but that view could change somewhat without changing actual examples of generative grammars. Indeed, when Chomsky started writing generative grammars in the 1950s, he had probably not even addressed the issue of language acquisition and the origin of the semantic component; the semantic component was tacked on to the syntactic component in the mid-1960s. A generative grammar is an abstract machine. It just sits and spits out sentences without worrying about how or when or why it was built. The kind of alternate approach we are exploring here holds that though this semantic project may excite us by producing sentences that look like pieces of general language, it cannot produce general language itself. The completion of the project—the production of general language—would require a pragmatics integral to and inseparable from semantics—which would make that semantics radically different from Chomskyan semantics. For the dimension called pragmatics (though not as usually conceived), which is typically relegated to an incidental status, is actually *constitutive* of meaning. Any position that denies the basic nature of the role of pragmatics and in so doing denies fundamental ambiguity by ignoring meaning-for and adhering to objectivist principles will ultimately come to grief when confronted with dynamic general language. (We need occasionally to remind ourselves of the embarrassingly obvious: The enterprise in which we are all involved is an intellectual rather than a political one, and if one theory can accommodate more of the manifest features of reality than another, then by that fact alone it posts a claim to supremacy.)

Let us speculate a bit about ways in which ethical obligations to others guide and constrain meaning. Think first about the issue of arbitrariness. The words on any level of a particular language are arbitrary in one sense—that a particular sound or inscription serves as this word or that may be merely conventional, although motivated by etymology and sometimes even by sound symbolism—but in another sense, they are not arbitrary at all. In a particular situation, as we set about to accomplish our purposes, we are constrained in our choice of words and forms of expression. We cannot communicate without using the forms of speech and vocabulary conventionally accepted by our audience, and which of those conventions apply when and where is determined by the need of the people to whom we are speaking or listening. This relativizes speech to relationships between individuals. The way we talk with Tom is different from the way we talk with Susan or a granddaughter or someone who is just learning our language. As has just been pointed out, for a Chomskyan, this is often a matter of degenerate usage, irrelevant to the possibility of language. But this relativism lies at the very heart of the possibility of language, because it is our view of the viewpoint of the other, however unfounded or inaccurate, that provides the fundamental, alinguistic, normative influences upon linguistic performance. And that fundamental, alinguistic influence on speech is obligation to the other. It is ethical.

Let us push the inquiry further. Imagine some object, such as a pad of paper. This, says Levinas in *Totality and Infinity*, is not in the first instance a cognitive object. Prior (in a logical sense) to being a cognitive object, it is an economic object: it is something I can grasp, possess, and take from or give to you. It has an economic meaning. (The economic dimension of the meaning escapes us when we just talk about semantics. The language of much linguistic theory is a language that peels off only a thin aspect of reality, leaves much of the rest out, checks up on itself, and confirms that it captured everything.) Now when engaged in taking this object or wanting it or giving it away or rejecting it, I acknowledge you or others as others, that is, as the being(s) I need to protect it from or give it to; I must do so in order to regard this as something either of us might possess. Therefore, I am first of all an ethical being who can be generous or selfish. This doesn't mean that ethics comes into play first chronologically, followed by economics, and subsequent to that, cognition. It means instead that cognition at its heart is essentially economic, and economics at its heart is essentially ethical.[32] An analytical priority is operative here, not a chronological one. To be a cognitive being in the peculiar language-using way of human beings is to be an ethical being. The priority of ethics and economics deserves further discussion. Levinas has written extensively on this topic.

To be an object of cognition is, at least potentially, to be an object that can be used, deployed in some fashion for some purpose. This is true for the pad of paper mentioned in the previous paragraph and even for abstract objects like numbers, which can be manipulated in various ways. And thus to be an economic object is simultaneously to be an ethical object, for the object can be used by oneself or by others in creative expression or in an act of spite or vengeance, as a gift or as a theft, and so forth. Insofar as we use an object ethically, we defer to, or at least caringly take into account, another's need—perhaps to understand our action, perhaps not to suffer from it, possibly to be sustained by it. Our felt ethical obligation is our perception of the other person's economic or cognitive need—or it may be our ethical need that allows another to fulfill his or her obligation.

So we may use a word in a wildly non-standard way because we know that is how another will understand it, or because it will amuse or please that person; or we may invent a metaphor that dislocates a word from its standard associations and thereby enriches its meaning for those who hear, just because the interests, purposes, or needs of the other suggest this. In these ways, we adapt, render more or less precise, or even create words, all because others ubiquitously influence our access to reality. It is unlikely that a race of people who grow up, live, and die, each in total isolation except for the first month of their infancy, would develop or maintain language. Even supposing that an individual of this race had contact with machines that could process domain-specific languages, there would be no *others*, thus no ethics and no economics. And, if Levinas is right about the priority of ethics and economics, there would be no basis for general language as we know it.

We adapt our language most often undeliberately and totally without calculation. No single and absolute 'standard usage' is presupposed that, once in play, serves as a platform for creative variation. On the contrary, to be in a position to speak at all is not merely to be endowed with sentence-production capacities, but also to view the situation or subject matter of which one speaks as being viewed by another or others. An approximation to 'standard usage' (which is a useful creation of lexicographers and grammarians) is an option, but not the only option which may be deemed appropriate in a particular social context. Therefore, metaphors and other neologisms can be produced spontaneously. Let us emphasize what we said before: Even if we're self-serving—that is, attempting to use other people for our benefit at their expense—then in order to do so we must recognize their otherness and take it into account in our unethical scheming in order to be intelligible to them. Our treatment of them as objects is detectably different from the way we would treat something that really is an object.[33]

We can now review how we have addressed three comments made earlier in the chapter. First was the comment that it is problematical to apply a concept acontextually or asocially. A concept from a domain is highly contextualized; that is, it is restricted to the context of the domain in question. Outside of any domain, in general language, we have seen that concepts exist only as a way of making ourselves intelligible to others. They must be constantly sustained by use in communication or they become archaic. Secondly, we claimed that how we view people is an ethical question with linguistic consequences rather than a linguistic question with ethical consequences. This follows from our Levinasian perspective. We do not use language independently of ethics in order to formulate our view of people. Instead, we formulate our language as we respond to the ethical demands that are placed on us as we interact with others. And thirdly, we indicated that pragmatics is constitutive of meaning rather than secondary to it. This also follows from the priority of ethics and economics over cognition. There is no general language—and therefore no possibility of creating a domain for some economic/ethical purpose—without a pragmatic context of interaction with others. Thus there is no meaning at all, neither the primary meaning of general language nor the derivative meanings in a domain, without pragmatics.

We can also finally address the question of the origin of fundamental ambiguity. In the way we have described, the alinguistic or prelinguistic obligation I have to the other, which guides and constrains my linguistic development and even my formation of categories, does two otherwise incompatible things at once: (1) it generates just the sort of fundamental ambiguities that we observe in speech and texts—ambiguities that cannot be included in advance on a list finitely long—*and* (2) by the same stroke it establishes stabilities of usage of just the sort that we observe—stabilities that make it possible for us to read and make at least some sense of texts in our own language that are centuries old. The ambiguities come from the surprises of otherness. The only way to avoid surprises would be to totalize all others, but then they would cease to be *others*. The stabilities come because acknowledging in one's speech the authority of others' need for intelligibility tends to subdue or override aberrations of use. All this contributes to the conditions of non-arbitrariness that, together with fundamental ambiguity, we believe to lie behind speech and writing in order for language to be as we observe it to be. The non-arbitrariness and the fundamental ambiguity, on this account, spring from the same source.

The account we have briefly sketched suggests a theoretical point of view from which reality possesses the feature of *inexhaustibly multiple categorizability*. This point of view accommodates the insights of Lakoff. He says, as we have seen, that the kinds of categories that dominate for us are those associated with our relative size, our upright orientation, our flexibility and specific gravity, and the power, dexterity, and/or keenness of our particular monitoring, interventionary, and manipulative equipment—that is, our senses and our appendages. These orientations, capacities, and limitations belong not just to the individual but to those who are other than the individual, since each speaker/hearer speaks and listens as one whose utterance or understanding may go summarily awry if it doesn't sufficiently accommodate the physical orientation and capacities of the other person (who accommodates himself or herself to others in the same sort of way). The account sketched here also shares something with Heidegger's work on the relation of purpose and meaning, according to which the purposes expressed in the categories of language are not peculiar to individuals but are those shared within the community. This idea is not far removed from the later Wittgenstein's view of practices. According to that view, we are essentially with others in that our language, repertoire of actions, and even moods and attitudes—in short, the patterns of behavior that express our individual identity—are all ultimately adapted from and can be appropriated by those others. Thus, according to this idea, our repertoires of speech and conduct are reposited throughout the community of speakers and within any individual within that community, and take the form of shared social ceremonials, practices, and institutions. (Social constructionists in psychology, influenced by Wittgenstein, Vygotsky, Veblen, and others, have developed this view insightfully and argued for it persuasively. See, for example, Rom Harré, *Personal Being* and Wilfrid Sellars, "Empiricism and the Philosophy of Mind".)

To this nexus of intuitions about the practical and social ground of speech upon which Lakoff, Heidegger, and Wittgenstein and others converge, we are adding the Levinasian idea that linguistic practices can be most concretely, least abstractly, described as patterns of individuals responding not simply according to socially available forms and not even just to one another, but responding to one another responding to one another. Practices are rooted in individuals relating to individuals relating to individuals.

4.6 Grounding and acquisition

Let us now further pursue the question of grounding. We have suggested that language is grounded in the need to make ourselves intelligible. But have we avoided the problem of the given? What can we say about the application of concepts to reality? How can we have concepts before we use them? What about acquisition of concepts in the first place? We suggest that an answer might be worked out in the following general direction.

In regard to the application of concepts we already possess, we would say that in our basic cognitive contact with reality, as we categorize this item or that, we simply and straightforwardly employ concepts. It is a serious mistake to think that we need to pre-identify whatever we apply concepts to. Otherwise we would need some mechanism to identify the object so that we can apply the concept to it, and then we need to pre-pre-identify the object so that we can apply that pre-identification mechanism, and we enter an endless spiral. Kant worked out this solution of straightforward application of concepts as it applies both to the general schemata of cognition, such as sequence, juxtaposition, and causality, and to empirical concepts such as those of size, shape, velocity, texture, and color. The very idea of an object is the idea of a conceptualized entity, and the separation of the abstract concept of that object and its concrete material is achieved only in analysis and not as a sequence of stages of cognition. Because *any* access to the object or even to *features* of the object (which for present purposes are themselves objects) involves the application of concepts, it makes no sense at all to speak of correlating a word or concept to an independent object. The *object* is not an object until the concept is applied to it. This incidentally is the position of Jean-Marie Zemb. He says that the answer to the question "What controls our conceptualization of the world: our view of it or the world itself?" is "Both".[34] We conceptualize the world in cognizing it but will run up against real-world limitations that may force us to revise.

The account of meaning we have been outlining shows how the speaker is engaged, as a condition of speech, in linguistic practices not only of asking and responding, of giving orders, of endorsing and vilifying, and so on, but of subscribing to and circulating a general categorization of reality. Our account suggests that the consistency with which we deploy concepts is as much a function of physical orientation and capability, expectation, purpose, compassion or impression management, and prevailing practice as of dictation by reality. Precisely because reality can be viewed in multiple ways—inexhaustibly multiple ways—it does not prescribe any one possible view over the others. Yet reality does play a guiding and constraining role, as evidenced by the fact that it cannot be viewed in any way whatever. (That a set of possibilities is openly infinite does not imply that it includes every possibility, particularly those that are blatantly wrong.)

Without all the other considerations we have mentioned, each rooted in the face-to-face relations of which Levinas has written, reality itself would have to dictate directly how it must be read. It would then seem necessary for us to pick up the world's signals in advance in order to know how to respond to it cognitively. In that case, a non-conceptualizing cognition, that is, a view of the world that does not involve applying concepts, would be required in order to apply concepts. And there would consequently be only one correct way to view the world, or at least only one basis for views, precluding fundamental ambiguity.

We can put this point another way: Any theory of the conditions of linguistic behavior derived from the objectivist tradition, such as a branch of Generative Grammar, precludes fundamental ambiguity and requires that the semantic component be capable of identifying which senses could possibly apply to a word even before the pragmatic component can bring in questions of use by humans, such as cognition. But since for objectivists face-to-face relations and human cognition cannot assist in this selection of candidate word senses, the selection must occur in a direct, non-mediated fashion. Hence any such theory will encounter the difficulty of correlating words to reality and the attendant problem of what we have oxymoronically called pre-cognitive identification of that reality.

We might extend this position to the economic and ethical dimensions of cognition. To apprehend an object is not only to conceptualize it, but to regard it also in functional, economic terms relative to one's purpose, hopes, anticipation of possibilities, fears, and capabilities. And this economic context is set in the even broader ethical context of the need, whether for their sake or one's own, to anticipate the possible responses of others. These dimensions all come to bear together with—*simultaneously with*—the application of concepts; as we said, the priority they enjoy is logical rather than chronological, and their distinctness exists in analysis and never in the objects of cognition themselves.

But if it all works in this way—if the non-conceptualizing cognition problem is indeed a side-effect created by exclusion of our face-to-face relations to other people—if we do not in fact compare our concepts to reality before applying them—how can we have any confidence in our application of concepts or correct them when this confidence is shaken? For the answer, we can borrow a page from Hegel and the pragmatists who developed their position out of the matrix Hegel created. If our conceptualization of reality is faulty, we shall discover this not by comparing it with unconceptualized reality, but in further experience, by additional applications of concepts.[35] This is how we actually run up against and are corrected by reality. Indeed, one good account of the strategy of science says that it consists in devising ways in which to push further experience toward a limit where, if possible, prior conceptualizations will be discovered to be inadequate. Reality may allow an inexhaustible range of characterizations, but it does not, we repeat, allow absolutely any characterization whatever, and indeed can be rather unforgiving of carelessness or irresponsible judgments. It plays its role in the refinement of concepts without the need for accessing reality prior to conceptualizing it.

We have discussed the application of concepts, but how do we acquire our first concepts as children? The approach we have been exploring seems particularly promising for language acquisition theory. John Shotter, a widely influential British psychologist, watched hundreds of videos of mothers with infants, and came after long study to the conviction that in the early months, mother and child do not form a simple dyad, the mother responding to the child and the child to the mother. Instead, the mother relates to the dyad consisting of the mother and the child; she relates to the child as responding to her. Thus she interprets even the child's random gestures and facial expressions as meaningful, which is to say, she interprets them as sensitive to her, and consistently over time gives the child a response that constitutes the child as responsive (Shotter 1984:57-62). Her conceptualization of the child is ethically governed. In acting according to the conceptualization, the mother guides the child in conceptualizing her in a similar ethically governed way. An infant can follow an object with its eyes very early on. And the infant can grasp an object and let it go and distinguish its mother from other humans. All this happens well before being able to speak, at least before being able to engage in a conversation, which shows that the child has some economic 'concepts', such as the possession of objects about the right size to hold in its tiny hand, well before much language is acquired. Ethically, the child may be thought to be rather selfish, but a child who has been comforted can learn to give a hug of comfort to someone else at a very early age. And most children can locate an object that is being looked at by someone else (a rather complex process that seems to involve recognition of the otherness of the person whose viewpoint is adopted in order to look in the direction of the object) before learning to speak. Though we believe much work needs to be done in this area, the approach that Shotter has pioneered is very promising, and the vast literature in child language acquisition needs to be reviewed with an eye to identifying concepts that a child typically acquires before acquiring speech. However, it is already clear that the ethical approach to language grounds our initial concepts in nuances of the face-to-face relation of mother and child and in the child's innate capacity to recognize motion and grasp small objects, rather than in direct contact with an unambiguous categorization of the world. Once a child has some initial concepts and begins applying them in simple human interactions, it is through continued interaction that words are linked to concepts. Of course, those concepts and those words evolve through further interaction, and that interaction is greatly enhanced through even modest linguistic ability. However it is that syntactic ability is obtained, it is through situated, not isolated, sentences, and syntax is certainly not the only or initial clue that people use in making themselves intelligible and in taking the expression of others as intended to be intelligible. This approach allows for fundamental ambiguity without the arbitrariness of radical relativism.

Human language is firmly grounded in the ethics and economics of the recognition of otherness. Linguistics, on this view, is not just a branch of mathematics and certainly not a branch of *individual* psychology. Language is a marvelous form of communication with many powers, such as the power to create domains of knowledge that allow language within the walls of a domain to look as if objectivism governs the universe. When we as authors began to see language in this new way, which we might call an *agentive view*, we experienced an intellectual excitement and emotional satisfaction. The long-standing objectivist approach did not need to be discarded, but simply put into perspective as a useful option for certain purposes. Domain-specific language can approach mathematical perfection while general language remains intensely human. We who study language can escape from many traps, including the trap of thinking we must choose between applying objectivism to all of language or rejecting it entirely (and all the results based on it).

4.7 Release from prison

In this chapter we have drawn upon certain insights of Lakoff, Heidegger, Wittgenstein, and especially Levinas and our own theoretical work to present a view of how language is possible, for both adults and children, through general cognitive and physical capacities (which may well be genetically determined) *and* through recognition of the 'otherness of other people'. Note that our proposed basis for the possibility of language, that which is given, is pre-linguistic: bodily capacity for sensory input, recognition of otherness, and innate cognitive capacities. On this view, general language is not arbitrary (being grounded in our obligations to others and limited by encounters with reality), yet it is ambiguous in a fundamental way. Thus, when dealing with language that is not restricted to a domain, we reject both objectivism and radically relativistic structuralism. Although we have presented the barest outline of a preliminary and tentative answer to the problem of concept/language acquisition, what is much more important than our opinion on this subject is careful attention to what we think should be a new question on the agenda of linguistics, the question of how we can account for the possibility of language as simultaneously grounded (non-arbitrary) and fundamentally ambiguous. We think that by allowing us to see language from a fresh angle, this new question of how language can be grounded yet ambiguous will bear more and more fruit in linguistics, translation theory, and natural language processing.

Taking this new question seriously frees us from the prison of objectivism and allows us, as we will see in the next chapter, to use computers for our benefit without spending our time on drudgery that the computer can do better or wasting our time on development projects that will surely gobble up resources indefinitely until they are declared failures.

The fundamental ambiguity of general language allows us to continue creating interesting and surprising new domains indefinitely. Since we are not prisoners of any particular domain but are free to create, enter, exit, and redefine domains, these domains are not actually prisons at all. Nevertheless, suppose that in some fantastical manner a human being were—in perception, thought, and expression—completely taken over by some particular domain language. This individual could consequently contemplate reality in one and only one way. No discovery would be possible, except of terrain not yet encountered, for everything that could be apprehended from a particular physical point of view would eventually be apprehended. The world would in this sense be all surface, no depth. Since this person would not discover truly novel aspects of anything, it is hard to see how metaphor would be possible—even the simplistic sort of metaphor that is immediately reducible to some literal expression or other. Would such a person not be trapped in a sort of psychological prison? We should be content, even grateful, to have unambiguous domain language (in which apparent ambiguities are superficial and can be resolved using homograph numbers) at *our* disposal as a tool for our benefit. What if general language were really only a certain kind of domain language and restricted *us* to a single basis for viewing the world? *We* would be at the disposal of this language.

Unambiguous general language would be the ultimate prison.

5 Implications

5.1 A review of our basis

Before pursuing some implications of what we have discussed in previous chapters, we will briefly review the basis we have developed for these implications, introducing some new material, including metaphorical stories,[36] as our primary claims are re-emphasized. This section may be useful as a reminder, but is not intended as a substitute for a thoughtful study of the previous chapters in forming a personal judgment on the claims made here.

5.1.1 An image with multiple interpretations

The other day I woke up with an image in my head, but I no longer knew what it meant. The image was simple—a horizontal, straight line with an oval above it that touched the line—and I was sure that it had meant something in my dream, but I had only a faint, fleeting recollection of the dream. You have probably felt the frustration of trying to bring back a dream.

I sat up and tried to grasp what the image might signify, even if it wasn't exactly what it had meant in my dream. My first impression was that it could be a balloon filled with water, sitting on a table and turned so that you cannot see the knot of the balloon.

I had the feeling that the image had something to do with humans, so I looked beyond balloons. My next impression was that it might signify another person encountered along the way during a stroll through a park. You don't know what to make of other people. You can try to squeeze them into a mold based on the way they are dressed, but you can't really get to know them unless you interact with them and let them come out of their mold. The line may represent the path you are walking along, and the oval may represent the mold that you put them into when you form a first impression.

That still wasn't quite right. Then a third impression came along. Perhaps the oval was a knothole in a piece of wood, and the line was the lower edge of the wood. But what did that have to do with people? Ah yes, that interpretation of the image reminded me of a story[37] about a visit to a tree house which had horizontal boards on all sides. It didn't matter that grown-ups who build houses generally put wood panels vertically. This tree house was more in the style of a log cabin. According to the story, a very imaginative boy, Harold, was invited into the tree house by Peter, the neighbor boy who had built the house. Peter closed the door and the small room became nearly dark, except for one beam of sunlight that shined through a knothole in one of the boards. That knothole was, of course, the oval in the image from my dream. Harold suggested playing a game in which he would pretend that he knew nothing about the outside world, and that he had always lived in the tree house in the dark. Peter, who had come to expect and enjoy Harold's crazy thought games, pointed out the dust particles that were floating in the beam, and they both watched them for a few minutes. Then Peter moved over so that the beam of light shined onto his face and began describing to Harold some of the things that were happening outside the tree house. Harold would not at first believe that Peter could see anything outside the tree house; totally engrossed in the tree-house world, he insisted that he could see the beam just as well as Peter could and that there was nothing to see but dust particles floating in the air. Then Peter helped Harold look along the beam of light instead of at it, and the outside world opened up to Harold.

There is no single correct interpretation of a picture (abstracted from objects), except, perhaps, within a domain. For example, on a Forest Service map, the oval might unambiguously mean a campsite and a small rectangle might mean that the campsite has a picnic table. In another domain, the same symbols may mean something entirely different. There is no well-defined limit to the number of possible domains in which an image could have particular domain-specific meaning and no limit to its possible interpretations in general language. The world is infinitely categorizable. But interpretations are not exactly random meanings either. Each is somehow motivated by the original image. The first interpretation of the image in my dream is motivated by its similarity with the shape of a balloon filled with water. The second suggests the unjustified oversimplification of a human to a stereotype which supposedly allows us to predict how that person will behave (a kind of extreme racism). And the third interpretation of the line and oval suggested on another level the story of the beam of light shining through a knothole into a tree house. One could say that the first interpretation is literal while the second is metaphorical, and the third is both literal and metaphorical. But note that contrary to a common assumption about metaphor, the metaphorical interpretations are not based on the literal balloon interpretation.[38] However, the beam-of-light story has a particular significance to the philosophy of language related to the second interpretation. As discussed in chapter 4, we concur with Levinas that selfhood is based on a recognition of otherness in the sense that other people also possess selfhood and thus are agents themselves. Without others, selfhood has no meaning. However, we can attempt to deny particular individuals their agency. One way is to stereotype another person and claim that a label is all we need to know about the other (as in the second interpretation of the oval). Another way to attempt to deny the agency of others is to pretend that they are not relevant to us by putting up barriers around us to shut out everything but our own little world (as in the story of the tree house). When we stop resisting the otherness of others and grant them the same agency we possess, then a whole new world opens up (suggested by looking along the beam instead of at it), an exciting world that is fundamentally ambiguous yet grounded in the ethics and economics of human relations (as explained in chapter 4), a world which opens up the possibility of dynamic general language. General language in turn opens up the possibility of creating domains for particular human purposes.

As long as we are comparing general language to a world, let us extend the metaphor to include domain-specific language. Start with our planet Earth and its various languages and cultures focused in various geographical areas; then think of the various satellites orbiting the earth as artificially created domains. Some domains, such as the domain of the maintenance and repair manuals for a piece of machinery sold worldwide, will be almost completely shared across several languages, just as one satellite can transmit to several areas of the earth. Even then there will be minor variations such as the voltage and frequency it expects when fed electrical power and the type of plug placed on the outlet to obtain that power. Other domains are tied to one culture, sometimes even within the same language, just as a weather satellite and a military satellite may be in the same orbit yet be incompatible. For example, the domain of Law in the United States and the domain of Law in Great Britain are two domains, whether you count British English and American English as one language or two. Translating between incompatible domains can be as challenging as translating between general languages.[39]

Human translators are able to handle both general-language and domain-specific texts. As a starting point, a translator must be competent in two or more general languages. Then, for each new domain, the human translator must gain new expertise. The same requirement applies to a machine translation system in that the lexicons, as well as any knowledge base the system may have, must be updated in order to produce high-quality translations from a new domain. But here the similarity ends. Human translators can produce high-quality translations of general-language texts that are dynamic— that is, full of metaphor, allusions, and intentionally unusual usage. Current machine translation systems cannot. Current techniques in machine translation produce fully automatic high-quality translation only rarely and only when applied to certain coherent bodies of similar texts that are all restricted to the same domain. The texts must be static in that they do not contain new metaphors, allusions, or grammatical constructions. Sometimes this restriction occurs naturally and the texts form a sublanguage. More often, the restrictions must be enforced with the cooperation of authors, resulting in what is called controlled language. Many have noted that MT works better in a narrow domain. The reason is obvious: everything is better-defined and less ambiguous than in general language. What is less obvious is whether the machine translation techniques that work quite well within a domain can gradually be extended to apply equally well to general language. Or will one encounter a phenomenon of diminishing returns or even an unscalable wall? Terrence Hook, who has developed a domain-specific Dutch-English machine translation system, made a typical comment. He said (personal communication) that when restricted to a domain, the output of his system is good enough to be used as is for some purposes. However, when, "on a rainy afternoon" he tries a passage from a newspaper, he gets gibberish. Is this only a temporary limitation of domain-specific systems? Will they gradually improve in their ability to handle general-language texts until they do as well on general language as they do on domain-specific texts? In chapters 3 and 4 we argued for the importance of the general/domain distinction and explored the assumptions behind various approaches to language. Our explorations enable us to answer the question about extending current techniques.

5.1.2 Techniques that do not extend to general language

A major shift has occurred in machine translation. John Hutchins, the acknowledged historian-in-residence of machine translation, has noted[40] that until about ten years ago the assumption was that systems should be general but that now the assumption is that systems, at least systems aimed at high-quality output, should be domain-specific. The issue among professionals is no longer whether current techniques in machine translation work equally well in a domain and on general text. They do not. The issue is whether current techniques can ever be extended to handle general language effectively. I have proposed that they cannot be extended to dynamic general language. Humans can adapt to domain-specific language, but current machines cannot extend to general language. This claim is highly controversial.[41] How could I be so bold as to make such a claim? The reason is based on (1) the fact that current techniques depend on philosophical underpinnings called objectivism and (2) my belief that general language does not conform to the assumptions of objectivism, thus invalidating current techniques as applied to general language.

George Lakoff, a prominent linguist and early supporter of Chomsky, long ago broke off from the Chomsky camp and has, as described in chapter 3, spent recent years exploring the assumptions of objectivism and developing a non-objectivist approach called *experientialism*. He summarizes objectivism as the belief that:

> rational thought consists in the manipulation of abstract symbols and that these symbols get their meaning via a correspondence with the world, objectively construed, that is, independent of any organism. (Lakoff 1987:xii)

This view has many implications. It implies that the human mind is an abstract machine and that any machine, including a digital computer, which is properly programmed is theoretically capable of thinking just as well as or even better than a human mind. Note that this view includes a strong form of mind-body dualism, which means that a human body is not at all necessary to human-like thought. Some researchers in Artificial Intelligence (AI), take what is known as the strong-AI position, which is that computers will someday be able to perform any intellectual task that humans can perform.[42] Marvin Minsky, a strong-AI proponent, recently wrote an article (1994) in which he estimates that the knowledge a human acquires over a lifetime amounts to not more than the equivalent of about three or four gigabits, which is less than the amount of information that can be stored on one CD-ROM [500 megabytes = 4 gigabits]. He then speaks of a nanotechnology that places individual atoms in desired positions and that will allow us to produce much smaller and faster computer chips than we now can build. He then states, speaking of future robots as our virtual offspring, our *mind-children*:

> Once we know what we need to do, our nanotechnologies should enable us to construct replacement bodies and brains that will not constrain us to work at the crawling pace of "real time". The events in our computer chips already happen millions of times faster than those in brain cells. Hence, we could design our "mind-children" to think a million times faster than we do. (Minsky 1994:90)

Minsky then notes that many scholars from a variety of disciplines "firmly maintain that machines will never have thoughts like ours, because no matter how we build them, they will always lack some vital ingredient". Minsky says he has no patience with such arguments because they are all flawed by assuming, in one way or another, "the existence of some magical spark that has no detectable properties".

Although over the years I have generally had little patience with Minsky and his outrageous claims,[43] he has a good point here. In a *post-religious* society such as ours, it does little good to use an 'undetectable magical spark' as the basis for an academic claim. Instead I have decided to focus on what hurdles would have to be overcome by a machine before it would even have a chance of handling dynamic general language as well as or better than humans. I do not claim that it will never be possible to build machines that can think like humans and, in particular, can handle dynamic general language as well as humans. Instead, I try to show that the *current* techniques of natural language processing (NLP) will never be extended to accomplish such tasks. Entirely new techniques will be needed. In particular, we will need techniques that avoid the assumptions of objectivism.

5.1.3 Avoiding objectivism

Both mainstream philosophy and mainstream linguistics have built into them assumptions based on objectivism. Here are some of those assumptions:

(a) Words (and fixed expressions such as multi-word terms) are mapped to a short list of discrete senses, often to a single sense. That is, a particular word has one or more well-defined meanings.

(b) Each sense exists independently of any particular word or sentence and has the properties of a mathematical set. For example, the sense of 'horse' that corresponds to an animal is a set of objects in the real world. Any particular object is either in the set (if it is a horse) or is not in the set (if it is not a horse). There is nothing in between. Since these senses are independent of particular sentences and independent of people, they correspond to the way the world is, to the way the world objectively divides itself up. Chomsky may favor a genetic basis.

(c) The meaning of a sentence treated in isolation can be obtained by combining word senses of the words of the sentence from the bottom up. If a word of the sentence is ambiguous then there may be multiple composite meanings for the sentence, unless all but one are weeded out by selectional restrictions.

These assumptions are embedded in the standard framework which divides language into syntax (including morphology), semantics, and pragmatics, with emphasis on syntax and semantics. According to this framework, linguistics is a branch of individual rather than social psychology. To someone committed to the mainstream view, this framework is perfectly standard and obviously true. There are many *flavors* within Generative Grammar, but they all share this framework and most work in machine translation is explicitly or implicitly based on it, even if it rejects the details of Noam Chomsky's current approach. All current approaches to linguistics that escape from the standard framework are intended for use by humans and are not computable; thus, while worthwhile, they are not, as we have pointed out, a viable basis for machine translation.

Computable approaches to language are based on all three basic assumptions listed as (a), (b), and (c). However, dynamic general language *violates* all three of the assumptions. It violates assumption (a) in that new word senses, sometimes called nuances, can be generated dynamically as needed in speech or writing, often for the purposes of a single text. Indeed, this dynamic aspect of meaning is found in all interesting writing, not just in great literature. Only in a well-defined domain can the meanings of words be pinned down. And that is because we humans create a domain specifically so that the senses of a term will be limited and discrete, with the goal being one concept per term and one term per concept in each language. This distinction between domain-specific language and dynamic general language was discussed in detail in chapter 3.

Dynamic general language also violates assumption (b) in that its categories are not mathematical sets tied directly to the way the world divides itself up. Lakoff (1987) gives abundant evidence to this effect from several disciplines. For example, he shows that categories of general language exhibit prototype effects in which some members are better members than others,[44] a behavior not allowed in mathematical sets. Again, in a domain, we divide up the world a certain way for a particular purpose. So from the point of view of the domain, the world can be seen as divided up into a neat ontology of domain concepts which are mathematical sets.

Assumption (c) is violated in that general language is always understood in a certain context. There is no such thing as the meaning of a sentence in isolation. Martin Kay (who, along with Yorick Wilks, was taught by Margaret Masterman, who sat at the feet of Wittgenstein) and his colleagues (1994) put it this way: "language is situated". When humans process general language, they do not delay consideration of pragmatic factors such as the situation. The syntax, then semantics, then pragmatics model applies only to domains in which the situation is constant and therefore implicitly taken into account at all levels.

So we see that dynamic general language violates all three assumptions on which most natural language processing is based. But controlled language restricted to a well-defined domain conforms to all three assumptions if we control it to be that way. At a dinner speech, Martin Kay once put it something like this: "Success in NLP has been seen primarily in cases where natural language resembles formal language". That comment, although intended to be humorous, is right on target and has a serious side. The syntax/semantics/pragmatics model of bottom-up composition from well-defined concepts is essentially a description of a formal language such as a computer programming language. Formal languages conform to all three assumptions while dynamic general language conforms to none of them. Thus, NLP techniques that are based on these assumptions apply to domain-specific text inasmuch as it resembles formal language and inasmuch as it does not exhibit the dynamic possibilities of general language.

Thus we can conclude that current NLP techniques will never be extended to handle dynamic general language, since to do so they would at least have to abandon the three basic assumptions of this section. Any set of techniques which truly abandoned these principles would look so different from current techniques that it would be inappropriate to call them an *extension* of current techniques. But what can we say about how these new techniques would look?

5.1.4 *What is needed*

Please recall that I am not saying that there are *no* techniques that can handle dynamic general language. I am saying that current computational techniques are insufficient. So what *would* be sufficient? First, the new techniques would allow for fundamental ambiguity. Fundamental ambiguity goes beyond superficial ambiguity in that it entails both an indeterminate list of possible senses for a word and an indeterminate relation between the senses and the real world. Most people in NLP to whom I pose the question of whether they believe in a universal set of concepts determined by the structure of the universe will respond that they do not believe in any such thing. Yet, their techniques, though they may not be aware of it, are based on this assumption. Again, within a domain, we can act as if there were no fundamental ambiguity so long as we have a group of people who have come to a shared understanding of the concepts of the domain. This shared understanding comes about through human experts who interact using a mixture of general language and specialized terms. General language provides the metalanguage for arriving at a common understanding. But this approach falls apart when applied to general language, because there is no metalanguage in which to discuss general language. Yorick Wilks[45] pointed out this problem when he asked how one can know whether everyone in a cooperative effort has the same understanding of the primitive concepts of an interlingua. This leads to the philosophical problem of the given, about which we have already spoken. How do we obtain the atomistic concepts that are used to build up more complex concepts? What gives them to us? Chomsky would say that they are genetically hardwired. Philosophers would say that if they are not hardwired and we do not have them already as infants, then we cannot get them through direct experience, since concepts are required to interpret our experience.

If the approach of this study is correct, a satisfactory solution must overcome the problem of the given yet allow for fundamental ambiguity. Chomsky's solution is unsatisfactory, since it does not allow for fundamental ambiguity. One criterion for a satisfactory solution is the test of dynamic metaphor. Current NLP techniques can easily handle frozen metaphor. We simply put a fixed expression in the dictionary. Although even there we run up against resolving ambiguities, such as the English request to go jump in the lake or the French request to go cook oneself an egg, which may be literal requests to perform a specific task or idiomatic requests to just leave and not come back, depending on the situation. Dynamic metaphor is much more challenging than frozen metaphor. Dynamic metaphor is created for the purposes of one text or even one sentence. Understanding dynamic metaphor involves taking into account the entire situation and those aspects of general knowledge that are relevant to the situation. It is extremely context-sensitive and thus contrasts with the objectivist processing, which assumes that the meaning of a sentence can be built up without taking into consideration the context at all. Some dynamic metaphors are so clever or poignant that they are frozen and preserved for future use. The prevailing wisdom is that metaphor is a secondary aspect of language that can and should be ignored until other problems are solved. Lakoff has shown that it is a pervasive aspect of language that needs to be solved up front. Certainly, for general language, we cannot afford to ignore metaphor. An interesting aspect of metaphor is that although one cannot prepare in advance a list of all possible metaphorical uses of a word, and although once a dynamic metaphor is created one cannot predict how it could be appropriately translated, every metaphorical usage is in retrospect motivated rather than random.

Ian Kelly supplied me with an interesting history of the senses of the word 'treacle' over the past two thousand years. At each change in sense, dynamic metaphor was involved, and each change was motivated, though some are surprising. The ancestor in Ancient Greek of the word 'treacle' referred to a wild animal. It then metonymically became the bite of a wild animal. This sense then broadened to become a general injury and later shifted to the medicine used to treat such an injury. Later still it narrowed to the substance put into a medicine in order to make it more palatable, and finally, in British English, to one such substance, molasses. Each step is logical and motivated for a human, but it would be asking too much of a machine based on objectivist assumptions to figure out the new meaning at any stage of the transition from wild animal to molasses. Some NLP projects have worked on understanding dynamic metaphor. They should not be expected to achieve human levels of performance unless they truly abandon their objectivist assumptions. But at least it should be possible to measure their performance in such tasks as translating texts that contain dynamic metaphor.

Is there anything else that would be needed in a viable approach for handling dynamic general language? Yes, it would be important to avoid falling into radical relativism when allowing for fundamental ambiguity. Radical relativism, typified by the Deconstructionist movement in literary theory, recognizes the problem of the given and solves it by saying that nothing is given. Concepts are not genetic; neither are they built into the structure of the universe. Everything is relative. The problem with this approach is that it does not explain how we can communicate. How do we know that our concepts have anything to do with the concepts in the head of the person we are talking to? In their own ways a number of philosophers, especially Wittgenstein, have argued that this is a misguided question. Our concepts are grounded not objectively but in our social interactions. This is a promising direction. Note that it implies that general-language linguistics is a branch of social rather than individual psychology.

Often it is said that a computer that could translate anything would have to understand what it is translating. But how do you tell if a computer understands? John Searle, a philosopher, proposed a puzzle (1980) in which it is assumed that techniques are somehow developed which allow a person sitting in a box to answer questions about a story by mechanically following a set of rules. The catch is that the story, the questions, and the answers are all in Chinese and the person is an English monolingual. Within a domain, say the domain of Chinese weather bulletins, this could probably be done if someone who speaks only English could follow rules similar to those used by the Meteo system to translate weather bulletins between English and French. Of course, it may take quite a while for the person in the box to produce an answer, but let us ignore that problem. The question is whether the ability to produce acceptable answers mechanically would constitute a demonstration that the person understands Chinese. Most people would say that the answer is obviously no, while strong-AI people would say that the answer is obviously yes.

Searle is on the side of those who think the answer is obviously no. He points out that if he were the person following the mechanical rules, he would eventually get out of the box and still not know any Chinese. He *would* still know English and understand questions posed to him in English, but he would not understand Chinese. He points out that some people have suggested that an adding machine *understands* arithmetic and that a door that opens automatically when someone approaches it and breaks a beam of light *understands* the instructions of the photocell. Searle points out that this sense of 'understand' is not at all the same as the sense in which we say a person understands Chinese. Searle then goes through several types of replies he has received to his argument from strong-AI types. One type of reply is that perhaps a person or computer that blindly follows the rules sitting closed up in a box does not understand Chinese, but if the rules were programmed into a small computer that was put into a robot, then the robot would understand, thanks to its ability to move about and *see* things. Searle replies that this implies that understanding is solely a matter of formal symbol manipulation, which is one of the tenets of objectivism. Searle counters the symbol-manipulation theory by noting that an essential element of understanding is conscious intentionality. Most people would accept this. The problem is how to detect whether a machine *intends* to do something or merely follows a series of instructions. Strong-AI proponents must logically accept a form of mind-brain dualism, namely that the mind, including its intentionality, can be successfully implemented in either a digital computer or in a human brain or, presumably, in 'Cartesian mental substance' if we ever run across any of that stuff, whatever it is. In any of these cases, the mind is entirely separate from the brain, which is what it means to claim a mind-brain dualism. Searle takes delight in pointing out, however, that the AI literature contains "frequent fulminations against 'dualism'". Searle rejects this form of dualism and expresses his belief that intentionality is a biological phenomenon. If this is so, he points out, we should no more expect a computer program to have intentionality than a computer software simulation of photosynthesis to produce sugar. The problem is that unless we can somehow detect intentionality and prove that it is a biological phenomenon, we have a stand-off between Searle and Minsky. They may agree that a computer needs understanding and that understanding entails intentionality, but that leaves unanswered the question of whether a computer can have intentionality. In line with my previous stance of attempting to identify specifically what would be needed for a computer to handle general language rather than just saying that it would need an undetectable spark, we should perhaps look for indirect ways to detect understanding and intentionality.

Marvin Minsky, in the same article where he pontificates about artificial brains, says something with which I agree, namely, that one thing which separates current machines from humans is the flexibility of the human mind. When a computer program encounters a situation for which it has not been explicitly programmed, it either stops or produces meaningless results. When humans encounter a new situation, they are often able to try various solutions until something works. This applies to Searle's Chinese Box puzzle. Flexibility is a detectable aspect of understanding and intentionality. Even METEO has occasional problems with a sentence, usually due to a typographical error or noise on the transmission lines. A human reviser handles these situations because they cannot all be systematized and therefore require the flexibility of the human mind. The human who blindly followed the instructions of METEO would exhibit no more flexibility or robustness than a computer. Therefore, neither a computer nor a human who follows instructions mechanically truly understands. We have now added an additional requirement to a machine that might handle natural language. It must exhibit flexibility in handling new situations. This flexibility would probably be related to the ability to handle dynamic metaphor. It seems that ways of testing flexibility could be devised.

Joseph Weizenbaum is well known for having written a computer program called Eliza that simulates a psychoanalyst. When it was first installed on a computer at a university, some people would 'talk' to it for hours on end through a computer terminal, exposing their darkest secrets and actually believing that it was a human psychoanalyst or at least that it really *understood* them. Weizenbaum was appalled.[46] He knew that the computer program didn't understand a thing they were saying. It simply looked for key words and put together minor variations on stock replies. For example, if a person said, "My parents are divorced", Eliza would reply something like "Tell me more about your family", using a table that lists 'parent' as a 'family' word. How was Eliza so successful in fooling intelligent people? First, it was dealing with a domain, the domain of the detached psychoanalyst gathering data. Eliza never said anything substantive, not even mundane things. It could not even answer a question like "How many days are there in a week?" It just asked questions to keep the person talking, and who doesn't like to talk when *someone* will listen? Eliza clearly fails the flexibility test of being able to handle a new situation.

It is instructive at this point to consider one other person who has written about mechanistic approaches to language. Roy Harris, in his book *The Language Machine* (1987), traces the history of the idea that human language can be put into a machine, going back to *Gulliver's Travels*, in which there is a section about a machine which randomly produces sequences of words. Young men are employed for the purpose of sifting through the random sequences for those sequences that have meaning and then putting these sequences together into books. This satire on a wrong way to create literature is surprisingly not too different from the deadly serious way that a Chomsky-style grammar randomly generates sentences in isolation to supposedly generate a human language, except that it is semantic rules that eliminate the millions of sequences that do not make sense instead of a roomful of humans, a process euphemistically called 'overgeneration' and 'selection'. Along the way from Gulliver to Chomsky, we find Saussure, who posited that there was a language machine in the brain in order to distinguish linguistics from language teaching. For him, the language machine was automatic, so no one had control. Thus there was no need to teach the inner workings of the language machine to humans and no danger of language teachers taking over part of linguistics. What is missing from Saussure is any mention of bilingual humans or social class differences in dialect. These were erased by the idealized *langue*. Saussure spoke out against prescriptivism, but, ironically, it was during Saussure's lifetime that the idea of a standardized national language arose, a triumph of prescriptivism, with theoretical support from Saussure's idealization of language. A national language is a creation which gives a false idea of uniformity and contributes to the view of language as a machine. Then Chomsky completed the project by making language into a machine that functions completely without human intervention. For Roy Harris, the view of language as a machine has contributed to the exclusion of a moral dimension from language and a devaluing of a search for solid truth and knowledge, the result being radical relativism. Another bizarre consequence of the language machine view is that communication is only an incidental aspect of language instead of its core.

There is a contradiction between the model of language as a machine that is independent of social interaction and the deepest yearnings of the authors of these models. Chomsky, in a documentary on his life and work, stated that although he has sought a connection between his linguistic theory and his political activism, which centers on manipulation of public opinion by the press, he has found none.[47] Shouldn't that lack of connection be worrisome at best? And Minsky, in his article about artificial brains (1994), makes the rash claim that "no popular ethical system yet, be it humanist or religion-based, has shown itself able to face the challenges that already confront us." He is clearly concerned about the meaning of life for himself and others. He even ends his article with a sermon-like plea: "Our job is to see that all this work shall not end up in meaningless waste". It seems that a good place to start would be to place social interaction at the core of language and give some of the long-established ethical systems a chance to work instead of dismissing them summarily.

Now we can combine the previous points of flexibility and social interaction to avoid both the problem of the given and radical relativism. We need a flexible grounding of language that avoids radical relativism and allows for social interaction at the core of language. This leads to the work of Levinas on the questions of interiority and totalization. As described in chapter 4, Levinas has shown that to be an interiority—that is, to have subjectivity, selfhood, conscience, and agency, which I believe to be an essential condition of consciousness and understanding—one must acknowledge the existence of other interiorities that cannot be totalized. Put in more familiar words, to be a living, thinking person, one must acknowledge the existence of other thinking, living persons who are peers and agents themselves and whose actions and motives cannot be perfectly controlled or predicted. Even an attempt to control other people is an implicit acknowledgement of their agency which you wish to destroy. Totalization involves bringing others (as well as objects) into your world and reducing them to objects by assuming them to be as predictable as objects. Totalization in an NLP system that interacts with people in any way would involve making a model of the person with which the system is interacting, and incorporating that model into the algorithm of the system, so that the computer actually interacts with the model, which is part of itself, not with the person.[48] An algorithm is a finite set of instructions such that each decision is binary (i.e., yes or no) and the process terminates in a finite number of steps. All computer programs (except those stuck in an *infinite loop*) are algorithms. Once we accept that although totalization of the inanimate physical world is desirable and largely possible, totalization of other people is neither ethical nor possible, then we can draw the startling conclusion that an approach to dealing with natural language that truly allows for social interaction could not be a totalized system and therefore could not be algorithmic! For entirely different reasons, prominent physicist Roger Penrose has suggested that the brain may operate non-algorithmically on the basis of faster-than-light processes of quantum mechanics. (1989)[49]

5.1.5 *Requirements for the possibility of language*

Let us return to the image at the beginning of this chapter. According to one interpretation, the oval represented a knothole in a tree house. The tree house could stand for a domain-specific approach. The walls of the tree house enclose and delimit the domain, taking up the image of walls in chapter 3. Useful work can be and is accomplished in machine translation with a domain-oriented approach based on the assumptions of objectivism. Subject matter domains with well-defined concepts and simple links to unambiguous terms, together with controlled languages restricted in syntax and semantics to a particular domain, can be created by humans who already possess general language. Computers can then be programmed to process domain-specific texts as if that is all that exists, staying inside the tree house and ignoring the knothole. However, before computers will have a chance of performing as well as humans on dynamic general language, they will at least have to:

(1) avoid the assumptions of objectivism,

(2) allow for fundamental ambiguity,

(3) handle dynamic metaphor,

(4) become much more flexible,

(5) and become an agent, recognizing other people as agents (which implies a non-algorithmic approach).

The final requirement for becoming an agent and seeing others as agents that regard oneself as an agent, thus permitting social interaction, is suggested by the step of looking *along* the beam of light shining *through* the knothole instead of *at* it. Until you take this step, it is impossible to know what the result will be. Once you do, a whole new world opens up. The addition of this final requirement of agency for the possibility of language is perhaps the major theoretical contribution of this book, along with the observation that domain-specific language differs radically from general language in that with sufficient control, these requirements can be lifted within the confines of a domain. This explains why some applications of NLP have produced better results than others.

The five requirements listed above form an initial mission statement for anyone who embarks on the development of a machine that can handle general language at the level of a human. They comprise my current thinking on a basis for the possibility of language. I hope that the reader is convinced that any basis would include at least these points. Although an on-going discussion is clearly needed[50] and there may be other, as yet unidentified requirements for the possibility of language, in the next section we will stop campaigning for these points and shift to an exploration of some consequences.

Someone who attempts to create a machine that can handle dynamic general language would be well-advised to review the work of Peirce (Semiotics), Zemb (Statutory Analysis), Halliday (Systemics), Lakoff (Experientialism), and other non-objectivist approaches to language, even though none is currently computable without making compromises to objectivism by retreating to a domain.

We should not complain about the heavy requirements I have imposed on an approach that could handle general language at human levels of performance. In 1984, many of us reviewed the vision of the world presented by George Orwell in his novel *1984* and were thankful that things were not as bad as he had predicted, at least in the world outside the Soviet Bloc. I had occasional contact with people on the other side of the Iron Curtain during the 1970s and 1980s and heard first-hand horror stories of oppression heaped on those who dared think on their own in a way that opposed the government then in power. In Orwell's world, the Party had invented Newspeak, a deliberately restricted language in which it was impossible to think thoughts that were not approved by the Party. Now we have seen the Iron Curtain fall. If all language could suddenly be treated like domain-specific language, then a new and far worse Iron Curtain would, in Orwellian fashion, forever keep us from thinking truly new thoughts, and we would become machines trapped in the straightjacket of objectivism.

5.2 Overview of implications

We have characterized some necessary, though perhaps not sufficient, conditions for the possibility of general language, especially the condition of agency. These conditions may be somewhat akin to a list of organic compounds that must be present in a primordial broth for God or Chance (according to the reader's preference) to create life in the form of cells that can reproduce. The conditions are fairly simple to state, once you have built up enough philosophy (or chemistry). But the final step to language (or life) is still not understood. The implications of the conditions for the possibility of general language versus domain-specific language are simple to state, but the effort to implement them will be substantial. It is not embarrassing that the most important conclusions and implications of this book can be stated on a page or two. It is to be expected. Of more interest is whether the arguments are convincing and whether the implications will take root.

The implications of this philosophical discussion for translation technology are simple. Most work in machine translation is currently headed in the right direction, but conflicts await downstream. Domain-specific approaches that use controlled language should be continued, and controlled languages should be made to conform to all the assumptions of objectivism so far as possible. Dialogue-based machine translation can guide the user into writing in a controlled language. Providing low-quality indicative translation for information only is unarguable since many find indicative translation useful, thanks to the flexibility of humans to adapt to the bizarre nature of indicative translation. *But further work on fully automatic high-quality machine translation of unrestricted text is a waste of time and money unless the issues in this book are carefully addressed*. If we ever reach a breakthrough in natural language processing which allows for the handling of dynamic general language, it will not be based on any extension of current techniques in machine translation. The electric lightbulb did not result from research and development on the candle (personal communication from Roger Harris). It will be a truly surprising, unpredictable breakthrough and therefore is not in the foreseeable future, even though it may come at any time. Therefore, funding for work in high-quality machine translation of general-language texts should be limited to basic research which attempts to develop approaches which satisfy the five requirements listed above, rather than to an extension of current techniques beyond domain-specific applications.[51] This is a heavy implication that will be hard for some to swallow.

But what about texts that require high-quality translations but are not domain-specific, that is, are not written in a controlled language restricted to a particular domain? Is there anything that computers can do to help *humans* with the translation of such texts? The answer is a resounding yes. A number of computer-based tools for human translators are on the market already, and many translators find them highly useful. Suppose it is agreed that research funding should be provided for both computer-based tools for humans and fully-automatic machine translation [for controlled languages or indicative quality]. How should the funding be allocated to these two aspects of translation technology? One method would be to look at the European Commission, which has perhaps the largest translation department in the world with twelve hundred full-time in-house translators. Over one million pages of text are translated per year by the Commission into publishable quality documents. About two hundred thousand pages of text are translated per year using machine translation. However, only about twenty percent of the machine translation (about forty thousand pages) is part of the million pages (i.e., about four percent). The rest of the machine translation is used for indicative documents that are not published.[52] Rather than reduce the load on human translators, machine translation has merely slowed the growth of the load on human translators and has addressed a previously unfulfilled need for indicative translation that can be obtained quickly without going through the translation department when high quality is not necessary. Since, after nearly twenty years of development and use of machine translation at the Commission, the lion's portion of text is still translated by humans, and since the breakthrough needed for high-quality machine translation of general text is tantalizing but still in the unforeseeable future, I propose that it makes eminent sense to move toward a three-way split of funding in roughly equal portions as follows: (1) various approaches to machine translation (other than full-automatic translation of general text); (2) computer-based tools for human translators; (3) basic research on approaches which satisfy the five requirements we have outlined for the processing of dynamic general language. There is no need to agonize over the limitations of current techniques. This three-way split provides for a division of labor according to individual inclination and opportunities, between refining the application of current techniques where appropriate and discussing radically new approaches to general language. Those who study general language need to have patience in doing basic research without slipping into objectivism (because of computation envy) or sliding into a relativist mode of discussion which lacks all grounding.[53]

Later in this chapter we will come back to translation technology, describing what is available and on the horizon, including terminology management and various tools based on matching up corresponding units of a source text and target text, and how translation technology can fit into the document production chain.

The implications of our philosophical discussion for translation theory are perhaps less obvious than for translation technology. According to Neubert and Shreve, (1994:9), "Much early work in translation studies is rooted in the linguistic tradition", but there are two recognizable trends which lead to a lack of consensus in translation studies. One is "the shrinking role of linguistics as the intellectual basis for translation studies". The other is "theoretical particularism" (1994:11), which they explain to be the creation of multiple supposedly global approaches to translation, each based on purely local understandings. Neubert and Shreve lament that the result has been translation conferences and translation studies literature that contain "an enormous amount of frustrating miscommunication",[54] and they rightly point out that translation studies is a young discipline and that young disciplines often have competing paradigms. Upon reflection, and in the light of Neubert and Shreve's comments, there is also a simple yet far-reaching implication of our philosophical discussion for translation theory. There should be two major branches of translation theory, one for dynamic general language and the other for domain-specific controlled language. Translation theory for general language would be intended for human translators (and future 'mind-children' of human translators, if Minsky is right). Translation theory for controlled language would be intended for developers of machine translation systems using current techniques. These two branches of translation theory are as irreconcilable as the assumptions of objectivism and the nature of general language. A third branch of translation theory based on the first two, with significant practical applications, would develop a methodology for analyzing whether a given text is suitable for machine translation and why. As we have pointed out earlier, most texts are a mixture of general vocabulary and specialized terms. Only a small portion of the text that is authored conforms to a naturally occurring sublanguage that is entirely restricted to a narrow domain and is sufficiently predictable to allow us to get away with pretending that objectivist assumptions apply perfectly to it. Likewise, only a small portion of text is free from specialized terms of any kind. Most text is a mixture, including some amount of LSP (Language for Special Purposes). It is not obvious whether a particular mixed text is likely to produce good results when submitted to machine translation. But it should be possible to develop methods that can be used by skilled humans to predict results accurately.

If the above suggestion were taken seriously and translation theory were split into three branches as described (focusing on machine translation, human translation, and text analysis respectively), much of the tension that is recognized in current translation studies should evaporate. Translation theorists would be able to participate in machine translation projects without feeling that they are degrading themselves or betraying translators. The role of mainstream linguistic theory in human translation studies would naturally shrink, while linguistics' role in machine translation studies would increase. And a new and useful job title, such as *translation analyst*, would appear.

Translation theory for controlled languages would be based explicitly on objectivist principles. The concepts of a domain, which forms the universe of discourse, would be organized into a semantic network, often called an ontology, by experts in the subject matter field together with a terminologist. An interlingua would be set up using formal logic to represent statements about the domain in a language-independent format. Then, for each language that one wants to translate into or out of, a linguist would define a formal grammar and an algorithm for mapping between sentences of the formal language and propositions in the interlingua. A computational linguist would design a system to interact with a human to author texts in the controlled language or to revise previously authored texts until they conform. An applied linguist and/or an instructional scientist would design training materials to help humans write in the controlled language rather than in natural language. Humans who are not flexible enough to learn to produce the controlled language would have to find employment elsewhere, just as in any other profession that requires particular skills.

The most important difference between this approach and the approach usually followed in machine translation research and development concerns what happens when a sentence does not translate well because it does not conform to the expectations of the system. Traditionally, the response has been to extend the grammar or lexicon or other component so that the sentence will work. The problem with this response is, of course, that rather than eventually getting the system *right* so that it can handle anything, the system becomes unwieldy, and an improvement in one area causes new problems in other areas. The new controlled-language approach would be entirely different. Instead of adapting the system to the language that is fed into it, the language is adapted to the system. If the problem is caused by a grammatical ambiguity, the authoring/revision system is tightened up to eliminate the ambiguity. If a term is used ambiguously and there seems to be no reliable way to have the analysis component resolve the ambiguity, the offending sense of the term would be outlawed and, if necessary, the human would be warned about which senses are allowable, perhaps by a pop-up message that appears when the term is used. The interlingual representation of a sentence in formal logic would be its meaning. The grammar of the controlled language would be designed so that each meaning of each sentence could be computed bottom up. The controlled language and the system would be refined until the system produces acceptable translations, that is, translations that require little or no revision. This century's massive effort (built on Chomsky's conception of Cartesian linguistics and other thinking even further back) which has been expended in the development of formal logic and Generative Grammar will finally pay off in the form of fully automatic high-quality machine translation of carefully restricted text.

The above scenario, although slightly exaggerated to distinguish it clearly from the traditional approach to machine translation, which, until recent years, attempted to extend an objectivist approach to handle more and more aspects of non-objectivist general language, is perhaps not just a pipe dream. A joint project that involves Caterpillar Corporation and the Carnegie Mellon University Center for Machine Translation is following essentially the plan we have presented. The domain is technical documentation for Caterpillar equipment for heavy construction. The machine translation system includes a knowledge base about Caterpillar concepts. The authors are required to use a controlled language which is checked by a computer program. Potential ambiguities are detected and resolved even before the source text is presented to the machine translation system. As of this writing, the Caterpillar project is not far enough along to be judged a success or failure. Assuming technical competence on the part of the developers, only one thing can go seriously wrong—a lack of gumption on the part of the entire team to restrict the controlled language until the system works, no matter how painful it is initially to the authors. Writing in a highly controlled language is an acquired skill.

Computer programmers write in a highly controlled language. They don't complain when the compiler points out a discrepancy between the language they write and the formal bounds of the programming language. Unfortunately, many computer programmers lack skills in technical writing. Controlled-language writers may have to come from the intersection of those who can write well and those who can program well. If the Caterpillar project is, for some reason, not a resounding success, other projects will duplicate the success of the METEO system but with controlled language instead of a naturally-occurring sublanguage.

A word of caution is in order. Not all domains are necessarily amenable to the controlled-language approach. We have already mentioned that law is not a shared domain. It is not obvious that a single conceptual ontology can be constructed that encompasses United States, British, and French law. The legal system of one political unit in one language may approach a domain. But even there, human judges are required to pass judgment on the meaning of a contract because humans often disagree. The concepts of sociology may not be sufficiently well-defined to support high-quality fully-automatic translation. Even in technical areas, what appears to be one domain may actually be two or more domains with the same name. Additional difficulties to be expected are (1) domains in flux where basic concepts are in the process of being created using dynamic processes of general language and (2) domains where traditions have fossilized ambiguities and overlapping concepts. In a domain such as Caterpillar equipment, management can impose the use of certain terms and the elimination of others according to the recommendations of the machine translation team. Such control is not always available to developers. In addition, written materials are not always present in sufficient quantity to justify the investment necessary to develop a machine translation system that produces high-quality output. Despite the apparent optimism expressed here, one must not lose sight of the demanding conditions I have enumerated. It is most likely that, so long as the world economy continues along the lines of the past few decades, just as in the European Commission, machine translation will only serve to slow the growth of the need for human translation, not eliminate it or reduce it. This means that translators need not fear machine translation. The need for human translation should continue to grow. Translators should not even hesitate to get involved with a machine translation team, either as a designer or as a post-editor. The only translators who may end up in difficulty are those who refuse to embrace computer-based tools and methods which can, while enhancing quality through consistency, reduce the time needed to translate the vast quantities of text that contain specialized terms but are not appropriate for machine translation.

We have now proposed answers to the open questions of translation mentioned in the preface. Machine translation produces generally poor results relative to the performance of skilled human translators because the techniques currently used are based on the assumption that natural language conforms to the objectivist view that currently prevails in mainstream linguistics and philosophy. In order to substantially improve the quality of machine translation, one needs either to control the language of the source text so that it acts as if it conforms to the assumptions of objectivism or to develop an entirely new approach to machine translation which avoids objectivism, includes sufficient flexibility to allow for fundamental ambiguity and dynamic metaphor (taking into account the situation and surrounding text), and both possesses and acknowledges agency.

In chapter 2, we asked whether it would be more challenging to send a manned spaceship to visit the planet of a nearby star or to develop a machine translation system that could translate as well as a competent human translator. Questions of funding aside, the answer depends on whether a major breakthrough is needed. For slower-than-light travel, we have the technology today to send a spaceship to the stars, so long as the passengers are dedicated and patient and willing never to come back, even though their children may return. The project would be more straightforward than a general solution to the machine translation problem. However, for faster-than-light travel, we would need a major breakthrough. Who knows which will come first, the general-language breakthrough or the faster-than-light breakthrough?

In the next section, we will back off from conquering the stars and general language. We will present the outlines of an approach to translation theory consistent with the general/domain distinction we have made and examine a few recent surveys of translation theories. Later in the chapter we will return to the implications of our discussion for current translation technology.

5.3 Some implications for translation theory

The general/domain distinction and our discussion of what makes language possible have implications for translation theory. I have suggested that there should be three areas within translation theory: human translation theory to provide guidance to humans in the translation of general-language and LSP texts; machine translation theory to guide in programming computers for the translation of controlled language texts within well-defined shared domains; and text analysis to help decide whether a given text should be translated by a human or computer. In this section, we will discuss human and machine translation theory, concentrating on human translation. In particular, we will discuss the need for translation specifications, offer some answers to some of the questions that were left open in chapter 1, and briefly review some current approaches to translation.

5.3.1 A multidimensional approach with specifications

Within a controlled language restricted to a domain, one can get away with thinking of meaning as transcendental, as something that can exist outside of the human mind and that can be encoded into a text and extracted from a text independent of the situation. Actually, domain-specific meaning exists only as long as it is continuously sustained by those people who are influential in the domain. But that does not matter as long as the situation is held constant, which amounts to staying within the walls around the domain. However, outside those walls, the myth of transcendental meaning breaks down, like the wicked witch who melts when she gets wet. When we talk about human translation of dynamic general language, we must avoid the myth of transcendental meaning, which is part of objectivism.

If we take agency seriously, as described in chapter 4, then it is impossible to force someone to respond to a text in a certain way.[55] Setting the emotional aspects of a response aside temporarily, it is even impossible to guarantee the unambiguous transfer of information. Even the phrase "transfer of information" betrays the error of slipping into *domain-think*. Outside of a totalized world such as a domain, there is no such thing as objective information. Human relations are basic. Even among friends, misunderstandings often arise. When we communicate, we walk a tightrope between assuming too much and assuming too little about the world of the other person. If we assume too much, the hearer is likely to fill in details that differ from the intent of the speaker; if we assume too little, then we offend the hearer by stating the obvious. There is no way to systematize the world of the hearer inside the world of the speaker without eliminating agency. This means the world of the hearer may be constantly evolving in ways we cannot predict. This may be why teenagers and parents often have trouble understanding each other, since the world of a teenager usually evolves too fast for parents to track. Even the process of a parent tracking the evolution may be offensive to a teenager who is intoxicated with the possibility of making more personal decisions.

If we avoid the myth of transcendental meaning and take agency seriously, then another myth disappears—the myth of the one correct translation. Unfortunately, many people who request and pay for translations believe in the myth of the one correct translation. They believe that translation is like a black box. All you have to put into it is a source text and a specification of what language it is to be translated into. You don't need to specify who the audience is or what the purpose is. You don't need to provide company-specific equivalents for specialized terms. You just put in the source text and out pops *the one correct* translation. This myth is widespread.

The major practical implication of all this for human translation is that a source text should always be accompanied by a set of specifications indicating preferences on the part of the requester. If a series of documents have the same specifications, then a reference to the codified specifications would be sufficient, but the details should always be retrievable. Actually, this need for specifications also applies to machine translation as well, but in that case they are built into the design of the system and the particular grammars and lexicons that have been implemented. As we continue our discussion of human translation we will explore what might be included in a *translation specification*, by which we mean a set of specifications as to how a particular translation should be done. Even a set of specifications does not determine a unique translation. It only allows a particular translation to be evaluated as consistent or inconsistent with those specifications.

A slightly frivolous follow-up to the section on mascots in chapter 1 can now begin, with your indulgence. Clearly, translation needs more than one mascot. For machine translation of controlled language, I propose the rhinoceros as mascot. A rhino is similar to a domain in that its thick skin is like a wall. And when a rhino gets pointed in the right direction (or a machine translation system gets set up properly) very little gets in its way as it charges. For human translation, I am currently considering the zebra as a mascot, since its stripes are for me a metaphor of the items in a list of specifications. But in line with the principle of agency, each human translator should be encouraged to choose a personal mascot.

With the division of translation theory into [overlapping] branches, one that deals with dynamic general language and the other with controlled languages whose properties resemble formal languages more closely than natural language, we are struck by the fact that most work on the process of translation applies only to controlled languages. Indeed, an enormous amount of work in linguistics and philosophy applies only to the controlled-language branch. However, the controlled-language branch of translation theory applies primarily to machine translation rather than human translation. This raises the valid question of whether there is actually a theory of human translation. With the exception of 'Think Aloud' studies in which the translator talks into a tape recorder about decisions he or she is making while doing a translation, most work on the process of translation has taken the form of a model of translation consisting of three modules: analysis, transfer, and production (often called synthesis or generation). Unfortunately, this model is heavily based on objectivist assumptions and does not really apply to human translation. It is central to controlled-language translation, not general-language translation. This perhaps explains why most human translators do not feel that translation theory is relevant to their daily work. Contrast this with an engineer. What civil engineer would think of building a bridge, other than an exact replica of a bridge that is functioning already, without using theoretical principles to predict stress on the materials and compare the stresses with the tested strength of those materials? What electrical engineer would build a new transformer without using a mathematical model to predict the power it can transfer without overheating? Yet a human translator feels no need to consult a theory of translation before or during the act of translating.

One might even ask whether it makes sense to speak of a *theory* of human translation at all.[56] A theory in the hard sciences is usually a mathematical model of some aspect of the physical world, a model with predictive power. However, if the discussion in this book is essentially correct, human translation of general language will never submit to a traditional mathematical model, since that submission would involve totalization and a shift to controlled language. We will not even try to speculate here what goes on in the mind of a translator during the act of translating. That project will be left for another time when extreme caution can be used to avoid falling into an objectivist explanation. Therefore, perhaps we should talk of an *approach* to human translation rather than a theory of human translation, but for the moment we will use 'approach' and 'theory' interchangeably when speaking of human translation.

One way to approach human translation is to speak of various dimensions of a text. Here I contrast dimension with layer or level. In a multi-level approach to language where the layers are morphology, syntax, and semantics, it is assumed that each successive layer is entirely derived from the preceding layer. In a multidimensional approach, each dimension can vary independently of the others, just as a three-dimensional box can be modified to become narrower, lower, or shallower without changing the other two dimensions.

In a domain-specific machine translation system designed to work on controlled language, it can make sense to talk about *the* translation of a document, since the same text coming through again should produce exactly the same translation the second time it goes through the same algorithmic process. However, it makes no sense at all to speak of *the* human translation of a text.

We have mentioned the strange myth of the one correct translation. Many people who pay for a document to be translated (we will refer to them as requesters) have the mistaken notion that it suffices to provide a source text in order to receive the one correct translation. According to this myth, if a second translation of the same text differs from the first, it is because at least one of the translators failed to translate properly. An accompanying myth is that it is not necessary to supply a terminology file with the source document since a good translator will know how the terms should be translated. These myths are filled with the assumptions of objectivism. Of course, once a domain has been mathematically modeled, including the setting up of a clean mapping of terms from one language to another via the concepts of the domain, it is not necessary to supply a bilingual terminology file with each document. Each document is treated just the same as every other. However, it is equally obvious that another closed world could be set up, based on the same domain, in which terms are translated differently. Indeed, this is the typical case. Each organization has proprietary terminology, whether they realize it or not. Often organizations do not take proprietary terminology into account, and the result is a document given out for translation in a naked state, without benefit of related documents and their translations or of a terminology file of organization-specific target-language terms linked with source-language terms. The results are usually embarrassing to everyone, unless the translator has done considerable previous work for the requester or happens to be clairvoyant.

The multidimensional approach to translation includes specifications as a key component in translation. The specifications are worked out between the requester and the translator or some intermediary, such as a representative of a translation agency or company. We will simply call the two parties the requester and the translator/intermediary. Rather than just describing the potential user, that is, the audience, of the translation and the purpose of doing the translation, the specifications should tell what the audience and purpose mean along various dimensions. Different types of text will imply the emphasis of different dimensions in the specifications. For example, the specifications for an LSP text will always include a terminology file or a reference to a previously supplied terminology file. This could be called the dimension of terminology. Included in this dimension is the question of what should be done when a term encountered in the text does not appear in the specified terminology file.

A true horror story may serve to affirm the importance of the dimension of terminology in LSP text.[57] The Canadian government purchased a military airplane, the CF-18. The extensive maintenance, operation, and repair documentation was translated from English to French for use on French-speaking air bases in Canada. The translation was extremely expensive. Some time later, the personnel at a French-speaking air base were asked if they had any difficulties with the French documentation for the aircraft. They said they did not since they did not use the French documentation. When asked why they had discarded the French documentation and instead used the English version, they replied that they could not understand the French documentation. Now these were native speakers of French, so additional explanations were in order. It was uncovered that the French translation had been done in pieces by many different translators, that no terminology file had been specified up front, and, predictably, the same English terms were translated various ways throughout the French version. The terminology problem was so severe that it was easier to use the English version than to try to understand the French version. This meant that a huge amount of money had been wasted because the principle of specifying the dimension of terminology had been violated.

Another dimension applicable to LSP texts is formal structure and order of units. Is there some unit of source text that should always have a corresponding unit in the target text? Typically, the requester wants a correspondence at the paragraph level. In other words, all the information in the target text relevant to a particular paragraph of source text should be placed in one paragraph and corresponding paragraphs should be in the same order. This parallelism of paragraphs does not always hold. Some translations, especially less technical translations, can involve putting information in a different order. On the other hand, a technical translation could be specified to correspond at the sentence level. A glossing of a text is just an operation, which could logically be called a type of translation, in which the level of correspondence is specified to be at the word level.

Another dimension of translation is register—that is, the level of language appropriate for a particular audience. An article on nuclear physics from the journal *Scientific American* that is to appear in a French magazine for twelve-year-old students must likely undergo a considerable change in register. Usually, it is obvious what register a translation should be written in. But it is only obvious if one knows the requester's purpose for doing the translation and the intended audience for the translation. Even then, there can be serious disagreements concerning register. For example, a number of years ago, a user rejected a carefully done translation because the register had been raised. The source text was in conversational English often using the past tense in a narrative. The translation into French used the *passé simple*, a tense which is found in formal written text but which is not normally spoken. The translator would have been perfectly capable of producing a text with a less formal register but did not. There was a serious disagreement about the usefulness of the translation because the requester, user, and translator had not come to an agreement concerning register *before* the translation began. Such discussions, however painful, are less painful when held before the translation is done than after. An alternative which may sometimes be acceptable is to have the translator do a short section of text as a prototype for evaluation by the requester and representative users. It may be easier to discuss specifications when a sample is in hand than before anything at all has been done with the source text.

Of course, a series of closely related texts for the same requester and intended user may not need an individually prepared set of specifications for each text. A set of specifications could be worked out once and applied to each text in the series. There is an old saying that it takes two to tango. I would say that it takes two mistakes for a translation to be done without specifications: (1) the requester must allow the work to be done without having agreed on specifications and (2) the translator/intermediary must agree to do the job without specifications. Once the requester is convinced of the need for specifications, it is the responsibility of the translator/intermediary to make the requester aware of the many dimensions that need to be considered in writing the specifications. The most delicate stage is when the requester is not yet convinced of the need for specifications. Attempts on the part of the translator/intermediary to educate the requester may be interpreted as incompetence, while a translator/intermediary who says that all that is needed is the source text may be telling the requester what they *want* to hear but not what they *should* hear.

Within the framework we have developed in this book there is no reason to assume that two people, in the absence of specifications, will translate a given text in the same way any more than two students will write the same essay on a film they have seen. And it is not enough for the requester to give just a statement of the purpose and audience. Many sets of specifications can be consistent with the same statement of purpose and audience. Would you consider paying someone to build a house without specifications in the form of architectural drawings? Would it be sufficient to specify that the house will be used for eating, sleeping, and entertainment for two parents and three small children? Many sets of architectural drawings would be consistent with that statement of purpose and audience.

Why do so many people leave translation to chance when they would not leave house building to chance? Perhaps they have unconsciously accepted some notions of objectivism which are pervasive in Western culture. They think of meaning as a property of a text, like juice that can be extracted from a fruit without damaging the fruit. The situation is assumed to be no more relevant to the meaning than the intent of the person who squeezes the fruit is relevant to what kind of juice comes out. This meaning then is thought of as something that exists independently of the fruit from which it is derived and can be used to create a new kind of target fruit with the same juice. If this analogy sounds a bit far-fetched, it is because I did not want to make it sound too convincing. It is, after all, a fairy tale. As we have seen, the only time a translation can be viewed as the re-incarnation of the context-independent meaning of the source text is when the context is so rigidly defined and constant that it becomes invisible, that is, within a shared domain for purely descriptive texts. Within the constructed world of a domain, it is okay to believe in fairy tales about meaning. A domain is an artificial world in which objectivist fairy tales come true. With a constant purpose—say, to inform someone about the maintenance and repair of a complex device—and with a constant audience—say, a technical service person—a single set of specifications can be set up, including an extensive terminology file, and translation can be viewed as a process of extracting the meaning of a source text and producing a target text that has the same meaning. However, outside a shared domain, this fairy tale breaks down. There are an infinite variety of specifications to choose from, and context must be considered at every stage. A meaning of a text never exists outside a text and independent of all people. It exists only in the mind of a speaker or hearer and is influenced by interaction with others. The closest thing to a meaning that can be taken seriously in general language is an invariant meaning of a word according to the tradition of Charles Peirce. However, for Peirce (personal communication with John Robertson), the invariant meaning does not become an actual word sense until human intelligence applies the invariant in a particular situation, a far cry from a context-independent objectivist unit of meaning.

Since a domain is only a fantasy world, there are many things which can impinge on it. Often a domain is not really shared. A little-known text by Rudolf Jumpelt (1961) presented a great deal of detail concerning asymmetries between English and German in various domains. For example, there is not even agreement on the details of the structure of the human ear in American and German medical traditions, which developed somewhat independently.[58] The description of diseases also differs substantially between English and Spanish.[59]

Machine translation theory applies to texts that are highly controlled and restricted to a single, shared, well-defined domain. Human translation theory applies to all other texts. We have mentioned only a few dimensions that should be included in the specifications for a human translation. Machine translation systems are usually designed to accept just one specification: the name of the domain-specific dictionary to consult first. Hutchins and Somers (1992:137-140) make an interesting comment that bears on the specifications used in machine translation, although they do not call them specifications. They point out two characteristics of most machine translation systems which they view as problems. First is 'pre-determination' as a methodology: this means that for a given intermediate representation of the meaning of a sentence, one and only one translation is produced by the system, assuming the dictionaries are held constant. Thus, only one set of specifications exists. But what are those specifications? They are tied up in what Hutchins and Somers call the 'structure-preservation' strategy (the second problematical characteristic), which they explain through the dimension of syntactic structure. Each target-language sentence is given the same syntactic structure as the corresponding source-language sentence, unless the target language does not allow that structure. Then specific adjustments are made to the structure according to rules that have been programmed. This results in a rather literal translation. As Hutchins and Somers point out, structure preservation is generally the *last* option for a human translator rather than the preferred strategy, at least for a human translator who leans away from the literal translation approach.

It is somewhat tempting to loosely identify the free versus literal tension that has existed over the years in translation theory with the general/domain distinction we have identified and with the human versus machine translation branches of translation theory that we are now discussing. Perhaps the reason the free versus literal tension has existed for so long is that people have tried to resolve it in the wrong way. Trying to decide which side is right and which is wrong is like trying to mix oil and water. They will keep separating because each has its own nature. However, if we recognize that both have a valid role, *free* as the normal specification for human translation and *literal* as the normal specification for machine translation, the tension evaporates. Of course, structure preservation works best for closely related languages. Machine translation between Japanese and English requires such massive adjustments of structure that machine translation systems between these languages usually use some intermediate representation which is *deeper* than a surface syntactic structure. Perhaps we should avoid the temptation of identifying the literal versus free tension too closely with the general/domain distinction. However, one thing is clear. Machine translation systems usually have one set of specifications programmed into them. Human translators need to be more flexible.

Truffaut[60] has pointed out that literal translation can be an appropriate and respectable specification for human translators, confirming our inclination to avoid the temptation of settling firmly on free translation for humans and literal translation for computers. For example, it can be an expression of modesty to approximate, without violating the syntactic possibilities of the target language and without wallowing in ugliness, the word order of a sacred expression. And the literal translation of a metaphorical story such as a parable can be an admission that the parable has multiple and unforeseeable applications for various readers at various points in their lives. Truffaut also points out that one should never separate meaning and style, whether the style be literal or free. The King James Bible does not lack in meaning because it retains references to mustard trees. Rather than choosing another metaphor for faith based on a more familiar plant, the translators invite the reader to learn about life in the Middle East.

Returning to the question of mascots, I have already mentioned my affinity to the rhino as a mascot for machine translation and the zebra for human translation. But the famous tower and its namesake the Babel fish should not be forgotten. We often see the Tower of Babel in promotional material for various computer products that are supposed to solve the world's language problems. Perhaps the strong-AI people should take the Babel fish as their mascot. However, one should perhaps be cautious when dreaming of eliminating the consequences of multiple languages. In the story about the Babel fish I referred to in chapter 1, it is pointed out that "the poor Babel fish, by effectively removing all barriers to communication between different races and cultures, has caused more and bloodier wars than anything else in the history of creation" (Adams 1979:60-61). I once read a science fiction short story about the Tower of Babel that had essentially the same theme.[61] The

Almighty comes to visit earth and punishes humans for their pride and arrogance by not only eliminating the diversity of languages but also by forcing everyone to understand each other's intent perfectly, thus causing instant pandemonium. It would be a particularly exacting God who would take this form of revenge on imperfect people who often do not have a genuine concern for the welfare of others, especially if I am right in projecting that the total removal of ambiguity would thrust us into an objectivist universe and eliminate our agency. Orwell predicted that a certain language can eliminate subversive thoughts. Either he was wrong, or he was trying to make us appreciate our agency by suggesting it could be taken away. Fundamental ambiguity does not spring from the language itself but from the agentive relationships between people who are engaged in dialogue. Douglas Adams (1979) may have been suggesting this when in the Babel fish story, just after Arthur starts to understand the Vogon language (thanks to the Babel fish in his ear), his companion, Ford, counsels him to be prepared for the "jump to hyperspace. It's unpleasantly like being drunk." Arthur asks, "What's so unpleasant about being drunk?" To which Ford replies, "You ask a glass of water". Arthur has to think it over to realize that he has interpreted 'drunk' to mean 'intoxicated', rather than 'swallowed'. When Arthur awakens after the extraordinarily unpleasant experience of jumping to hyperspace, he understands what Ford had been trying to explain with the 'drunk' metaphor. The Babel fish has not eliminated ambiguity; it has just greatly broadened the circle of people with whom he could engage in a discussion and have misunderstandings or understandings.

Derrida, in his article "Des Tours de Babel", as edited by Joseph F. Graham (Derrida 1985), tells us that the Tower of Babel "does not merely figure the irreducible multiplicity of tongues; it exhibits an incompletion, the impossibility of finishing, of totalizing, of saturating" (1985:165). This is a reference to Derrida's general position against an objectivist grounding of language. As pointed out in chapter 4, we reject an objectivist grounding but also reject the radical relativism of saying that there is no grounding at all. As suggested by Levinas, language is grounded in constant interactions between humans who are responding to ethical obligations to each other, yielding to or resisting the perceived needs of the other. But with that proviso, we can begin to appreciate the value of Derrida's comment that the distinction between the original and its translation (1985:196) in French law is based on a supposed distinction between content and expression [or form]. Derrida points out that a translation of a translation is legally considered to be derived from the original, not the intermediate translation, as if a translation had no life of its own. Gentzler (1993), in his chapter on Deconstruction, claims that deconstructionists reverse the direction of thought and posit "the hypothesis that the original text is dependent on the translation". However, my reading of Derrida on this point is that he is not fully reversing the direction of thought but rather challenging the form/content hypothesis of objectivism. It needs to be challenged. Why should a translation not be considered a text in its own right? It is the result of a creative effort on the part of the translator, unless the translator is pretending to be a machine, in which case French law has a point. It even becomes understandable that one's interpretation of a source text would be influenced by reading a translation of it, just as it could be influenced by reading a commentary on it. According to Marilyn Gaddis Rose (personal communication), "The translation gives the originary text an afterlife and shows the first language the accrued importance of that text." We must be constantly vigilant in avoiding any theory of human translation that has in it hidden objectivist assumptions, such as the notion that a text has a fixed meaning independent of the reader.

In chapter 1, we saw some examples of asymmetry between languages. In light of our conclusion that human languages are not all grounded on the same objective categorization of reality, we should be more surprised by *symmetry* than *asymmetry* between languages. Some factors that promote a degree of symmetry between English and French are the languages' common Indo-european ancestry and the interaction across the English Channel. But despite their physical and historical proximity, each language retains its distinctive perspective based on internal social interaction. For example, a 'channel' in general is a *détroit* or *bras de mer* in French; yet in the case of the English Channel, it is neither of the two but rather *La Manche* (literally, 'the sleeve')—but *manche* cannot be translated as 'channel' in any other context. And the narrowest point of the channel, the Strait of Dover to the British, is called the *Pas de Calais* by the French, with Dover and Calais being the English and French cities at either end of the underground tunnel (sometimes called the *Chunnel*) connecting France and England by rail. *Vive la différence!* How one's attitude can change. I distinctly remember walking on the sandy beaches of the English Channel near the town of Saint Brieuc in the mid-1960s, during my first visit to France, puzzling over the fact that many words in English did not have one-word equivalents in French. At that time, it seemed strange that English and French were so different. Now it seems strange that they are so much the same.

Of course, all human languages have something in common: *humans* and the *planet Earth*. Skilled field linguists like Kenneth Pike are able to use their knowledge of humans to go into a remote area and quickly learn to speak the local language even though the people have had little contact with the outside world. Pike uses objects like rocks, sticks, and local fruits along with gestures of eating and giving and taking (which are reminiscent of the pre-linguistic economic concepts of children) to elicit utterances from the locals. He transcribes phonetically what he hears and starts looking for patterns such as phonemes and morphemes. Here again, the universality of his method is based not on some supposed self-categorization of the universe but on the neurophysiology of the human auditory system. We can only listen to one sound at a time, and our inner ear performs a preliminary formant analysis within a fairly narrow range of frequencies. All this limits what can constitute a sound in a human language. Alien creatures could conceivably be deaf to the range of frequencies of human speech but communicate via ultrasound. What we still do not understand is how we are able to instantly and unconsciously identify the invariant phoneme in many slightly different instances of a sound. When a human looks at a set of sounds represented as speech waveforms, he or she is unable to identify which are instances of the same phoneme, even though the same waveforms, when sent through a sound card on a computer, are indistinguishable from live speech. Humans apparently process speech based on what some linguists have called *relative* invariance.[62] The salient characteristic of relative invariance is that the same absolute speech waveform could be interpreted as one phoneme on one occasion and another phoneme on another occasion, depending on who is speaking. When we first hear someone speak who has an unusual accent, we somehow analyze their personal system of phonemes and sense how they contrast with each other rather than with some absolute standard for a given phoneme. For example, the words 'rack' and 'rock' differ only by one phoneme. One person's 'rack' could sound like another person's 'rock' but each person will likely make some kind of distinction between the two words, since a complete merger of the two phonemes would cause considerable confusion in English. The ability of humans to detect and produce relative invariance may be related to their ability to use metaphor. We do not understand either human ability, and until we do, we will probably not understand how it is that humans translate between asymmetrical systems.

But humans can and do translate between asymmetrical systems. A skilled translator can choose to make a translation sound very natural or sound foreign. In chapter 1, we mentioned a children's story about a boy in Tahiti who steals a piece of fruit and later makes amends. We discussed a case in which the translation is intended for children in Wisconsin and asked whether the fruit (which was a mango) should become some typical Wisconsin fruit (such as an apple) in the translation. Now we can answer the question: it depends on the specifications. One of the richest dimensions of human translation is the treatment of culture-specific objects. If the primary purpose of the story is to teach a moral principle that the Wisconsin child can immediately grasp, then the specifications might include an instruction (along the dimension of culture) to be target-culture oriented and substitute locally familiar items. On the other hand, if the primary purpose of the story is to teach the Wisconsin children about life in Tahiti, then the specifications would probably include an instruction to leave the mango but to weave in explanatory material (via parenthetical expressions, appositives, drawings, sidebars, etc) that will help the Wisconsin children learn about the Tahiti-specific objects. On the other hand (for those who have three hands), the specifications may include instructions to leave the Tahiti-specific objects even if the purpose is to teach a moral principle. Why? Because a little foreign ring to the story may help keep the attention of the children. Such delicate questions will probably be worked out between the requester and the translator, possibly with revisions after work on the translation has begun and new issues arise.

Other dimensions besides treatment of culture-specific objects are raised by the stolen-fruit story. It must be decided where the action is taking place. The default, that which would be assumed unless specified otherwise, is that the action would take place in the same place as the original story, Tahiti. But if the dimension of naturalness in the specifications instructs the translator to produce a text that sounds as if it were written in English with no hint of it being a translation, then either the characters in the story need to become English-speaking people living in Tahiti or the place of the story needs to be shifted to an English-speaking place, such as Hawaii if one wants to keep the mangos, taking advantage of the fact that mangos are not unique to Tahitian culture. But what if the story includes a highly culture-specific item such as ceremonial tattooing as found in certain polynesian cultures? A tattoo does not have the same cultural significance in American culture, where it is a symbol of rebellion rather than submission. Clearly, it is possible to write a set of specifications which are contradictory. For example, one could request a translation which does not read like a translation (along the dimension of naturalness) but which retains source-culture specific items.

Writing up specifications is not problem-free, but it is much less emotional than arguing about whether a given translation is good or bad in the *absence* of specifications. Once things have advanced to the stage of criticizing an actual text, it is easy for a translator to be influenced by a desire to protect professional worth rather than a desire to please the requester. However, a discussion of specifications which will influence the translation of the text can be vigorous without being taken as a personal attack. Specifications, if taken seriously, can help the requester determine exactly what he or she expects from the translation. They should result in either a commitment on the part of the translator to produce the translation as specified, a give and take in which the requester agrees to different specifications than originally requested, or even a refusal on the part of the translator to be constrained by an undesirable set of specifications. Of course, specifications will nearly always include a price and delivery date, along with delivery format and method (such as paper, diskette, or electronic mail). Unfortunately, these are often the only specifications that are discussed in advance. A realization up front that the requester's specifications are unacceptable to the translator is distinctly preferable to the production of a target text which is unacceptable to the requester.

A special case is a literary translation that is completed on the translator's own time. Here the requester and the translator are the same person. No one is putting out money for the translation, and the translator can afford to let the specifications evolve as the work progresses. Even so, it might be useful for the translator to record decisions made about various dimensions of the translation in order to maintain consistency, especially if the text is long, or to be better able to write about the translation later on.

Specifications are often limited to a brief discussion of price and delivery date. Unless the requester and translator are the same person or the text is one in a uniform series with the same requester and translator, and satisfaction on both sides concerning previous texts (in which case there is an implicit set of specifications), it is extremely important to write up an explicit set of specifications. This is often neglected. Many requesters do not even realize that specifications are needed; and some translators are too timid to insist on clear specifications. Most of the translation that is paid for each year is of LSP texts, and, as we have seen in the sad CF-18 airplane story, substantial amounts of translated LSP text are unusable. Much of this waste could be avoided through the use of specifications.[63] Perhaps the most basic specification for the translation of an LSP text (besides the well-understood elements of price, time, format, and method of delivery) is the treatment of the dimension of terminology. First, the terms in a text should be identified, preferably at authoring time. Then, the equivalents for the terms should be specified. The word 'equivalence' is often avoided in translation theory, but in the case of one-to-one links between source and target terms, it does apply.

There are several sources for term equivalents. When available, normalized terminology should be used, such as the terminologies produced by ISO and the Canadian Government.[64] This terminology work is done by experts in various domains. When a term is specific to the organization producing the source text or when no standard translation equivalent is available, then the organization should provide an equivalent to be used in all their texts. When a standard equivalent is not available for a given term, then it must be clear in the specifications whether the requester or the translator/intermediary is to do the necessary terminological research. Importantly, there should be an agreement about the format in which new terminology, including unexpected terminological questions encountered during the translation, should be returned to the requester.

There is a tendency among translators to be secretive about some aspects of their terminology files. Clearly, some requester-specific terminology can be confidential if it concerns documentation for a product which is not yet on the market, but that is easily resolved by including in the specifications a list of terms to be kept confidential until the product is released. But that is not the problem to which I refer. Some translators will even avoid sharing their terminology files with the requester of a translation. I used to think this attitude was based strictly on a desire to keep a client by making it difficult for the requester to give future business to another translator. However, discussions with colleagues have suggested other possible reasons, such as fear of criticism from terminologists for not having maintained sufficiently sophisticated terminological entries or lack of separation between the terminology research done for various clients. A perfectly valid reason for not sharing certain entries in a personal file is that they are not standard correspondences between terms but instead are insightful and personal text-specific equivalents for phrases of general language. Whatever the reasons, withholding information between the requester and the translator/intermediary on matters of standardized terminology that concerns them both is incompatible with the multidimensional specification approach we are presenting. It can reinforce the false notion of translation being a black box into which only a source text is placed and out of which only a target text appears.

Terminology is part of the specifications for a translation, and terminology management software is making it feasible to quickly extract the entries that are specific to a particular client. Instead of being something hidden and somehow magic, terminology should be an open part of the contract. It has been estimated that for LSP texts, terminology research can account for up to sixty percent of the time required to produce a translation.[65] If the requester and the translator/intermediary can talk about terminology in a business-like fashion, then it can be brought out in the open that if the requester is willing to supply a terminology file containing the requester-specific target-language equivalents to be used for a given text, then the requester should pay a lower price than if the translator is expected to do the terminological research, which may include consulting with engineers or other members of the requester's organization. If the requester-specific bilingual terminology is supplied and the only terms not supplied are those which have generally accepted equivalents and should be known by any translator who is competent in the domain, then the translator should be able to produce the translation much faster than if time has to be taken out for terminology research. The requester should thus receive a discount representing a portion of the time savings generated by supplying the terminology file. The translator/intermediary should still receive as much as or more per hour of work when the terminology is not supplied by the requester. Thus everyone wins. Of course, economic penalties should be attached to a failure on the part of the translator to use the requester's terminology consistently and to a failure on the part of the requester to supply a complete terminology file as part of the specification. A translator should get more business because they produce high-quality results, not because they are able to hold a client hostage.

Upon reflection, it becomes obvious to a requester that the burden of maintaining an organization-specific terminology file is normally upon the requester side, not the translator/intermediary side—unless the requester plans on using the same translator for all future work. The reason is that inconsistent use of terminology is fatal. The CF-18 story we have told is not an isolated incident. It is unusual only in the amount of money that was wasted on a single translation project. For an LSP text to be useful, the terminology must be used consistently. If one portion of the documentation for a complex device calls a certain widget a 'reverse ratchet converter' and another part of the documentation calls the same widget an 'inverted slot-arm transmission' confusion and delays, if not dangerous mistakes, can result. If a team of maintenance persons is trained to repair a complex device using one set of terminology and then a new edition of the maintenance manual comes out using substantially different terminology for the same objects, the resulting confusion and delays become financial losses for someone. Paul Engle has proposed that "The lives of every creature on the earth may one day depend on the instant and accurate translation of one word" (in Gentzler 1993). Although the Iron Curtain has fallen, there are still more than enough ICBMs pointed at both sides of the Atlantic to have a good shot at destroying all vertebrate life on earth. Let us hope that Engle's fear is unfounded but encourage that terminology be taken as seriously as his related aphorism "Translate or Die" suggests it should be.

Failure to learn from mistakes is a greater sin than making them in the first place. In chapter 1, we told about the trouble caused by the way 'side arm' was translated in an official military document. The military cannot foresee every translation problem that might occur, but once a problem does occur, it has a solemn responsibility to find a solution and record it in a terminological database to be consulted during future translations.

The terminological dimension of translation contributes to the meaning of a sentence in context. If the purpose of a translation is to provide factual information such as the installation, operation, maintenance, or repair of a physical device or a software package, then it is likely that the specifications will include a request to make sure that each term that is included in the source text is somehow accounted for in the target text, either by an equivalent target-language term or by a pronoun representing it. Such a request can be couched in objectivism because it is useful to pretend that objectivism applies to domains. At first it seems obvious that every translation should at least include references to all the same objects as the source text. Matching terminology includes this dimension. But in translation of promotional material, the specification to refer to all the objects mentioned in the source text is often dropped. The product will be referred to directly or indirectly, but the arguments for purchasing the product may be changed radically. A beverage that is exported to Israel would not sell well if promotional material retained a ham sandwich as an example of a food that goes well with the beverage. The translation of the title of a film may refer to a different aspect of the story than the original. There are interesting cases such as the French film *La Totale* which was remade in the U.S.A. as *True Lies* and then translated back into French as, literally, 'The Chameleon'. The original French title may refer to the total chaos brought into the life of a woman whose husband turns out to be a secret agent. It would be tempting to say that translated film titles and promotional material are not really translations. Perhaps there is a case for claiming a distinction between re-authoring and translation. But then where do you stop? We must be cautious not to take the first step down a spiral staircase that eventually leads to an invalidation of all general-language translation and limits us to the mythical world of context-independent and human-free objectivist bottom-up meaning.

Suppose that the purpose of a given translation is to be informative, and suppose that the requester wants the information in the source text to appear in the translation so far as possible. Further suppose that the text is not sufficiently constrained to use machine translation and that the specifications do not include a request to approximate the source syntax. Is there some technique that can be used by human translators to check their work, beyond checking to see that all terms have corresponding items in the translation? One promising avenue is to use Statutory Analysis. This type of analysis, which has been elaborated by the French linguist and philosopher Jean-Marie Zemb (see Melby 1988), involves dividing each statement into three parts: **thema**, **phema**, and **rhema**. The thema consists of those elements that are claimed to exist and times that qualify those claims of existence; the rhema is a claim made about the thema; and the phema is the relation between the thema and the rhema. For example, in the sentence "I gave my boss a piece of my mind today", the thema is the speaker (the employee) and the time (today); the rhema is the act of telling the employer what the employee thinks of him or her; and the phema is affirmative. In the sentence "I didn't see John yesterday" the thema consists of the speaker and John; the rhema is the act of seeing; and the phema is negative. The analysis into thema, rhema, and phema assigns a logical status (hence Statutory Analysis) to sentence elements independent of traditional syntax. There is no necessary connection between thema/rhema/phema and traditional subject/predicate. This allows a translator or reviewer a methodology for checking to see whether at least the logical status of a troublesome and complex sentence is the same in the source text and target text. The syntax of the source and target sentences can be radically different while their logical status (according to Statutory Analysis) is usually the same. This methodology could also be helpful in translator training as a framework for pointing out some types of translation errors to student translators. Note that Statutory Analysis does not claim to represent all the information in the text or the meaning of the text. It is not a layered approach in which all the meaning of a text flows from layer to layer. It is not hampered by objectivist assumptions. It is not claimed to apply to all sentences. It is a dimension of language which can be a helpful diagnostic.

There are many other dimensions of translation that are worth discussion besides terminology, logical status, register, naturalness, culture, and place. The translation of a screenplay for the purposes of dubbing typically has specifications that include matching the length of corresponding utterances with preferences for similar lip movements, even at the expense of what in other circumstances would be a less desirable translation, but not at the expense of a blatant contradiction with the visual or the loss of elements crucial to the plot. The translation of a software program, sometimes called localization or internationalization, is an intricate task that involves an extensive set of specifications for such items as length of messages and culturally sensitive icons. Truffaut[66] has rightly noted the importance of another dimension, musicality, in the sense of suprasegmental intonation higher than the phrase level, sometimes extending beyond the sentence to discourse level. It is often expected of a human translation that the text will sound pleasant according to poorly understood but intuitively felt conventions of the target language. Clearly, the list of dimensions cannot be closed. The suggestion by I. A. Richards, a well-known theorist of literary criticism, that translation "may very probably be the most complex type of event yet produced in the evolution of the cosmos", is often quoted (Richards 1953:250). Any contenders?

5.3.2 More discussion of issues from chapter 1

Several issues were raised in chapter 1. Perhaps we are ready to further address them. The long-term debate between literal versus free translation was briefly sketched, including the recent contribution to the debate by Venuti, who argues that a translator should not even try to be invisible. We have already noted that the debate cannot be resolved simply by linking literal translation with domain-specific texts and free translation with general-language texts, even though there is a tendency to produce freer translations of general texts. Within machine translation, there is not much room for maneuvering so long as the principles of pre-determination and structure preservation are followed. Within human translation, chapter 1 asked whether there might be some other perspective from which there is no need to decide the question once and for all. The multidimensional specification approach allows us to stop asking whether translation, in general, should be free or literal. No one will ever give an argument so compelling as to convince everyone that all translation should be one way or the other. The desire to resolve the free versus literal debate is probably generated by the assumptions of objectivism. Whenever meaning is viewed as something that can exist independently of the speaker, hearer, and situation, there will be a desire to identify the one proper way of decoding that meaning from the source text and encoding it into the target text. In the agentive view of language, there are meaningful interactions between people, but extracting the meaning of a sentence is like performing an autopsy. You can find all kinds of things that were part of the living body, such as the heart and kidneys, and you can find all kinds of things that were part of the sentence, such as the words and punctuation, but the life of the body is not something we have been able to isolate and neither is the meaning. The translator has the same dilemma as the monolingual writer. The reader is not present. Translating is somewhat like leaving a message on an answering machine. You have to imagine yourself speaking to the absent person as if he or she were there. What are you trying to accomplish by speaking with the person? What will maximize your chances of success? There is no dimension of meaning as such in our approach to translation. But as we have seen, all dimensions can contribute to meaningful interactions. Syntactic structure is a dimension. Typically, the specifications will include an instruction to use target-language syntax. If there is a reason to mimic source-language syntax as much as possible, that can be specified. All will depend on the purpose of the translation. Granted, most purposes for translating are not advanced by an attempt to mimic the source-text syntax. But that is not the same as saying that all human translation should be free rather than literal. All human translation should be literally conformant to the specifications and free from objectivist constraints.[67]

The multidimensional approach provides a relatively unemotional method for evaluating translations. The only bad translation is one that does not conform to the specifications. However, a translation may be undefined, rather than good or bad, if the specifications are unclear or incomplete.

Multidimensional specifications are the basis for our approach to human translation. Controlling language until it can be treated according to objectivist assumptions is the basis for our approach to machine translation. We have not described a basis for the third area, text analysis to decide whether a text is suitable for machine translation. This area must be somewhat experimental in that what counts is how well a machine translation system does on a particular text, not what text analysis says will happen. The approaches to text typology developed by text-linguistics and elaborated by Snell-Hornby (1988) and by Sager (1993) seem relevant here.

It seems that the agentive approach to language is consistent with the somatic approach of Robinson (1991). There is no transcendent, disembodied meaning in human translation. In machine translation, we create an artificial world within which we can get away with pretending that there is transcendent meaning. For Robinson, as for Lakoff (1987), the human body is the starting point for meaning. The senses are not irrelevant to understanding. George Steiner, the respected translation theorist, once commented that a blind person should be able to produce translations indistinguishable from those of a seeing person. Practicing translators who teach translation have found otherwise.[68]

Some might complain that we have not actually presented a theory of human translation. The analysis/transfer/generation approach to machine translation describes a process of machine translation. We have described no process for human translation, only an approach to planning and evaluating translation using specifications based on multiple dimensions. Along with many of my colleagues, I yearn for a better understanding of human translation. I hope for further insights into what happens inside us when we make the jump from one language to another. We certainly take many dimensions into account, but how? Meaning exists only in a particular situation. Therefore, I repeat the caution that meaning as such is not even one of the dimensions we include in specifications for human translation. If that disqualifies our approach from being a theory, so be it. If the admission price to theory-hood is reduction to an algorithmic process, the price is too high. I refuse to oversimplify and misrepresent by saying that a translation is a text with the same meaning as the original.

In chapter 1, I asked how it would be possible to communicate if meaning were *not* transcendental. Now, from the perspective of chapter 4, I can ask how it would be possible for people who are communicating thanks to their agency and their acknowledgment of the agency of others to continue to be agents and continue to communicate if meaning *were* transcendental.

Current computers are limited in their ability to translate dynamic general language. If current objectivist techniques are ever extended so that computers and humans translate all texts equally well, then the central thesis of this book is false. If entirely new techniques allow future computers to achieve Minsky's dream of equalling or exceeding all human intellectual abilities, including translation, then (if I am right) those computers will possess agency and view humans as either friends or enemies. In the meantime, let us use our agency to produce human translations that enlighten, uplift, and nourish, even if machine translation is only able to inform.

5.3.3 A brief look at some approaches to translation

What approaches to human translation are being taught and used? We have suggested the importance of multidimensional specifications. How does our approach fit in with other approaches? We will look at just a few and only briefly. We should keep in mind the frequently-heard complaint among those who earn their living by translating that translation theory does not seem to be helpful in earning their daily bread. I believe that multidimensional specifications is not just an academic exercise but can save money by avoiding costly misunderstandings. As we look at other approaches, let us be careful not to combine approaches willy-nilly and produce a bothersome monster rather than a useful tool for translators.

Earlier in this chapter we noted that Neubert and Shreve (1992) have observed a decline in the influence of the linguistic approach (by which they mean Generative Grammar and its objectivist assumptions) in translation theory. We would support this decline when it comes to human translation theory but not in machine translation theory. However, Gentzler (1993) points out that the decline is not universal. He describes the influence of Chomsky on Nida, who has published on aspects of a linguistics-based translation theory throughout the 1960s, 1970s, and into the 1980s. According to Gentzler, the influence of Nida's approach is still very strong today: "In terms of its importance in the field, Nida's science cannot be underestimated, for his approach is being disseminated in the classrooms of both Germany and the United States" (1993:47). Gentzler notes that Wilss, a noted German translation scientist, has also been influenced by Chomsky. We have already noted that Generative Grammar has been highly influential in recent approaches to machine translation. All this is ironic in the light of Chomsky's disclaimer in *Aspects of the Theory of Syntax* concerning translation. Gentzler quotes Chomsky, who asserts that

> The existence of deep-seated formal universals ... implies that all languages are cut to the same pattern, but does not imply that there is any point by point correspondence between particular languages. It does not, for example, imply that there must be some reasonable procedure for translating between languages. (1965:30)

Gentzler interprets this statement by Chomsky as an expression of caution about the applicability of one grammar to several languages. There are other possible interpretations. Chomsky may have believed that his approach would eventually provide a basis for translation but wanted to cover up an embarrassing aspect of his theory not emphasized in *Aspects*. It is a fact that Chomsky's approach to Generative Grammar in 1965 included the notions of deep structure and surface structure linked by transformations and that those transformations worked only in one direction, from deep to surface. There was no "reasonable procedure" for going from surface structure to deep structure.[69] This may sound bizarre, but it is true. Chomsky justified the irreversibility of transformations on the basis that his was a model of competence rather than performance. Not only did his theory not provide a reasonable procedure for translating, it did not even provide a reasonable procedure for analyzing a sentence into its deep structure. Of course, this gap in Chomsky's approach has not kept translation theorists from using it as a basis for translation theory, nor has it kept machine translation practitioners from developing programmable procedures for going from surface structures to deep structures and back to surface structures. There is even a branch of Generative Grammar called Lexical Functional Grammar which pointedly departs from Chomsky by including reversibility as a basic tenant. Head-driven Phrase Structure Grammar, another branch of Generative Grammar, also provides for more computationally tractable and thus more reasonable procedures for processing [controlled] languages. Even Chomsky's recent branch of Generative Grammar, Government and Binding, is being used at a number of centers as a basis for parsing text.

Evidently, the linguistic approach to translation is alive and well in machine translation and, at least in some schools, in human translation. How and when can it be useful? One case may be when the human translator wants to avoid making grandiose claims about understanding the source text and all its implications. We have noted that great literature is usually full of dynamic metaphor. When a book deserves re-reading several times over one's life and stimulates new insights with each reading, how can a translation capture all the life of the original? One viable stance is to admit that the translation is only one interpretation of the original but that it is a literary work with a value of its own. Another stance is to try to help the reader come closer to the original text by retaining some or all of the metaphors of the original even if they seem strange in the target language. This may require additional commentary by the translator and extra work by the reader. The agentive view of language suggests that neither approach is wrong. The translator can try to present a text which is easily digestible in the world-view of the projected reader or invite the reader to stretch and partially enter the world of the author. The only thing that would be wrong would be to fail to indicate in the specifications which option is being taken.

Gentzler discusses the introduction of the notion of 'polysystem' into translation studies. Even-Zohar and Toury use this term to describe the various literary systems (from poetry to editorials to children's fiction) that co-exist in a language. This notion should be useful in the area of text analysis. Toury emphasized in the 1970s and 1980s, based on his reading of the later Wittgenstein, that there is not just one correct translation (Gentzler 1993:129) since every translation privileges some aspects of the text at the expense of others. This is an early attempt to break away from the objectivist basis of the linguistic approach and is clearly compatible with multidimensional specifications. However (1993:131-132), Toury also assumes that it is possible to construct a *tertium comparationis*, essentially an interlingua that objectively captures the meaning supposedly shared by source and target texts. He even appeals to Chomsky's *Aspects* for authority. This internal contradiction is not surprising or unusual. It has taken me nearly twenty years from the time I sensed a serious problem in linguistic theory to the current uncovering of some of my own objectivist presuppositions.[70] And I expect to uncover more in the future.

Gentzler also discusses deconstruction and points out that most translation theories have not really taken it into account. Although deconstruction has provided some valuable insights in translation (see our previous discussion of Derrida), the agentive view suggests that deconstruction has gone too far toward radical relativism. Translation theory should be founded on real communication between real people. People talk and write and translate all the time. There is evidence of understanding and misunderstanding. We should be burdened neither with the search for transcendental meaning nor the despairing view of language as ungrounded.

Sager provides a wealth of information that is compatible with a multidimensional specification approach. He points out that "It is now widely recognized that the human translator does not provide a possible model for a translation machine" (Sager 1993:20). I have attempted to explore why. His book is especially useful in that it acknowledges the entire range of language from 'completely natural' to 'almost artificial' (1993:27). He does not directly address the issue of the underlying assumptions of current techniques in machine translation or their inherent limitations, but he is one of the few to explicitly address the question of text analysis for the purpose of deciding whether human or machine translation is more appropriate (1993:185-209).

Vermeer (in Snell-Hornby 1994:11) has devised the term 'skopos' to describe the ultimate aim of a communicative act. He talks about a 'meta-meaning' but avoids the trap of assuming that it is simply a property of the source text. He says that it "arises out of the commissioner's [our requester's] intention to have communication established with someone else in a given situation by the help of a translator". The notion of skopos seems compatible with an agentive view of language. The agentive view even provides a philosophical foundation for skopos.

Neubert and Shreve, whom I have referred to several times, have helped move translation studies away from an overdependence on a linguistic approach. They emphasize the text as opposed to the sentence in isolation.

They correctly point out that machine translation is highly dependent on the linguistic approach. They also make an intriguing and insightful comment that "Mutual knowledge means that a communicating partner is able to *know that the other knows too*" (Neubert and Shreve 1992:55). There is a minor inconsistency in their writing (an inconsistency of which I am also occasionally guilty) in that they have not rooted out all traces of objectivist assumptions tied to the linguistic approach, and they have not turned completely away from the conventional way of talking about the *meaning* of a text as if it were an object that is extracted from the source text and recoded in the target text. This does not detract from their discussion of textuality, including intentionality, acceptability, situationality, informativity, coherence, cohesion, and intertextuality. Their work should be highly valuable to the training of translators and the evaluation of translations.

Robinson (1991), to whom we have also referred, is particularly careful to uncover the philosophical foundations of the linguistic approach to translation. He does not attempt, as we have, to find an alternative grounding for language, but his particular contribution is complementary to our project. He discusses various 'tropes', by which he means turnings back and forth by the translator to face sometimes the author of the source text and sometimes the projected reader of the translation in a dialogue that is highly personal and human.

Hopefully, the reader senses that over the past thirty or forty years, translation theory has reached a turning point. In this extremely brief span, relative to the history of translation, we have gone from domination to failure to a breaking away: domination by a linguistic approach; failure of the linguistic approach to come through with results in machine translation when applied to tasks that require an understanding of general-language texts; and a breaking away from the linguistic tradition in human translation. In this same span we have seen the rise of the mainframe computer and its partial replacement by personal computers. Recent advertisements by mainframe computers no longer attempt to ignore personal computers, hoping they will go away. They have formed a partnership. Translators need to form a partnership with machine translation. We have seen that the trends in machine translation are to high-quality translation through controlled language in a domain and to low-quality translations to meet certain needs that are not appropriately met by traditional human translation. Other books are available (such as Hutchins et al 1992 and Arnold et al 1994) which provide more detailed introductions to the workings of machine translation. We have seen that human translation theory is headed away from the linguistic approach and toward what humans have been doing all along—communicating in particular situations for specific purposes. The practical contribution to translation theory and practice of our philosophical ruminations is an emphasis on specifications. The theoretical contribution is an outline of how language is possible. We have proposed that with the bulk of the human translation needs of the world involving LSP texts, everyone needs to pay more attention to appropriate exchange and use of terminology without returning to a linguistic approach for the non-term units of the text. To translate LSP texts effectively, translators need to build on the basis of word processing and use computers in new ways as tools to extend memory, reduce drudgery, and improve communication. But it is not enough even if all *translators* take the general/domain distinction seriously. Everyone who deals with language is affected.

5.4 Some implications for translation technology

A major implication of our study of the nature of language is that current machine translation techniques will never be extended to handle dynamic general language the way humans do. If you need a text translated, you should at least hesitate before accepting without question a sales pitch for a machine translation system. Consider the following excerpt from a brochure advertising a handheld computer that comes in two models, one that translates both ways between English and French and another that translates both ways between English and Spanish. The computer is advertised as being appropriate for short documents such as newspaper articles, memos, and letters. The brochure continues by explaining that it is

> the world's first portable language computer that actually understands and translates complete sentences. [It] lets you type in **any** sentence, phrase, or word and get an immediate and accurate translation.... It actually analyzes each sentence to determine each word's part of speech and contextual meaning. The resulting translation is highly accurate and grammatically correct—complete with proper meaning, capitalization, punctuation, and syntax. The Language Computer's 50,000 entry dictionary and advanced algorithms allow it to distinguish different meanings of the same word and to substitute a phrase or expression that conveys the proper meaning for those words and phrases it does not recognize.

A naive person who needs a text translated and who is used to a modicum of truth in advertising should be rushing out to buy the device. Besides, it runs on just two AAA-size batteries.

In order to contrast hype with reality, we have included an appendix containing sample translations produced by some machine translation systems on the market.

But the implications of our study are not all negative. Technology applies to translation appropriately in at least the following three circumstances: (1) to produce fully-automatic indicative translations for individual non-translators; (2) to produce publication-quality translations using machine translation when there is a high-volume of machine readable text consisting of rigidly controlled language restricted to a narrow domain; and (3) to provide computer-based tools for human translators.

In all cases, the level of success in applying technology to translation depends on an analysis of the source text, the objectives of the requester, and the profile of the user; this results in a set of specifications. In the first circumstance mentioned in the preceding paragraph (indicative translation), the requester and user are the same person. This option is already available in the European Commission over their internal network. It is becoming available on various telecommunications networks such as CompuServe (U.S.A.), Minitel (France), and the Internet. And individuals can purchase low-cost machine translation software for their personal computer.

An important aspect of the specifications is the dimension of terminology. We have already explained how important it is to use terminology consistently in LSP text. But effective terminology management is not trivial. Before describing computer-based tools available now for human translators and looking to the future, we will explore some of the benefits of saving and processing both the source and target texts in electronic form.

5.4.1 Bitext and translation

Nearly all texts, both source texts and translations, are now prepared in electronic form using some kind of word processing software. And most translations correspond to the source text roughly sentence by sentence, with some source sentences corresponding to two sentences in the translation and some pairs of source sentences corresponding to one sentence in the translation. Most translations follow the order of the sentences in the source text, not because that is the only way to translate, but because it makes it easier for the translator to check over the translation to see if anything important is missing. If these conditions hold (source and target texts in electronic form, sentences usually paired and in the same order)—and they usually do for LSP texts—then it makes sense to create a bilingual database of paired source and target texts. Each pair of texts is then aligned so that corresponding segments (usually one or two sentences) are linked together. Each segment is a translation unit linked to its corresponding translation unit in the other text. A pair of texts thus aligned is called a bitext (for 'bilingual aligned text').[71] A collection of bitexts is called a bitext database.

A bitext database is a rich resource. Although there is no link between words of the source text and words of the target text, it can be assumed that whatever LTUs there are in the target text, if any, corresponding to the source text, they will be somewhere in the target segment to which the source text is linked. Some of its uses are for terminological/phraseological research, translation of a revision of a previously translated text, and terminological validation of a translation.

For terminological/phraseological research, the bitext database must be indexed by every word, keeping the source text and target text distinct, and preferably marking user-selected groups of texts in the index as well. Then software must be written to allow the user to type in an LTU and find all occurrences of it in the bitext database. Suppose the bitext database is English and French. Then if the English side is interrogated for occurrences of the LTU 'operating system', any English segment containing those two words will be shown, along with the corresponding French segment. In this case, the LTU may be the term for the system software on a computer but the system may also retrieve instances of the two words that do not form an LTU, such as in the sentence "We found one operating system and one disabled system". But since it is a human who interprets the results of the search, it does not matter that there are some false responses. At least the response is vastly narrowed down from a manual reading of the entire bitext database. Indeed, for a bitext database consisting of millions of words of text, it would be completely infeasible to search it manually. An electronic search for a combination of words can be done in a few seconds, and typically a substantial portion of the responses is relevant. Besides looking for terms, troublesome phrases can be researched even if they are not what would normally be considered a term. For example, suppose a translator wonders how the metaphorical use of the expression 'bridge the gap' has been rendered by other translators. A bitext database research can provide the answer almost instantly. A possible extension to a basic search is allowance for more complex search patterns, such as a word followed by anything but a certain word followed by another specified word before the end of the sentence. A useful preprocessing task is to reduce all the words of the text to their base form, that is, the form that appears as a headword in a dictionary, for placement in the index or else expansion of a search request to include inflected forms.

A bitext database with indexing and retrieval software as just described can be called a bilingual concordance system. The idea has been around for a long time, and recently, automatic alignment techniques have evolved quickly, making it practical to create large bitext databases.[72] Terminological and phraseological research on a bitext database can produce results that are extremely useful to a translator or terminologist even if the alignment is occasionally faulty. At worst, some of the target-language segments retrieved will not correspond to the source-language segment they are linked to and thus be a minor inconvenience for the human who must determine that they are to be ignored.

A bilingual concordance system is a good use of technology in translation because it allows a translator to find useful information in previous translations without requiring any understanding of the texts on the part of the computer. Thus it applies to the vast quantity of LSP texts that consist of a mixture of general language in a certain style with terminology from one or more domains and are not sufficiently restricted to be suitable for machine translation when high quality is needed.

A second use of a bitext database is what is often called a 'translation memory'. This is a specialized function for translating a minor revision of a previously translated text. Suppose that a set of documentation is translated and later revised, with only ten percent of the sentences changing and the overall style and terminology remaining consistent with the previous version. It would be extremely wasteful to have a human retranslate the entire text when most of the sentences of the previous translation could be used as is. Therefore one uses the computer to reduce unneeded translation.

There are two approaches to translation memory based on a bitext database of the previous version and its translation. The approach which is commonly implemented at present is to process the revised text sentence by sentence and determine whether the sentence appeared in the previous version of the source text; if so, the translator is allowed to insert the corresponding previous translation segment instead of re-translating. Another approach is to have the computer produce a target text consisting of the entire previously translated text except for those segments that have changed in the revision. Either way, the translator only translates the revised sentences. Even there, a translation memory system can sometimes be useful if the revised source sentence differs from the previous version only by a detail such as a change in date. The translation memory system can substitute the date from the new source segment into the old translated segment and propose the revision to the translator with the option of editing it further. This requires software to find source segments that do not match exactly, but it does not require human-level similarity processing. The worst cases in translation memory are failure to retrieve a relevant source segment and retrieval of an irrelevant segment. So long as they do not happen very often, a translation of a revision of a document can be produced in much less time than by expecting the translator to consult the previous text and its translation and use cut and paste features of a word processor to produce the same result.

Translation memory is a good use of technology in translation, and although the idea has been around for a long time, it is just now being used extensively.[73] When it applies (that is, in the case of the translation of a minor revision of a previously translated document), it is extremely useful. A variation on a revision of a document is a minor revision of the messages in a software package for a new 'release' of the software. Like a bilingual concordance, it does not require that the software understand the text, and the human translator remains in control. It can even be useful outside of revisions of documents when translating extremely dull, repetitive texts that repeat entire sentences and paragraphs from the same or other documents. Another variation on translation memory is to make standard reference books that contain standard translations available to the translator for insertion into a translation.

A third use of a bitext database is for translation checking. The first two applications, a bilingual concordance and a translation memory, are for use *during* translation. The third application, a translation checker, is used *after* translation. A translation checker draws on a bitext database consisting only of one text and its translation along with positive and negative checking files. The positive checking files contain normalized terminology which the translator is expected to use in the translation. Each source-text segment is checked for occurrences of any of the terms in the positive list. When a term is found, the corresponding target segment is scanned to see if its normalized target-language term exists somewhere in the target segment. If not, the human translator is alerted and decides whether there is actually a problem in the translation or whether it was a false alarm, such as a pronoun standing for the term in the target text. Each source-text segment is also scanned for items from the negative file. This file contains a list of translation errors that human translators have been observed to make and which can be detected through a simple comparison of words, such as using a false cognate.[74] Potential errors of this type are also brought to the attention of the human translator.

An additional benefit of such a checker is that if a whole segment of text is missing from the translation by some oversight or accidental deletion, it will probably be detected if there are enough normalized source-target term pairs. It can be imagined that missing segments could also be detected by a third file of one-to-many translation mappings. A target segment should contain at least one of the listed options for each of the source terms. If none are in the corresponding target segment, then the human translator would again be alerted and would look for a problem.

Translation checking is another good use of technology in translation because it reduces the tedium of checking translations. Human translators who review the translation of another translator can use translation checking as a tool. Human translators, unlike computers, understand the source text, and they have only occasional misunderstandings unless they take work in a domain for which they have not properly prepared themselves. Their errors are usually only errors of carelessness, and computers can help detect such errors. The translation checker need not be comprehensive or perfect to be useful, so long as it does not give too many false alarms.[75]

There is a caution that applies to all applications of bitext databases. They are not replacements for good terminology work; they are only tools for a human terminologist. Normalized terminology still needs to be recorded in a terminology file, and terminological research should only be done on a bitext database of high-quality texts and translations; otherwise it can perpetuate bad translations. It would not just be inefficient for each translator to use a bilingual concordance to look for the translation of each term—it would be disastrous, because the database will likely be full of conflicting correspondences for terms that should be treated consistently. The bitext database should be consulted only when a term is not found in the appropriate terminology files. In that case, it can be extremely valuable, but the results of terminology research should be recorded in a terminology file for future use. A translation memory can be very useful for the translation of a minor revision of a previously translated text, but if the revision involves a change in the normalized correspondences for terms, it is no longer a minor revision, and in that case the blind use of a translation memory system could produce a monstrosity consisting of new segments using one set of correspondences and old segments using another set. A human translator would be hard pressed to produce such a bad translation without the translation memory. One possible solution is to have the translation memory system include a type of prechecking in which the bitext of the previous source and translation is checked against the current file of normalized terminology for conflicts.

There is an additional difficulty that applies to bitext databases. Sometimes the texts will come from more than one word processing system. In this case, viewing the texts becomes problematical; also, programs that convert from one format to another are notorious for skipping and scrambling portions of text. A related difficulty is the representation of non-English characters and their transmission via various media.

For those interested in the problem of characters, I have published a paper which discusses the representation of characters and possible solutions for exchange.[76] For those already familiar with the problem I will simply mention that one solution is to use SGML entities for interchange and Unicode for local representation and processing. The use of SGML as the underlying basis for the presentational markup of a text, with word processing software maintaining an SGML markup and dynamically converting it to a presentational markup and allowing the user to work in WYSIWYG (what-you-see-is-what-you-get) mode, is the best long-term solution for increasing the effectiveness of technology in LSP texts, both those that are sufficiently restricted to be appropriate for machine translation and those that are sufficiently restricted to be appropriate for a bitext database but are best translated by a human.

Over a decade ago, I first proposed a multi-level translator workstation that combined software tools for translators (commonly called a translator's workbench) and computer hardware to support them.[77] It is gratifying to finally see more translators using translator workstations and more effort being put into the development of software tools for translators. My original design included a first level for situations (unfortunately still all too common) in which the source text is not available in machine-readable form, a second level in which the source text is available in machine-readable form, and a third level at which there is a link to machine translation. Some recent systems, such as IBM's Translation Manager and the Eurolang Optimizer, allow for an optional link to machine translation. This allows, as I proposed, the translator to work in the same environment, whether translating text using various tools or revising the output of a machine translation system. There should be an additional function specifically designed to facilitate the revision of a human translation by another human translator.[78]

5.4.2 On the horizon

We have described some applications of technology that are on the market or under development. They are all useful because they do not assume that language conforms to objectivist assumptions, except when dealing with normalized terms from a well-defined domain that are used according to the specifications, and when processing translation segments that correspond between source and target texts because the specifications require them to correspond. These applications focus on particular aspects of text that humans have agreed to restrict; thus they are not expected to understand the text. Machine translation only has a chance of producing high-quality output when a human translator could also produce high-quality output without understanding the domain or the text being translated. In that case, most translators would prefer to have a computer do the work than to suffer the boredom. What trends are on the horizon for applying technology to translation?

The first trend is clearly toward the increased availability of text in machine readable form and the increased use of various bitext database tools such as the ones I have described.

The second trend is toward more use of descriptive markup such as SGML as the underlying markup for text.

The third trend is the increased sharing of terminology (Wright 1995).

The fourth trend is toward domain-specific controlled-language applications of natural language processing. Some projects in this area to watch over the coming years are the Dialogue-Based Machine Translation system being developed at the University of Grenoble; the huge VerbMobil project in Germany, which is intended to produce a domain-specific prototype of a handheld speech-to-speech machine translation system that would be used to help people speak in their language and be heard in another language; and the CYC project in Texas. It would be very easy for someone to forget the domain-restriction of the VerbMobil system and expect it to work like the Universal Communicator of Star Trek and similar devices in other science fiction. Despite my personal attraction to the characters and situations in the Star Trek series, the writers have made a serious theoretical error based on the false objectivist assumption that general language uses metaphor only as a sideline that can usually be ignored. In one episode of *Star Trek: The Next Generation* ("Darmok"; second episode in the fifth season), a people is encountered who use metaphor extensively. The Universal Communicator breaks down. All of us are such people; a Universal Communicator that cannot handle metaphor will never work. The CYC project, a major effort in AI, has dramatically changed its design to treat a set of domains rather than attack dynamic general language head-on.[79]

The fifth trend is, I hope, to take our conditions for the possibility of language seriously as a starting point and continue look for ways to deal with dynamic general language that do not let objectivism in through the front or back door. This is basic research and extends far beyond the horizon. We may have only identified a small part of what is needed to make dynamic general language processing possible, which is only a jumping off point for the project of understanding how humans translate when they are not acting like machines, which is just the beginning of building machines that act like humans.

5.5 Alternatives and risks

It has been estimated that about fifteen billion U.S. dollars are spent on translation every year. And as international trade increases, the need for translation is increasing. But good translation is hard work and therefore expensive, and alternatives to human translation have always been sought. We have discussed machine translation as an alternative to human translation under certain circumstances. We will conclude with a note of caution about being overly enthusiastic about alternatives to human translation, using technology or other means.

One of the most successful alternatives to translation has been to learn a lingua franca as a second language. Latin served the purpose for centuries, then French, and now English and Spanish. But second languages typically do not replace first languages unless a cultural group loses its identity and is absorbed into another culture. In Latin America, Spanish is an economic passport, yet native American Indian languages survive as first languages. Few are still seriously pushing Esperanto or any other language as the first language for the whole world. And despite the ubiquity of a dialect of English which is often called 'International English', there is a growing need for translation into the first language of the user of a text.

The importance of one's first language is easy to understand in light of the view of language we have presented here. Language is not just a part of a culture; it may be more accurate to say that culture is a part of language. One might object, pointing out that people from different cultures can communicate in a lingua franca, and thus culture could not be part of the lingua franca. But let us be careful. What do people talk about in a lingua franca? They may talk about some technical domain at a professional conference. In that case, they are not using dynamic general language. They may talk as tourists. Tourism is a domain that locals learn for straightforward economic reasons. They do not typically speak of cultural matters. When we use technology as an alternative to translation, we should not lose sight of the fundamental distinction between dynamic general language and controlled domain-specific language. Domain-specific language is made possible by creating an objectivist-like world using general language. General language is made possible by acknowledging the agency of others. It is made rich by human flexibility. We can handle new situations, including the interpretation of dynamic metaphor. We thrive on fundamental ambiguity, which is essential to our agency. We use the metaphor of objectivism to create domain-specific artificial languages as tools.

Jean-Marie Zemb has said that to understand language, we need, besides words and grammar, a third element: human thought.[80] Human thought, as opposed to whatever computers currently do in their millions, even billions, of circuits, includes agency and all else that makes language possible. We have a right to make tools and benefit from them. Why would we want to become unthinking slaves to our own tools? Our discussion of the possibility of general and domain language has implications beyond translation. If we lose sight of the general/domain distinction and, in the name of progress or efficiency, think of all words as terms or otherwise attempt to limit our use of language, including translation, to what computers can currently do, we may place our humanity or someone else's at risk. If, however, we remember the distinction and what makes each type of language possible as we build tools, we can enrich our humanity.

Appendix

A.1 Samples of machine translation

There is a children's poem about a boy who, when he was good, was very, very good, but when he was bad was awful. That seems to describe machine translation.

Here is a sample of raw machine translation supplied by a sales representative of the METAL system, developed by Siemens Corporation and the University of Texas at Austin.[81] It was selected as an example of a sentence that worked reasonably well for not being restricted technical language. The information with the sample indicates that the analysis phase took about three minutes and the transfer/synthesis phase took about one minute.

MT sample 1

• *German source text*	• *English output from METAL*
Er ging nun an die Küste, fand am Strande ein Boot und ein altes Netz, das er flickte, und segelte aufs Meer hinaus, um Fische zu fangen.	It now went to the coast, found a boat and an old net which it patched at the shore and sailed it in the sea out in order to catch fish.

Here is a sample of raw machine translation given on a promotional flyer for Globalink's Power Translator Professional system.

MT sample 2

• *French source text*	• *English output from Globalink PTP*
Veuillez nous créditer du montant indiqué sur le relevé ci-joint.	Please credit us the amount indicated on the statement enclosed.

Here is a sample text supplied to Systran by an unidentified customer. Systran offers the text and its target-language examples as particularly satisfying MT output.

MT sample 3

- *English source text*

(a) The purpose of the Advanced Technology Program (ATP) is to assist United States businesses to carry out research and development on pre-competitive generic technologies. These technologies are: (1) enabling, because they offer wide spectrum of potential application and form an important technical basis for future commercial applications; and (2) of high value, because when applied, they offer significant benefits to the U.S. economy. Pre-competitive technology is defined in 295.2(n) and generic technology is defined in 295.2(e).

(b) In the case of joint research and development ventures involving potential competitors, the willingness of firms to commit significant amounts of corporate resources to the venture indicates that the proposed research and development is pre-competitive. For joint ventures that involve firms and their customers or suppliers, or for single firms not proposing cooperative research and development, a quantified description of the expected applicability of the technology and adequate assurances that the technology being developed will be utilized widely can provide evidence that the proposed research and development is pre-competitive.

- *French output from Systran*[82]

(a) Le but du programme de technologie de pointe (triphosphate d'adénosine) est aider des entreprises des Etats-Unis d'effectuer la recherche et le développement sur des technologies génériques précompétitives. Ces technologies sont: (1) permettant, parce qu'elles offrent la gamme étendue d'application potentielle et forment une base technique importante pour de futures applications commerciales; et (2) de valeur élevée, parce qu'une fois appliqués, ils offrent les avantages significatifs à l'économie américaine. La technologie précompétitive est définie dans 295.2(n) et la technologie générique est définie dans 295.2(e).

(b) Dans le cas des entreprises communes de recherches et de développement faisant participer les concurrents potentiels, la bonne volonté des sociétés d'investir des quantités significatives de ressources de corporation dans l'entreprise indique que la recherche et le développement proposés est précompétitif. Pour les entreprises en participation qui impliquent des sociétés et leurs clients ou fournisseurs, ou pour les sociétés simples ne proposant pas la recherche et le développement en commun, une description mesurée de l'applicabilité prévue de la technologie et à assurances proportionnées que la technologie étant développée sera utilisé largement peuvent fournir l'évidence que la recherche et le développement proposés est précompétitif.

• *German output from Systran*

(a) Der Zweck des Programms der neuen Technologie (Atp) ist, Staatgeschäfte zu unterstützen, Forschung und Entwicklung auf vorwettbewerblichen generischen Technologien durchzuführen. Diese Technologien sind: (1) ermöglichend, weil sie breites Spektrum der möglichen Anwendung anbieten und eine wichtige technische Grundlage für zukünftige kommerzielle Anwendungen bilden; und (2) von hohem Wert, weil, wenn sie angewendet werden, sie bedeutenden Nutzen der US-Wirtschaft anbieten. Vorwettbewerbliche Technologie wird in 295.2(n definiert) und generische Technologie wird in 295.2(e definiert).

(b) Im Fall gemeinsamer Forschungs- und Entwicklungswagnisse, die mögliche Konkurrenten mit einbeziehen, zeigt die Bereitwilligkeit der Unternehmen, bedeutende Mengen der korporativen Betriebsmittel am Wagnis festzulegen an, daß die vorgeschlagene Forschung und die Entwicklung vorwettbewerblich ist. Für Beteiligungsgeschäfte, die Unternehmen und ihre Kunden oder Lieferanten miteinbeziehen oder für die einzelnen Unternehmen, die nicht kooperative Forschung und Entwicklung vorschlagen, können eine quantitativ bestimmte Beschreibung der erwarteten Anwendbarkeit der Technologie und ausreichende Versicherungen, die die Technologie, die sich entwickelt wird, verwendet wird, weit Beweis zur Verfügung stellen, daß die vorgeschlagene Forschung und die Entwicklung vorwettbewerblich ist.

• *Spanish output from Systran*

(a) el propósito del programa de la tecnología avanzada (ATP) es asistir a los negocios de Estados Unidos realizar la investigación y el desarrollo en tecnologías genéricas precompetitivas. Estas tecnologías son: (1) permitiendo, porque ofrecen amplia gama del uso potencial y forman una base técnica importante para los usos comerciales futuros; y (2) de alto valor, porque cuando están aplicados, ofrecen ventajas significativas a la economía de los E.E.U.U.. La tecnología precompetitiva se define en 295.2(n) y la tecnología genérica se define en 295.2(e).

(b) en el caso de la investigación y del desarrollo comunes aventura la participación de competidores potenciales, la buena voluntad de firmas de destinar cantidades significativas de recursos corporativos a la empresa indica que la investigación y el desarrollo propuestos es precompetitivos. Para empresa a riesgo compartido que implican las firmas y sus clientes o surtidores, o para las solas firmas que no proponen la investigación y el desarrollo cooperativos, una descripción cuantificada de la aplicabilidad prevista de la tecnología y los aseguramientos adecuados que la tecnología que es convertida será utilizada extensamente pueden proporcionar evidencia que la investigación y el desarrollo propuestos es precompetitivos.

• *partial French output from Intergraph Transcend*

(Un) Le but du Programme de Technologie Avancé (ATP) devrait aider les affaires d'États-Unis pour exécuter pour faire des recherches sur et le développement sur les technologies génériques pré-compétitifs. Ces technologies sont: (1) rendre capable, parce qu'ils offrent le spectre large d'application de potentiel et forment une base technique importante pour l'avenir applications commerciales; et (2) d'haute valeur, parce que quand s'appliqué, ils offrent des profits significatifs à l'économie américaine. La technologie Pré-compétitif est définie dans 295.2(n) et la technologie générique est définie dans 295.2(e).

Now here is what happened with several machine translation systems when we put in short texts from a French magazine specialized in astronomy and space exploration.

MT sample 4 (from *Ciel et espace*, n. 296, November 1994, p. 3)

- *French source text*

En attendant la future station spatiale internationale, c'est dans le domaine des satellites, des lanceurs et des stations au sol que s'affrontent les différentes puissances mondiales.

Une scène où les États-Unis jouent le premier rôle devant une Russie fragilisée et une Europe lézardée.

Où l'on voit également s'affirmer de nouveaux talents et de nouvelles ambitions.

- *English output from a major MT system*

The one is of the satellites, the promoters{thrower} and the breaks{position/stop} meanwhile the future spatial international break{position/stop}, in the domain{field/property} in{on/to} the ground that the powers different confront each other world-wide.

A scene{stage} where the United States play the first list{role} before{in front of} fragilisée Russia and a lézardée Europe.

Where does someone also see herself{himself/themselves} asserting of new talented and new ambitions.

- *English output from Systran*

While waiting for the future international space station, it is in the field of the satellites, the launch vehicles and the stations on the ground that clash the various world powers. A scene where the United States plays the first part in front of weakened Russia and lézardée Europe.

Where one also sees affirming new talents and new ambitions.

• *English output from Globalink Message Translation System*

In the meantime the future international spacial station, it is in the area of satellites, promoters and stations to the ground that confront the different world powers.

A scene where U.S. play the first role ahead a Russia @@fragilise'e and an Europe loungeed.

Where one sees equally to assert new bruise and new ambitions.

MT sample 5 (more text from *Ciel et espace*)

• *French source text*

Les astronomes qui travaillent dans le domaine visible se heurtent tous au même adversaire: la turbulence.

L'atmosphere de la Terre rend un peu myopes mêmes les meilleurs de leur télescopes.

Un seul remède : l'optique adaptative.

Cette technologie haut de gamme est d'ores et déjà testée en vraie grandeur.

Examples : l'observation de la surface des astéroïdes, ou encore les étoiles laser de Robert Fugate.

• *English output from a major MT system*

The astronomers who work in the obvious{visible} domain{field/property} all clash with the same opponent: the turbulence.

The atmosphere of Earth returns a little myopes same the best ones of their telescopes.

A single remedy: the adaptatif optics{point of view}.

This haut de gamme technology is tested from now on in real{true} grandeur{greatness/height/magnitude/size}.

Examples: the observance{observation} of the surface of the astéroiedes again{still} the laser asterisks{star} of Robert Fugate.

• *English output from Systran*

The astronomers who work in the visible field run up against all against the same adversary: turbulence. The atmosphere of the Earth makes a little short-sighted same the best of their telescopes. Only one remedy: adaptive optics. This top-of-the-range technology is tested right now full-scale. Examples: observation of the surface of the asteroids, or the stars laser of Robert Fugate.

• *English output from Globalink Message Translation System*

Astronomers that work in the visible area knock all at the same adversary: the turbulence.

The @@atmosphere of the Earth renders a same myopic bit best of their telescopes.

An alone remedy: the optic @@adaptative.

This high range technology is @@ores and already tested in true magnitude.

++Examples: the observation of the surface of asteroids, or again laser stars of ++Robert ++Fugate.

MT source text 6 (from a short article "Fishy Repair Jobs" in *Scientific American*, October 1994 p. 15, slightly edited to simplify)

• *English source text*

Two reports, one involving rats and the other humans, suggest that during sleep our brains remain quite busy, furiously consolidating important memories that have accumulated during the day.

• *Spanish output from METAL*

Dos informes, un implicando ratas y el otro humans, sugiere que nuestros cerebros siguen existiendo bastante durante el sueño busy, consolidando furiously recuerdos importantes que se han acumulado durante el día.

For several nights after the rats' maze exercises, their hippocampal neurons displayed similar firing patterns; the rats were apparently playing back their memories of running the maze.

The major difference was that the firing was more rapid, as if the memories were being run on fast-forward.

The firing occured[83] during slow-wave sleep, a phase of deep (but not dreamless) sleep marked by low-frequency pulses of electrical activity in certain regions of the brain.

Varias noches después de los ejercicios de laberinto de las ratas, su neurons de hippocampal mostraba patrones de encendido similares; las ratas estaban volviendo a tocar aparentemente sus recuerdos de correr el laberinto

La diferencia esencial era que el encendido era más rápido, como si los recuerdos estuvieran siendo corrida encima rápido forward.

Los occured de encendido durante la onda lenta duermen, una fase de sueño profundo (pero no dreamless) marcado por impulsos low-frequency de actividad eléctrica en ciertas regiones del cerebro.

- *Spanish output from LOGOS*

Dos informes, unas ratas de implicación y los otros humanos, sugieren que, durante el sueño nuestros cerebros permanecen completamente ocupados, las memorias de agrupación furiously importantes que acumularon durante el día.

Para varias noches después de que el laberinto de las ratas hace las ejercicios, sus neuronas hippocampal han visualizado modelos de disparo similares; las ratas estaban volviendo a poner sus memorias de aparentemente la publicación de laberinto.

La principal diferencia era que los disparos eran más rápidos, como si ejecutan las memorias estaban en el rápido hacia adelante.

Los disparos occured durante el sueño a lenta onda, una fase de profundidad (pero no el dreamless) el sueño señalado con impulsos de frecuencia bajo de la actividad eléctrica en ciertas regiones del cerebro.

• *Spanish output from Systran*

Dos informes, las ratas de participación uno y los otros seres humanos, sugieren eso durante sueño que nuestros cerebros siguen siendo absolutamente ocupados, furiosamente consolidando las memorias importantes que han acumulado durante el día. Por varias noches después de las ratas el laberinto ejercita, sus neuronas hippocampal exhibió patrones similares de la leña; las ratas jugaban al parecer detrás sus memorias de funcionar el laberinto. La diferencia principal era que la leña era m'as rápida, como si las memorias fueran funcionadas en rápido-delantero. La leña ocurrió durante lento-agita el sueño, una fase del sueño profundo (pero no dreamless) marcado por pulsos de baja frecuencia de la actividad eléctrica en ciertas regiones del cerebro.

• *French output from Systran*

Deux rapports, les rats on impliquants et les autres humains, suggèrent que cela pendant le sommeil nos cerveaux restent tout à fait occupés, furieusement consolidant les mémoires importantes qui se sont accumulées pendant le jour. Pendant plusieurs nuits après les rats le labyrinthe s'exerce, leurs neurones hippocampal a montré les modèles semblables de mise à feu; les rats jouaient apparemment en arrière leurs mémoires de courir le labyrinthe. La différence principale était que la mise à feu était plus rapide, comme si les mémoires étaient courues sur rapide-vers l'avant. La mise à feu s'est produite pendant lent-ondulent le sommeil, une phasedu sommeil profond (mais non dreamless) marqué par des pouls de bassefréquence d'activité électrique dans certaines régions du cerveau.

- *German output from Systran*

Zwei Reports, mit einbeziehende Ratten man und die anderen Menschen, schlagen vor, daß das während des Schlafes unsere Gehirne ziemlich beschäftigt bleiben und furiously wichtige Gedächtnisse vereinigen, die während des Tages angesammelt haben. Für einige Nächte nach den Ratten trainiert das Labyrinth, ihre hippocampal Neuronen anzeigte ähnliche Zündungmuster; die Ratten spielten anscheinend zurück ihre Gedächtnisse des Laufen lassens des Labyrinths. Der Hauptunterschied war, daß die Zündung schneller war, als ob die Gedächtnisse auf Schnellvorwärts laufen gelassen wurden. Die Zündung trat während langsam-wellenartig bewegen Schlaf, eine Phase des tiefen (aber nicht dreamless) Schlafes auf, der durch Niederfrequenzimpulse der elektrischen Tätigkeit in bestimmten Regionen des Gehirns gekennzeichnet wurde.

- *Portuguese output from Systran*

Dois relatórios, os ratos se de envolvimento e os outros seres humanos, sugerem que isso durante o sono nossos cérebros remanescem completamente ocupados, furiously consolidando as memórias importantes que acumularam durante o dia. Por diversas noites após os ratos o maze exercita, seus neurônios hippocampal indicou testes padrões similares do acendimento; os ratos jogavam aparentemente para trás suas memórias de funcionar o maze. A diferença principalera que o acendimento era mais rápido, como se as memórias eram funcionadas em rápido-para diante. O acendimento ocorreu durante lento-acena o sono, uma fase do sono profundo (mas nao dreamless) marcado por pulsos low-frequency da atividade elétrica em determinadas regiões do cérebro.

• *Italian output from Systran*

Due rapporti, ratti di coinvoluzione si e gli altri esseri umani, suggeriscono che quello durante il sonno i nostri cervelli rimangono abbastanza occupati, furiously consolidando le memorie importanti che si sono accumulate durante il giorno. Per parecchie notti dopo i ratti il labirinto si esercita, i loro neuroni hippocampal ha visualizzato i modelli simili di infornamento; i ratti stavano giocando apparentemente indietro le loro memorie di funzionamento del labirinto. La differenza principale era che l' infornamento era più veloce, come se le memorie stessero facende funzionare su veloce-di andata. L' infornamento si è presentato durante lento-fluttua il sonno, una fase di sonno profondo (ma non dreamless) contrassegnato dagli impulsi a bassa frequenza di attività elettrica in determinate regioni del cervello.

• *Spanish output from Globalink Message Translation System*[84]

Dos informes, uno involucrando ratas y el otro @@humans, sugiere que durante el suen~o nuestros sesos permanecen bastantes ocupados, furiosamente consolidando memorias importantes que han acumulado durante el di'a.

Para varios noches despue's de los ejercicios de laberinto de ratas, sus @@hippocampal las neuronas mostraron modelos similares de descarga; las ratas aparentemente jugaban el dorso sus memorias de correr el laberinto.

La diferencia importante era que la descarga era ma's ra'pido, como si las memorias @+siendo la corrida sobre ra'pido - delantero.

La descarga ocurrida durante lenta - ola de suen~o, una fase de profundo (pero no @@dreamless) el suen~o marcado por pulsos de baja frecuencia de actividad ele'ctrica en regiones ciertas del seso.

• *French output from Intergraph Transcend*

Deux rapports, un rats qui impliquent et l'autre humain, suggérer que pendant le sommeil que nos cerveaux restent tout à fait occupé, furieusement consolider les mémoires importantes qui ont accumulé pendant le jour.

Pour plusieurs nuits après le exercices de labyrinthe des rats, leur hippocampal neurons montrés similaires les modèles qui vident; les rats rejouaient apparemment leurs mémoires de courir le labyrinthe.

La différence majeure était que le vider était plus rapide, comme si les mémoires étaient courues sur rapidement-en avant.

Le vider a arrivé pendant le sommeil de lent-vague, une phase de profond (mais pas dreamless) dort marqué par les pouls de fréquence bas d'activité électrique dans les certaines régions du cerveau.

A.2 A sample indicative translation scenario

We discussed the possibility of using machine translation for correspondence between people who have little or no knowledge of one another's language. Clearly, such an endeavor makes sense only if both parties are highly motivated. It probably makes sense only if each is studying the language of the other. Here is a fictional exchange of letters between Mike, who speaks only English, and Gloria, who speaks Spanish (for German and French speakers, we have translated the English letter into those languages as well). For reference, word counts of the source texts and translation times for some output texts are given. All Microtac translations were done on a 66 MHz 486 DX2 PC with 16 Meg of RAM.

MT sample 7 (a letter from Mike to Gloria)

• *English source text (229 words)*

Dear Gloria:

Thanks a lot for your last letter. I was visiting my Grandmother in Chicago when it came, so I didn't see it for a few days. Sorry it took me so long to get back to you.

School is really killing me right now. My Calculus class gives me loads of homework, and some nights I end up staying up till two or three in the morning just to get it done. Then when the alarm goes off the next morning, I can hardly open my eyes and stagger to the shower. I suppose things aren't much easier for you, are they?

It feels like winter here already. Just before Thanksgiving we got dumped on--seven inches of very wet, very messy snow. The roads were slippery, and I saw several cars off the road on my drive home

• *Spanish output from MicroTac Spanish Assistant for Windows 1.00a (1:09 minutes)*

Estimado Gloria:

Gracias mucho por su última carta. Visitaba a mi Abuela en Chicago cuando vino, para que no lo vi por unos días. Afligido tomó me tan largo volver a usted.

Escuela es verdaderamente matanza yo ahora mismo. Mi clase del Cálculo me da cargas de tarea, y unas noches que acabo arriba quedan arriba hasta dos o el tres del mañana sólo hacerlo hace. Entonces cuando la alarma va apartado el mañana próximo, puedo abrir apenas mis ojos y tambaleo a la ducha. ¿Supongo cosas no son muy más fácil por usted, está ellos?

Toca como invierno aquí ya. Sólo acción de gracias anterior que hicimos descargó en--siete pulgadas de nieve muy mojada, muy desarreglada. Los caminos eran from work. Good thing I learned to drive in snow a long time ago! After the big storm some of the snow melted, and then the temperature plummeted, so the ice on the roads got even worse.

One good thing, though: the storm left a thick blanket of powder up at the ski resorts. Most places are reporting about an 80 inch base, which is phenomenal for this early in the season. Any chance you could come up here over New Year's?

Hope things are going well.

Mike

resbaladizos, y vi varios carros apartado el camino en mi hogar del paseo de trabaja. ¡Cosa buena que aprendí a manejar en nieve un tiempo largo hace! Después de la tormenta grande algunos del nieve fundió, y entonces el [plummeted] de la temperatura, así el hielo en los caminos se puso igual peor.

Una cosa buena, aunque: la tormenta salió una manta espesa de polvo arriba al esquí acude. La mayoría de lugares informan acerca de un 80 base de la pulgada, que es [phenomenal] por este temprano en la estación. ¿Cualquiera oportunidad que podría aparecer aquí encima de Nuevo año?

Espere que cosas van bien.

Mike

• *German output from MicroTac German Assistant for Windows 1.00a (1:14 minutes)*

Geehrter Gloria:

Vielen Dank für Ihr letzter Brief. Ich besuchte meine Großmutter in Chicago, wenn es gekommen ist, also ich es nicht gesehen habe für einige Tage. Traurige es hat genommen, ich so lange werden hintere zu Ihnen.

Schule ist wirklich Tötung ich richtige jetzt. Meine Rechnungsart stuft mir Lasten von Hausaufgaben gibt ein, und einige Nächte, die ich aufwärts ende, bleiben bis zwei oder drei bekommen am Morgen nur, es tut. Dann wenn der Alarm geht weg der nächste Morgen, ich kann kaum meine Augen öffnen, und wankt zur Dusche. Nehme ich an, sind Dinge nicht viel leichtrer denn Sie, ist sie?

Es fühlt sich wie Winter hier schon. Nur vorher hat Erntedankfest, das wir bekommen haben, weggeworfen auf--sieben Zölle von sehr nassem, sehr dreckigem Schnee. Die Straßen waren rutschig, und ich habe mehrere Autos weg gesehen die Straße auf meinem Antrieb-Heim von Arbeit. Gute Sache, die ich gelernt habe, fahren in Schnee eine lange Zeit vor! Nach dem großen Sturm ist einigem vom Schnee geschmolzen, und dann hat die Temperatur abgesunken, so das Eis auf den Straßen ist ebene schlechtere geworden.

Eine gute Sache, aber: der Sturm ist gegangen eine dicke Decke von Pulver oben an den Schi-Urlaubsorten. Die meisten Stellen berichten, über einen gründet 80 Zoll, welch ist für diesen früh phänomenal in der Jahreszeit. Irgendeine Chance, die Sie hier an Jahr heraufkommen können?

Hoffnung-Dinge gehen gut.

Mike

• *French output from MicroTac French Assistant for Windows 1.00a (1:20 minutes)*

Gloria:

Merci un terrain pour votre dernière lettre. Je visitais ma Grand-mère à Chicago quand il est venu, donc je ne l'ai pas vu pour quelques jours. Désolé il a pris je donc long reculer à vous.

École est vraiment meurtre je maintenant. Mon Calcul classe me donne des charges de devoirs à la maison, et des nuits je fin hausse reste jusqu'à deux ou trois le matin seulement obtenir le fait. Alors quand l'alarme part le matin prochain, je peux ouvrir à peine mes yeux et chancelle à l'averse. Est-ce que je suppose est-ce qu'objets ne sont pas beaucoup de plus facile parce que vous, est ils?

Il sent comme hiver ici déjà. Immédiatement avant jour de l'action de grâces nous avons obtenu avons déchargé sur--sept pouces de neige très mouillée, très en désordre. Les routes étaient glissantes, et j'ai vu plusieurs voitures éteint la route sur mon conduit au maison de travaille. Bonne chose qui j'ai appris à conduire dans neige un long temps il y a! Après la grande tempête quelque de la neige a fondu, et alors le [plummeted] de la température, donc la glace sur les routes a obtenu même plus pire.

Une bonne chose, pourtant: la tempête a laissé une couverture épaisse de poudre au ski a recours. La plupart endroits rapportent environ un 80 base du pouce, qui est phénoménal pour ce tôt dans la saison. Toute chance qui est-ce que vous pouvez vous lever ici à Année?

Espérez qu'objets vont bien.

Mike

- *Spanish output from Systran*

Gloria Querido :

Gracias mucho por su letra pasada. Visitaba a mi abuela en Chicago cuando vino, así que no la vi por algunos días. Apesadumbrado me duró tan para conseguir de nuevo a usted. La escuela realmente me está matando ahora. Mi clase del cálculo me da cargas de la preparación, y algunos las noches I termina encima de permanecer para arriba hasta dos o tres de la mañana apenas para conseguirla hecha. Entonces cuando el alarmar sale la mañana

próxima, puedo abrirme apenas los ojos y escalonarlos a la ducha. Supongo que las cosas no son mucho más fáciles para usted, son ellas? Se siente como invierno aquí ya. Momentos antes de Thanksgiving conseguimos descargados en-siete pulgadas de nieve muy mojada, muy sucia. Los caminos eran deslizadizos, y vi varios coches del camino en mi impulsión casera del trabajo. Buena cosa que aprendí conducir en nieve hace un rato largo! Después de que la tormenta grande algo de la nieve derritiera, y entonces la temperatura cayó a plomo, así que el hielo en los caminos consiguió incluso peor. Una buena cosa, aunque: la tormenta dejó una manta gruesa del polvo para arriba en los recursos del esquí. La mayoría de los lugares están divulgando alrededor de una base de 80 pulgadas, que es fenomenal para esto temprano en la estación. Cualquier ocasión usted podría venir para arriba aquí concluído el nuevo año? Las cosas de la esperanza van bien.
Micrófono

• *Spanish output from Globalink Message Translation System*

Estimado Gloria:

Gracias un lote para su u'ltima carta. Yo fui visitar mi Abuela en Chicago cuando vino, tan Yo no vi lo por unos pocos di'as. Triste me tomo' tan anhelar regresar a usted.

La escuela se mata realmente me ahora mismo. Mi Calculus la clase me da cargas de tarea, y algunas noches Yo acabo por permaneciendo arriba hasta dos o tres en la man ~ ana simplemente para conseguir hizo. Entonces cuando el alarma va fuera la pro'xima man ~ ana, Yo puedo abrir apenas mis ojos y tambaleo a la ducha. ??

Yo supongo cosas no es mucho ma's fa'cil para usted, son ellos?

Tiene ganas de invierno aqui' ya. Simplemente antes de Di'a de Gracias nosotros conseguimos descargado sobre -- siete pulgadas de muy mojar, nieve muy desordenada. Los caminos eran resbaladizos, y Yo vi el @+varios automo'viles fuera el camino sobre mi hogar de paseo desde el trabajo. La cosa buena Yo aprendi' para manejar en la nieve hace mucho tiempo! Despue's de la tormenta grande alguna de la nieve derretio', y entonces la temperatura cayo', tan el hielo sobre los caminos consiguio' parejo peor. Una cosa buena, aunque: la tormenta @+dejar una manta gruesa de polvo arriba en los recursos de esqui'. La mayori'a de los lugares informan sobre una 80 pulgada de base, que es fenomenal para esta temprana en la temporada. ?? Cualquier oportunidad usted podri'a venir arriba aqui' sobre Nuevo An~o?

Las que cosas de esperanza vayan bien.

Mike

• *partial French output from Intergraph Transcend*

Cher Gloria:

Merci beaucoup pour votre dernière lettre. Je visitais ma grand-mère dans Chicago quand il est venu, donc je ne l'ai pas vu pour quelques jours. Désolé il m'a pris si long pour vous retourner à.

L'école vraiment me tue maintenant. Ma classe de Calculus me donne les chargements de devoirs, et quelques nuits je finis par veiller jusqu'à ce que deux ou trois dans le matin seulement pour le recevoir fait. Alors quand l'alarme saute le matin prochain, je peux ouvrir à peine mes yeux et titube à la douche. Je suppose que les choses ne sont pas beaucoup plus faciles pour vous, n'est-ce pas?

MT sample 8 (Gloria's reply to Mike's first letter)

• *Spanish source text (140 words)*[85]

Querido Mike:

Qué suerte que me hayas invitado a visitar para el año nuevo. Te iba a preguntar que si tenías planes, pues necesito ir a Denver por esa fecha para una entrevista. La Universidad allá busca algún estudiante que sepa español y que asista a la Universidad Autónoma de México para ayudar con el desarrollo de un programa de intercambio de estudiantes. ¿Sería posible quedarme con tu hermana cuando venga?

Lamento que sufras tanto con el cálculo. Como siempre te he dicho, tu verdadero talento es escribir poesía. ¡Lástima que hayas abandonado la literatura a favor de la ingeniería! Podías haber sido un gran escritor, pero ¡ni modo!

Ya mero estudio para mi último exámen del trimestre. Espero que salga bien, mas me siento algo desesperada. A ver qué pasa.

Me saluda a Jenny--y nos vemos pronto.

Gloria

• *English output from MicroTac Spanish Assistant for Windows 1.00a (1:05 minutes)*

Dear Mike:

That luck that had invited me to visit for the new year. I/he/she/it/you was you going to ask that if you had plans, I then need to go to Denver for that date for an interview. The University there any student searches for that I/he/she/it/you know Spaniard and that I/he/she/it/you attend the Autonomous University from Mexico in order to help with the development of a program of exchange of students. Would it be possible stay with your sister when do I/he/she/it/you come?

Lament that I/you suffer so much with the calculation. As always I have said you, your true talent is to write poetry. Pity that had abandoned the literature in favor of the engineering! You could have been a great writer, but neither manner!

Already grouper study for my last [exámen] of the [trimestre]. I wait for that I/he/she/it/you succeed, [mas] sits down something desperate. To see what you/he/she/it pass.

You/he/she/it greet me Jenny--and we are seen soon.

Glory

• *English output from Systran*

Querido Mike:

That luck that you have invited to me to visit for the new year. It was going to ask to you that if you had plans, because I need to go to Denver by that date for an interview. The University there looks for some student who knows Spanish and that she attends the Independent University of Mexico to help with the development of a program of interchange of students. Would be possible to have left I with your sister when she comes? Moan that you undergo so much with the calculation. As always there am saying to you, your true talent is to write poetry. ¡La'stima that you have abandoned literature in favor of engineering! You could have been a great writer, but ¡ni way! Already mere study for my last examination of the trimester. I hope that it exits well, but I feel something desperate. To see what it happens. It salutes to Jenny--y we see ourselves to me soon.

Gloria

• *English output from translation by a college student with a BA in Spanish (5:23 minutes)*

Dear Mike:

What luck that you invited me to visit for New Year's! I was going to ask if you had plans, 'cause I need to come to Denver around that time for an interview. The university there is looking for a Spanish-speaking student from the

Autonomous University of Mexico to help develop a student exchange program. Could I maybe stay with your sister when I come?

Too bad that Calculus is so tough! Like I've always said, your real talent is writing poetry--it's a shame that you abandoned literature for engineering! You could have been a great writer. Oh well!

Right now I'm studying for my last test of the semester. Hopefully it will be okay, but I'm a bit desperate. We'll see what happens.

Say hi to Jenny for me. See ya soon.

Gloria

A.3 Types of text and pre-editing

Machine translation vendors are typically quick to point out (as we have) that the type of source text can profoundly affect the output from their system. Highly literary pieces, such as poetry, metaphor, and so forth, do not translate well by machine.

In some cases it is possible to pre-edit the text that is processed by machine translation. Globalink offers the following editing guidelines to users of their Message Translation System:[86]

We suggest that you "pre-edit" your message/text before using the system. Try to be as clear and simple as possible in your sentence structure. That is, if a sentence is long and complicated, break it into two or more distinct shorter sentences.

If a sentence places the verb at some distance from the subject, we suggest that you repeat the subject to insure that the verb is conjugated properly.

Example: We enjoyed our stay here and hope to return one day.
Better: We enjoyed our stay here and we hope to return one day.

Try to eliminate ambiguous elements in the sentence, if possible. For example, if you are using a word which can be interpreted as more than one part of speech, (i.e. the word could be a noun OR a verb), and you could use an alternative word or words which could be interpreted as only one part of speech, use the latter to achieve a clearer translation.

A large number of idiomatic expressions have been entered as such in the semantic unit portion of the system's dictionary. However, due to the complexity and endless variety of language, it is always advisable to check the message/text you want translated for such ambiguous or colloquial expressions to insure the best possible translation by the system.

Example: You'd better verify your flights before your departure.
Better: You should verify your flights before your departure.

Example: I have to get ready for our party.
Better: I have to prepare for our party.

In particular, a commonly-used English language structure which should be avoided is the phrasal verb, which is a verb followed by a preposition which work in combination with one another. Very often, a single verb alternative will work better in the system.

Examples: use "happen" instead of "come about"
"continue" instead of "go on"
"return" instead of "come back"
"find" instead of "come across"

Finally, avoid omitting words, such as "that" or "which," when they introduce dependent clauses. Although these terms are commonly omitted in speech, they are necessary for the system to function optimally.

You should also note that where the system cannot translate words in your message/text, those words will be indicated by a double @@ directly in front of those words.

Note also that you can indicate to the system that you do not want to translate certain terms, such as product names or personal names that the system would try to translate. For example, the system would translate the female name "May" but the sentence syntax would be adversely affected. To prevent such occurrences, type the string *sstrx* followed by a space before your word or expression and a space then *sstrx* after the word or expressions you do not want the system to translate.

Of course, not all texts lend themselves to such editing. Imagine being given the following source text:

> "Have it compose a poem—a poem about a haircut! But lofty, noble, tragic, timeless, full of love, treachery, retribution, quiet heroism in the face of certain doom! Six lines, cleverly rhymed, and every word beginning with the letter *s*!!"
>
> "And why not throw in a full exposition of the general theory of nonlinear automata while you're at it?" growled Trurl. "You can't give it such idiotic—"
>
> But he didn't finish. A melodious voice filled the hall with the following:
>
> Seduced, shaggy Samson snored.
> She scissored short. Sorely shorn,
> Soon shackled slave, Samson sighed,
> Silently scheming,
> Sightlessly seeking
> Some savage, spectacular suicide.

Machine translation vendors would definitely avoid such text. (So would many human translators, no doubt.) Incredibly, the above text *is a translation*, from the Polish, by Michael Kandel (from *The Cyberiad*, by Stanisław Lem, 1974, pp. 50-51). The irony is that the poem was supposedly composed by an 'electronic bard'! When we have new techniques that allow FAHQT of UT, maybe such computerized poets will also be a reality.

Endnotes

[1] The military events described here are documented in an article in *US News and World Report*, May 23, 1994, pp. 26-30. No political statement is intended. The translation difficulty is independent of the military objectives of any group.

[2] Vermeer (1994:7) suggests that Saint Jerome (the patron saint of translators, who died on 30 September, probably in 420, and who has been credited with starting the 'literal' versus 'free' debate) may have been misunderstood. He may have actually been describing morpheme-by-morpheme translation versus word-for-word translation and not proposing 'free' translation as used today. Thus we may have a translation problem within translation theory.

[3] Ferdinand de Saussure, whose course in general linguistics was published posthumously in 1916, is considered to be the founder of modern linguistics. He established the synchronic study of language (as opposed to the tradition of historical linguistics, which was primarily diachronic) and the distinction between an idealized object called *langue*, in which there are no individual variations, and actual speech, which was called *parole*. Europeans writing in English tend to refer to him as de Saussure while American linguists refer to him simply as Saussure.

[4] My description of Systran is based on the stages given in Hutchins and Somers (1992).

[5] The companies behind these two products, Globalink and MicroTac, have merged.

[6] Richard Kittredge originated the term sublanguage and has written an article about it (1987).

[7] The AMTA-94 conference, the first conference of the Association for Machine Translation in the Americas, October 5-8, 1994, Columbia Inn, Columbia, Maryland.

[8] General-language dictionaries written by lexicographers start with a word or other lexical unit and list its senses; they are usually in alphabetical order based on a headword. Technical dictionaries written by terminologists start with the concepts of a given domain and list the terms that are associated with those concepts in one or more languages. Ideally the entries are placed in some logical order that reflects the network of concepts, as viewed by experts in the field of work associated with the domain being treated. A 'lexiconcept' (suggested by colleague Chris Larsen in a personal communication) would probably be viewed by lexicographers as a word sense rather than the word itself; terminologists who do not believe lexicography and terminology can be mixed would view 'lexiconcept' as an oxymoron, while terminologists who believe in mixing would consider it a concept; but neither group of terminologists would consider 'lexiconcept' a term or a word. To those who work within the linguistic model called Stratificational Grammar, the term 'lexeme' may be equivalent to LTU, and to my colleagues

at the GETA project in Grenoble, 'lexical unit' is equivalent to LTU, but unfortunately, neither term is viewed as a cover term by lexicographers or terminologists.

[9] A watch of any kind (i.e., flood, severe thunderstorm, etc.) indicates that conditions are favorable for the development of the problem; the potential exists. A warning means that the weather problem has been observed and is approaching.

[10] This text was taken from the December 1991 issue. Every issue of every computer magazine includes similar examples.

[11] In 1990, I presented this study as a series of lectures as a visiting professor at the Collège de France, and in 1991 it was published in *Les Cahiers de Lexicologie*.

[12] English-French asymmetry has been studied extensively. See, for example, Garneau (1985).

[13] There is a hole in English related to nuts. Lithuanian has a specific verb for the stage at which nuts begin to form after the tree blossoms, for which we have no equivalent in English (personal communication with Sue Ellen Wright).

[14] Even in English there are anomalies. James McCawley points out (personal communication) that although *you're welcome* is usually an acceptable reply to *thank you*, an exception is the *thank you* in response to a compliment.

[15] *The Petit Larousse* 1995.

[16] One might object by pointing out that *faire un geste de la tête* is symmetrical with the expression *shake one's head*, and thus we do not have true asymmetry. However, one cannot make a complete list of all the expressions in which *geste* might occur and how each will be translated.

[17] There are still many users of DOS, a non-graphical user interface, in the world. Some of them will hang on for a long time. And why not, if DOS applications work for them? But the GUI opens up the computer to a portion of the population that has been intimidated by computers until now.

[18] James McCawley (personal communication) has suggested another example. If one is talking about the perfective, *have* can precede but not follow the progressive *be*, so one might assume that (a) *They have been smoking pot* is acceptable but (b) *They are having smoked pot* is not. However, (b) is acceptable if considered analogous to *They are having scrambled eggs*. One could give both readings to (b) without violating the principle of treating sentences in isolation, simply by putting two entries in the lexicon under *have*, one as an auxiliary and one as a main verb. The crucial issue is whether *all* contextual influences can be reduced to lexical entries and features. My experience with machine translation suggests this is not the case.

[19] Although one may not agree with Chomsky's advocacy of anarchy, his political views are certainly not boring. In the documentary film *Manufacturing Consent*, Chomsky remarks in an interview that he has never found a connection between his political activism and his

linguistic theory. Perhaps this is because his politics, which deals with human rights, could only be described linguistically by an approach that goes beyond the bounds of Chomskyan linguistics.

[20] No offense is intended here to any watchers of soap operas, because there is a non-boring aspect of soap operas that transcends the plot, namely that many watchers care very much about the players on the television screen and treat them as real people with real pain. But even a soap opera fan would probably not argue that his or her favorite series is a source of novel plot development.

[21] Lakoff, as a proponent of Generative Semantics in the 1960s, challenged the autonomy of syntax, but was pushed out of the mainstream of Generative Grammar. In *More than Cool Reason*, Lakoff points out that his own recent work is in some ways a continued exploration of the consequences of changing this assumption.

[22] In the real world of LSP (Language for Special Purposes) texts, we still find a great deal of ambiguity. In this book, domain language refers to the extreme case in which there is little or no ambiguity. The boundaries between general, LSP, and domain-specific texts are not clean.

[23] Jackendoff, in his recent work (1990), seems to be challenging the principle of autonomous syntax. However, he remains in practice within the confines of treating sentences in isolation and the assumptions of objectivism.

[24] As mentioned in the acknowledgement, Terry Warner is co-author of this chapter. Thus the meaning of the personal pronoun 'we' often shifts in this chapter to mean Terry Warner and myself rather than being a mechanism to include the reader.

[25] In a written exchange between James McCawley and Noam Chomsky (see *Behavioral and Brain Sciences* 3, 1990) McCawley states, "While an innate language faculty might well make available both the hypothesis 'object precedes verb' and 'object follows verb', with selection (—'reinforcement') deciding which one wins, it is implausible to suppose that it makes available to the learner a range of hypotheses as to the meaning of *assassinate* that includes 'kill in order to remove from political power'".

Chomsky replies: "As for the particular case McCawley mentions—namely, fixing the meaning of *assassinate*—I am aware of no alternative to the view that the concepts that enter into the meaning and conditions on their interconnections are available prior to the acquisition of the word, and that some of them (e.g., the 'aitiational' elements) are primitive. If so, then the innate language faculty does make available a range of hypotheses as to the meaning—a narrow range, presumably, if the word is learned easily on the basis of limited evidence as to use. McCawley regards this as 'implausible', without, however, explaining why or suggesting a more plausible alternative".

Note that Chomsky admits that he is not aware of an alternative to his very objectivist view that the language faculty, as opposed to, say, social interaction, makes available a narrow range of possible meanings for a word.

[26] For an explanation of reductionism, see Robertson (1993).

[27] Emmanuel Levinas is a philosopher who lives in Paris; he was originally a Lithuanian Jew. His writings are not primarily oriented toward linguistics or translation. He is much concerned with an understanding of how the Holocaust and other inhumanities can occur. But his writings have inspired us and others to rethink issues in many disciplines.

[28] Of course, many besides Levinas disagree with Chomsky's view of language as a branch of individual psychology. For example, we read, "Language acquisition occurs in the social context of discourse" (Bruner 1983:58).

[29] Ethical obligation in Levinas may be related to thirdness in Peirce (personal note from John Robertson).

[30] It is also possible that some people never develop a normal sense of otherness, and that they so thoroughly view others as *objects-to-be-used* that they actually feel no ethical obligation. We are not referring here to the supposed ability of a member of the Mafia to compartmentalize in order to view some people caringly, such as their own family members, while unconsciously resisting any ethical obligation to people (viewed as obstacles) who are outside. We are referring to young people who are described as *stone killers*.

When asked why he shot three people and stabbed one person in a fast-food store, for example, Jeffrey Farina said: "I had a boring day". One victim died; Jeffrey is scheduled to be executed for his crimes. Researchers have found that most such stone killers under twenty-one years of age were physically abused as children. Significantly, it was found that they are diminished in both their ability to feel empathy for others and in their verbal competence. The vast majority of people in all cultures cringe when they hear such stories, not because they have been taught to cringe but because they recognize the otherness of victims and have empathy for their pain. Unfortunately, the number of young stone killers has been increasing in the past ten years.

The details on Jeffrey and other information came from an article in *US News and World Report*, January 17, 1994, pp. 33-37.

[31] The relevance of this passage was pointed out to us by Lyn Mattoon.

[32] Not just Levinas thinks of economics as having an ethical basis. *Economy* comes from the Greek *οἰκία* or *οἰκὸs* ('house'), and for this reason economics must be *clean*, since one wants to keep one's house in order. Also, if economy is amoral, it becomes robber-capitalism or robber-socialism; moral economy multiplies goods just as Christ could feed thousands with five loaves and two fishes (personal note from Adam Makkai).

[33] We may unconsciously continue to treat those around us as others despite the self-deception which justifies our inhuman treatment of them; or, if we honestly think someone is an object because they are pretending to be so (such as a person who stands still in a window acting like

a mannequin), the language we use with them will detectably change in the unlikely event that we speak to the object-person at all.

[34] See also Makkai (1993:71-72).

[35] David Meyer (personal communication) suggests that this is the way neural nets learn, which is encouraging if one is looking for a new computational model that can handle general language without restricting it into a domain language. However, it is not clear whether neural nets as currently constructed recognize otherness.

[36] The approach of this section is based on a paper delivered at the Cranfield Machine Translation Conference held November 12-14, 1994, at Cranfield University, UK.

[37] The version of the story that I heard was originally suggested by C. S. Lewis's "Meditation in a Toolshed" (Lewis 1970:212-216).

[38] Terry Winograd (1987) provides an additional example of the fact that meaning is not always neatly divided up into a literal base meaning and figurative extensions. Suppose one asks the question "Is there any water in the refrigerator?" In the context of a typical American family, this would be a question about whether there is a pitcher in the family refrigerator containing enough cold water (above zero degrees Celsius but probably below ten degrees) to pour into a glass and have a good drink. However, a scientist asking another scientist this same question may be asking whether there is any substance in the laboratory refrigerator containing any H_2O that might interfere with an experiment that uses microwaves. Which is the *literal* meaning? If one tries to list all the possible meanings in all conceivable contexts, this is an admission that meaning is indeed dependent on context. If one argues that the literal meaning is the one that is most likely in a *normal* context, then this is also an admission that meaning is dependent on context, in this case, the context we have called the Utterly Boring World. There really is no meaning that is independent of all context.

[39] There are, of course, even variations in the legal system between states of the United States and between England and Scotland in Great Britain. Further complications arise when considering U.S. territories such as Puerto Rico and dependencies of the Crown such as the Isle of Man and the Channel Islands.

[40] John Hutchins commented on the shift from general machine translation systems to domain-specific systems at the 1994 Cranfield conference mentioned earlier in these endnotes. At that same conference, Peter Wheeler, who, in the past ten years, has gone from working at the European Commission with Systran, to working for Logos (a machine translation developer), to being an independent consultant, confirmed the accuracy of the remarks made by Hutchins.

[41] At the first conference of the Association for Machine Translation in the Americas, a member society of the International Association for Machine Translation, held in Columbia, Maryland, October 6-8, 1994, a panel discussion treated the topic of the future of machine translation. Several panel members expressed their belief that current systems would gradually be extended to handle general language.

[42] At the Cranfield conference mentioned earlier, I took a straw poll during a debate on the limits of machine translation in which professionals from all over the world were participants. About ten percent of the participants indicated that they take the strong-AI position.

[43] An outrageous observation at this point would be that there seems to be something about people whose names end in 'sky' (pronounced 'skee') that leads them off the deep end.

[44] One of the best-known examples of prototype effects is that a robin and a penguin are both birds but a robin is a *better* example of a bird.

[45] Wilks made this point in an unpublished paper presented at the 1994 Cranfield conference mentioned earlier in these endnotes.

[46] I learned how chagrined Weizenbaum was when I heard him give a lecture on the topic in the 1970s. Wilks (personal communication) disagrees with my view of Weizenbaum.

[47] This statement was made in a video clip of Chomsky which is part of the film *Manufacturing Consent*, a documentary on the life of Chomsky that has been shown on university campuses and art film theaters around the country.

[48] This suggests another way to detect understanding. Ask someone to make friends with the computer program and to ask it for advice and try to determine whether the computer program really cares about the person or is just "going through the motions". This would test both flexibility and interiority.

[49] Penrose has recently published another book that deals with human intelligence, *Shadows of the Mind*. Colin McGinn, reviewing this book in the January 6, 1995, edition of the *Times Literary Supplement* (page 12), notes that the first half of Penrose's book sets out to show that one manifestation of human consciousness, mathematical understanding, cannot be reduced to the following of formal algorithmic procedures. McGinn agrees with Penrose that "the algorithmic picture of human thought is implausible", but he disagrees with the reasons Penrose gives. McGinn's view is that algorithms substitute for understanding but do not reproduce it. He also draws on Searle's Chinese Box argument that we have mentioned elsewhere in this book. There seems to be an increasing interest in discovering the nature of human thought without assuming it to be computational in the traditional sense of consisting of the algorithmic manipulation of symbols.

[50] Some have suggested that connectionism (the building of neural networks) will allow human-like capabilities in machines. I have no way of knowing whether this will happen or not. But current connectionist techniques will probably not form the basis for an artificial brain. For one thing, current neural networks can be programmed on everyday digital computers and therefore are fully algorithmic. Also, there is no reason to assume that a neural net will achieve general-language abilities with much fewer neurons than a human brain, yet present neural networks simulate only a tiny fraction of the number of neurons in a human brain, and it is not obvious that current techniques can be so drastically extended.

[51] It will be difficult for some to accept the claim that current techniques are limited in their potential. General language and domain-specific language are profoundly different in the way they *can* be treated. Because the significance of this difference has not been previously appreciated, a supposition has circulated that all language is essentially the same and that general language can be modeled on domain language. That this supposition has spread far and wide is not surprising. It is based on a highly successful tradition which includes the Galilean mathematical paradigm of reality, the quest for a language machine, and the objectivist conception of language as a system of sentences that possess their sense wholly independently of their actual use (called their 'force') in a situation, that is, independently of all consideration of pragmatics. The supposition has also been supported by such developments as formal language theory tied to automata theory, formal logic, and the extraordinary expansion of the use of computers. However, we think that a careful consideration of the matter along the lines we have shown in this book will instead support the historical fact that domain languages are created by people to restrict general language for specific purposes. Domain languages could not come into being any other way. They can only be created within the framework of a functioning general language. Even though they can be treated as if they were autonomous, they are not and cannot be. After having been *created* out of general language, they cannot suddenly become the *creator* of general language.

[52] This information about translation at the Commission was presented by a Commission representative at the Cranfield University conference on machine translation held in November 1994.

[53] For someone like me, raised in an atmosphere of objectivism, it is easy to get caught up in a desire to have a computational solution, that is, an algorithmic solution that can be programmed on present-day computers to run entirely by itself. Even though I have come to believe that such a solution is not possible, there is a persistent feeling in the background that any theory that is not computational is not worthwhile.

[54] Later in their excellent book (to which we will return), Neubert and Shreve may inadvertently contribute to the miscommunication. They rightly point out that much work in translation studies in the United States does not benefit from seminal European works which have not been translated into English. But then (in endnote 71) they criticize Robinson (1991), whom I refer to in chapter 1 because of his grasp of philosophical traditions underlying the linguistic approach. They say he implies on page 134 of his book (in a passage that we will shortly quote) that he rejects translation studies, because he thinks that the very mechanical process he describes is germane to current mainline translation theory and professional practice, while in fact it ceased to be accurate sometime before the 1970s. I think Robinson is reaching back over thousands of years of Western thought, accurately describing what we have called objectivism and the linguistic and philosophic theories based on it (which are very much alive and mainstream). Robinson makes it clear throughout his book that neither he nor his colleagues translate that way. Whether Robinson is aware of the seminal works (likely available only in German) to which Neubert and Shreve refer is less certain. In contrast with their previous admission of lack of consensus in current translation studies, in the endnote they claim that Robinson is "somewhat isolated from the main thrust of international translation theory". Who can say, in a fragmented discipline, what that main thrust is?

[55] Christianity, as presented in the Bible, avoids the myth of transcendental meaning. Jesus repeatedly explained that not everyone would understand his teachings, only those who "have ears to hear". If He could not present language in a way that would force everyone to understand it with one, correct transcendental meaning, then who could expect to? Throughout the Judeo-Christian tradition, it is emphasized that people must choose to look at life with a certain perspective in order to understand what God expects of them. This perspective is usually called an attitude of faith, and it allows someone to understand the word of God. It is perhaps relevant that in the Epistle of John, Jesus is likened to the word of God rather than to a physical object that operates independent of attitude. Words are effective to the degree that those using them share a certain perspective. Faith is the perspective that allows Christianity to be effective.

[56] This idea came up in a discussion with Michele Kaiser-Cooke.

[57] This story was told at the TAMA conference in Vienna, November 24-25, 1994.

[58] The ear asymmetry was brought to my attention by Michele Kaiser-Cooke.

[59] Personal communication from Muriel Vasconcellos, formerly of the Pan-American Health Organization.

[60] From an unpublished lecture delivered in Barcelona by Louis Truffaut, president of the Geneva School of Translation and Interpreting.

[61] "Bible Stories for Adults, No. 20: The Tower" by James Morrow.

[62] One linguist who uses this term is my colleague John Robertson, who draws on the work of Roman Jakobson and C. S. Peirce.

[63] An immense worldwide campaign is needed to educate requesters about the importance of specifications and to encourage accredited and certified translators to insist on specifications.

[64] There are international organizations that encourage the normalization of terminology, such as Infoterm and TermNet in Vienna.

[65] Over the years, I have often heard forty percent cited by technical translators as a typical percentage of the time for a job spent in terminology research. The sixty percent figure was suggested in discussions at various conferences not as a typical percentage but as an occasional high figure.

[66] From an unpublished draft of a lecture presented in Lausanne in November 1994 by Louis Truffaut.

[67] There is an apparent exception. Some people say that a translator can sometimes do a decent job of translating a technical text without understanding it. In that case, the human is simply performing machine translation and hoping for useful results.

[68] Personal communication from the president of the Geneva School of Translation and Interpreting (Louis Truffaut).

[69] A colleague, Alan Manning, has pointed out that finding the deep structure of an utterance is a useful exercise in hypothetical inference. Since there is *no proven method for deriving deep structures from their surface representations*, students must guess at a deep structure, then mentally test their model to see what the proposed deep structure is capable of generating.

[70] I just recently uncovered an objectivist interference in my thinking about ethics. I assumed that if one chose to do right in a given situation, it was equivalent to doing "the right thing", which implies that there is only one right thing to do in a given situation, a very mechanical view of the world and somewhat parallel to looking for the one right translation of a text. It then dawned on me that a version compatible with the agentive view is that of all options at a given point in time, each is either right or wrong, which implies that many things could be right in a given situation, just as many translations can be compatible with the same source text and specifications.

[71] The term bitext was devised by Brian Harris, University of Ottawa.

[72] I published one of the first papers on bilingual concordance systems in the LACUS Forum (1981). It described a bilingual concordance system that ran on a mainframe computer. The principal difficulty was that the segmentation and alignment were done manually, so it was too labor-intensive to apply to large volumes of text. I knew at the time that an automatic alignment procedure was needed, but I got involved in other tools for translators and did not return to the alignment question. Later in the 1980s, I spoke with Martin Kay, who was (as usual) thinking along similar lines. He and others worked on a procedure for automatic alignment of bilingual texts from *Scientific American*. One approach, which has become known as the Gale-Church algorithm, was based on the simple observation that over the length of an entire text, longer source-text sentences usually translate as longer target-text sentences. Using global statistical methods, a preliminary alignment is done without even splitting the sentences into words. Some mistakes are made, but the beauty of the method is that the mistakes are local. A mistake made because a sentence of source text corresponds to two sentences of target text does not throw off the whole alignment procedure, since it is not a sequential matching procedure but rather an overall pattern matching of lengths. The original statistical algorithm was implemented by several groups, and additional methods involving limited bilingual dictionaries have been added to the statistical method to fix local errors. A final interactive step allows a human to correct remaining errors if desired, but for some applications, a bitext database can be useful even if a few sentences per hundred are misaligned.

[73] The first implementations of translation memory, to my knowledge, resulted from ideas that originated at the translation institute at Brigham Young University in the 1970s (the same institute where we developed the interactive machine translation system described in chapter 3). By 1981, there were two implementations, one I developed at the university, called a 'Suggestion Box' system, and the other, called 'repetitions processing', developed at ALPS Inc. (later AlpNet Corporation), which was formed by some people at the translation institute when the machine project ended in 1980. The AlpNet translation memory system, embedded in a product called Autoterm™, was sold to IBM with source code. IBM developed it further,

using consultants who later formed Trados corporation, and the IBM system eventually became Translation Manager™. Trados has since developed its own version of translation memory, and others started picking up on the idea and developing similar products a decade later.

An unresolved practical issue in translation memory systems is whether they are best implemented as an add-on to an existing word processor or as an integral part of a proprietary editor which allows text to be imported from and exported to word processors.

[74] An example of a false cognate between English and French is to use *libraire* instead of *bibliothécaire* as an equivalent for 'librarian'.

[75] Translation checkers are just coming onto the market. A prototype translation checker was described by Pierre Isabelle at the October 1994 meeting of the AMTA. Work on translation checking by ISSCO (U. of Geneva) was also reported on at a recent meeting of LISA.

[76] The paper was originally presented at a terminology conference in Ottawa and later revised for publication in three parts in the Sci-Tech Newsletter of the American Translators Association.

[77] See my COLING paper (1982).

[78] For a description of the translator workstation from the perspective of an individual translator working directly with requesters or through an agency, see my chapter on the translator station in the book titled *Professional Issues* in the *ATA Scholarly Monograph* series.

[79] The shift in attitude at the CYC project was made more vivid by a pair of meetings with the director of the project, several years apart. In the first, there was an insistence that it was feasible to identify the universal set of concepts. In the second, the insistence had shifted to finding useful applications of domain-specific and culture-specific ontologies.

[80] From an interview with Professor Zemb videotaped by the University of Nancy.

[81] From a handout available at the machine translation exhibit area of the AMTA meeting in Columbia, Maryland, October, 1994.

[82] For stylistic consistency, we removed some spaces from Systran's output (i.e., two spaces after a colon were changed to one).

[83] We inadvertently introduced this typographical error into the source text. Note its varying effects on the samples of MT output.

[84] Globalink MTS only recognizes ASCII text. Accented characters become two-character sequences (i.e., é → e').

[85] After translating this source text, we noticed two non-standard usages in this Spanish text. The first paragraph should probably conclude "cuando vaya" instead of "cuando venga". The second sentence of the third paragraph should probably read "Espero salir bien", rather than

"Espero que salga bien". These errors do not violate Spanish grammar, but they are not typical of native Spanish usage.

[86] This comes from an e-mail message sent by *help@glnk.com* to new users of Globalink MTS.

Bibliography

Adams, Douglas. (1979) *The hitchhiker's guide to the galaxy*. New York: Harmony.

Adams, Hazard and Leroy Searle, eds. (1990) *Critical theory since 1965*, third ed. Tallahassee: University Presses of Florida.

Anderson, Stephen R. *(Review of) The computer and the mind: an introduction to cognitive science*, by Philip N. Johnson-Laird, Cambridge, MA: Harvard Univ. Press, 1988. Lg. 65.800-11.

Anttila, Raimo. (1975) Revelation as linguistic revolution. *First LACUS forum 1974*. South Carolina: Hornbeam Press.

Arnold, Douglas, L. Balkan, Lee Humphreys, and S. Meijer, eds. (1994) *Machine translation: introductory guide*. Cambridge, MA: Blackwell Publishers.

Baker, G. P., and P. M. S. Hacker. (1984) *Language, sense and nonsense*. New York: Basil Blackwell, Inc.

Bar-Hillel, Y. (1960) The present status of automatic translation of languages. *Advances in Computers*, 1, pp. 91-163.

Barbe, Katharina. (1991) Linguistic models of irony. *The Sixteenth LACUS Forum 1990*, ed. Angela Della Volpe. Lake Bluff, IL: LACUS.

Botha, Rudolph P. (1989) *Challenging Chomsky: the generative garden game*. New York: Basil Blackwell, Inc.

Bracken, Harry M. (1983) *Mind and language: essays on Descartes and Chomsky*. Vol. 14 in *Publications in language sciences*, eds. Ger J. de Haan, Leo Wetzels, and Wim Zonneveld. Dordrecht: Foris Publications.

Brower, Reuben Arthur, ed. (1959) *On translation*. Harvard University Press. Cambridge.

Bruner, Jerome. (1983) The social context of language acquisition. *Approaches to language*. Roy Harris, ed. Oxford: Pergamon Press.

Byte, December 1991, pp. 17 and 32.

Chomsky, Noam. (1957) *Syntactic structures*, sixth ed. The Hague: Mouton.

Chomsky, Noam. (1966) *Cartesian linguistics: a chapter in the history of rationalist thought*. Vol. 1 in *Studies in language*, eds. Noam Chomsky and Morris Halle. New York: Harper & Row.

Chomsky, Noam. (1980) *Rules and representations*. New York: Columbia Univ. Press.

Chomsky, Noam. (1982) *The generative enterprise: a discussion with Riny Huybregts and Kenk van Riemsdijk*. Dordrecht: Foris Publications.

Chomsky, Noam. (1986) Knowledge of language: Its nature, origin, and use. *Convergence*, ed. Ruth Nanda Anshen. New York: Praeger.

Davidson, Donald. (1989) The conditions of thought. *The mind of Donald Davidson*, eds. Johnnes Brandl and Wolfgang Gombochz. Atlanta, GA: Rodophi Press.

Damasio, Antonio R. (1994) *Descartes' error: emotion, reason, and the human brain*. New York: G. P. Putnam.

Davis, Harley G. and Talbot J. Taylor. (1990) *Redefining linguistics*. New York: Routledge.

de Beaugrande, Robert. (1987) Special Purpose Language as a complex system: The case of linguistics. *Special language: From humans thinking to thinking machines. Papers presented at the 6th European Symposium on LSP at the University of Vaasa*, eds. Christer Laurén and Marianne Nordman. Philadelphia: Multilingual Matters, Ltd.

Derrida, Jacques. (1985) Les tours de Babel. *Difference in translation*, ed. Joseph Graham. Ithaca: Cornell University Press.

Descartes, René. (1960) *Discourse on method and Meditations*. Trans. Laurence J. Lafleur. Indianapolis: Bobbs-Merrill.

Dreyfus, Hubert L. (1992) *What computers still can't do: a critique of artificial reason*. Cambridge, MA: MIT Press.

Eco, Umberto, Marco Santambrogio, and Patrizia Violi, eds. (1988) *Meaning and mental representations, advances in semiotics*. Bloomington: Indiana Univ. Press.

Gaddis Rose, Marilyn. (1993) Foreignizing or domesticating: debating norms goes with the territory. *Keystones of communication: proceedings of the 34th annual conference of the American Translators Association*, ed. Edith Losa. Medford, NJ: Learned Information.

Garneau, Jean-Luc. (1985) *Semantic divergence in Anglo-French cognates: a synchronic study in contrastive lexicography*. Lake Bluff, IL: Jupiter Press.

Gentzler, Edwin. (1993) *Contemporary translation theories*. New York: Routledge.

Gunnar, Megan R. and Michael Maratsos. eds. (1992) *Modularity and constraints in language and cognition*. Vol. 25 in *The Minnesota Symposia on Child Psychology*, Hillsdale, NJ: Lawrence Erlbaum Associates.

Hagège, Claude. (1981) *Critical reflections on generative grammar*. Trans. Robert A. Hall, Jr. Vol. 10 in *The Edward Sapir monograph series in language, culture, and cognition*. Lake Bluff, IL: Jupiter Press.

Harré, Rom. (1984) *Personal being: a theory for individual psychology*. Cambridge, MA: Harvard University Press.

Harris, Roy, ed. (1983) *Approaches to language*. Oxford: Pergamon Press.

Harris, Roy. (1987) *The language machine*. New York: Cornell University Press.

Harris, Roy. (1990) The integrationist critique of orthodox linguistics. *Proceedings of the sixteenth LACUS forum 1989*, ed. Michael P. Jordon. Lake Bluff, IL: LACUS.

Harris, Zellig. (1956) Co-occurrence and transformation in linguistic structure. *Language*, 33.

Heidegger, Martin. (1962) *Being and time*. Trans. John Macquarrie and Edward Robinson. New York: Harper & Row.

Hewson, Lance and Jacky Martin. (1991) *Redefining translation: the variational approach*. London: Routledge.

Hofstadter, Douglas R. (1980) *Gödel, Escher, Bach: an eternal golden braid*. New York: Vintage Books.

Horning, Beth. (1991) Language busters. *Technology review*, October 1991, pp. 51-57.

Hutchins, W. J. (1986) Machine translation: Past, present, future. *Computers and their applications*, ed. B. L. Meek. New York: Halsted Press.

Hutchins, W. J. and Harold Somers. (1992) *An introduction to machine translation*. London: Academic Press.

Isabelle, Pierre. (1992) *Proceedings of the fourth international conference on theoretical and methodological issues in machine translation*. Laval, Québec: CCRIT.

Jackendoff, Ray. (1990) *Semantic structures*. Vol. in *Current studies in linguistics*, ed. Samuel Jay Keyser. Cambridge, MA: MIT Press.

Jones, Karen Sparck. (1986) *Synonymy and semantic classification*. Edinburgh: Edinburgh University Press.

Kay, Martin. (1973) The MIND system. *Natural language processing (Courant computer science symposium 8)*, ed. R. Rusten. New York: Algorithmic Press.

Kay, Martin, Jean Mark Gawron, and Peter Norvig (1994) *Verbmobil: a translation system for face-to-face dialog*. *CSLI lecture notes* no. 33.: Stanford University.

Kittredge, Richard. (1987) The significance of sublanguage for automatic translation. *Machine translation: theoretical and methodological issues*, ed Sergei Nirenburg. Cambridge: Cambridge University Press.

Lakoff, George and Mark Johnson. (1980) *Metaphors we live by*. Chicago: Univ. of Chicago Press.

Lakoff, George and Mark Turner. (1989) *More than cool reason: a field guide to poetic metaphor*. Chicago: University of Chicago Press.

Lakoff, George. (1987) *Women, fire, and dangerous things: what categories reveal about the mind*. Chicago: University of Chicago Press.

Landau, Barbara and Lila R. Gleitman. *Language and experience: evidence from the blind child*. Vol 8 in *Cognitive science series*, ed. Eric Wanner. Cambridge, MA: Harvard Univ. Press.

Langacker, Ronald W. (1990) *Concept, image, and symbol: the cognitive basis of grammar*. Vol 1 in *Cognitive linguistics research*, eds. René Dirven and Ronald W. Langacker. New York: Mouton de Gruyter.

Larson, Mildred L. (1984) *Meaning-based translation*. Lanham, MD: University Press of America.

Levin, Samuel R. (1977) *The semantics of metaphor*. Baltimore: Johns Hopkins Univ. Press.

Levinas, Emmanuel. (1969) *Totality and infinity: an essay on exteriority*, 6th ed. trans. Alphonso Lingis. Pittsburgh: Duquesne University Press.

Levinas, Emmanuel. (1987) *Philosophy and the idea of infinity. Collected philosophical papers*. trans. Alphonso Lingis. Dordrecht: Martinus Nijhoff Publishers.

Lewis, C. S. (1970) *God in the dock: essays on theology and ethics*. Ed. Walter Hooper. Grand Rapids, MI: William B. Eerdmans Publishing Company.

Locke, W. N., and Booth, A. D. (1955) *Machine translation of languages*. Cambridge, MA: MIT Press.

Longman dictionary of contemporary English. (1978) London: Longman Group Limited.

Lyons, John. (1968) *Introduction to theoretical linguistics*. Cambridge: Cambridge Univ. Press.

Lytle, Eldon G. (1974) *A grammar of subordinate structures in English*. The Hague: Mouton.

Lytle, Eldon G. (1980) Junction Grammar: Theory and application. *The sixth LACUS forum 1979*. Columbia, South Carolina: Hornbeam Press.

Makkai, Adam. (1993) *Ecolinguistics: ¿toward a new **paradigm** for the science of language?* New York: St. Martin's Press.

Melby, Alan K. (1980) A comparative book of Junction Grammar. *The sixth LACUS forum 1979*. Columbia, South Carolina: Hornbeam Press.

Melby, Alan K. (1981) Linguistics and machine translation. *The seventh LACUS forum 1980*, ed. James Copeland and Philip W. Davis. Lake Bluff, IL: LACUS.

Melby, Alan K. (1985) Generalization and prediction of syntactic patterns in Junction Grammar. *Linguistics and philosophy: essays in honor of Rulon S. Wells*. Amsterdam/Philadelphia: John Benjamins Publishing Company.

Melby, Alan K. (1988) Statutory analysis. *The fourteenth LACUS forum 1987*, ed. Sheila Embleton. Lake Bluff, IL: LACUS.

Melby, Alan K. (1991) *Des causes et des effets de l'asymétrie partielle des réseox sémantiques liés aux langues naturelles*. Les cahiers de lexicologie. Vol LVIII.

Melby, Alan K. (1994) The possibility of language. *The twentieth LACUS forum 1993*, ed. Valerie Becker Makkai. Chapel Hill, NC: LACUS.

Mills, Carl. (1991) Continuous (meaning) and discrete (form) in language, cognition and society. *Proceedings of the sixteenth LACUS forum 1990*, ed. Angela Della Volpe. Lake Bluff, IL: LACUS.

Minsky, Marvin. (1994) Will robots inherit the earth? *Scientific American*, 271(4), pp. 86-91.

Nagao, Makoto. (1989) *Machine translation: how far can it go?* Trans. Norman D. Cook. Tokyo: Oxford University Press.

Neubert, Albrecht, and Shreve, Greg. (1992) *Translation as text*. Kent, OH: Kent State University Press.

Nida, Eugene. (1947) Principles of translation as exemplified by Bible translating. *On translation*, ed. R. Brower. 1959. Cambridge: Harvard University Press.

Nida, Eugene, and Charles Taber. (1969) *The theory and practice of translation*. Leiden: Brill.

Nirenburg, Sergei, ed. (1985) *Proceedings of the conference on theoretical and methodological issues in machine translation of natural languages*. Hamilton, NY: Colgate University.

Orwell, George. (1949) *1984*. New York: Harcourt, Brace.

Oxford english dictionary, second ed., vol. 2. (1989) Oxford: Oxford University Press.

Palmer, Martha Stone. (1990) Semantic processing for finite domains. *Studies in natural language processing*. Cambridge: Cambridge Univ. Press.

Penrose, Roger. (1989) *The emperor's new mind*. New York: Oxford University Press.

Piattelli-Palmarini, Massimo, ed. (1980) *Language and learning: the debate between Jean Piaget and Noam Chomsky*. Cambridge, MA: Harvard Univ. Press.

Port Royal Logic, second ed., (1851). Trans. T. S. Baynes. Edinburgh: Sutherland and Knox

Pourtales, Guy. (1966) *Berlioz et l'Europe romantique*. Paris: Gallimard.

Radford, Andrew. (1988) *Transformational grammar: a first course*. Vol. in *Cambridge textbooks in linguistics*, ed. B. Comrie, et al. Cambridge: Cambridge University Press.

Reich, Peter A. (1986) *Language development*. Englewood Cliffs, NJ: Prentice-Hall.

Richards. (1953) Toward a theory of translating. in *Studies in Chinese thought*, ed. Arthur Wright. Chicago: University of Chicago Press.

Robertson, John. (1993) "One soul shall not be lost": the dangers of reductionism. James L. Barker lecture, College of Humanities, Brigham Young University.

Robinson, Douglas. (1991) *The translator's turn*. Baltimore: Johns Hopkins University Press.

Rudolf, Jumpelt. *Die Übersetzung naturwissenschaftlicher und technischer Literatur*. Berlin-Schöneberg: Langenscheidt.

Sager, Juan C. (1993) *Language engineering and translation: consequences of automation*. Amsterdam: John Benjamins.

Schulte, Rainer, and John Biguenet, eds. (1992) *Theories of translation: an anthology of essays from Dryden to Derrida*.

Searle, John. (1980) *Minds, brains, and programs*. Vol. 3 in *The behavioral and brain sciences*. Cambridge: Cambridge University Press.

Sellars, Wilfrid. (1963) *Empiricism and the philosophy of mind. Science, perception and reality*. New York: The Humanities Press.

Shaumyan, Sebastian. (1987) A semiotic theory of language. *Advances in semiotics*, ed. Thomas A. Sebeok. Bloomington: Indiana Univ. Press.

Shotter, John. (1984) *Social accountability and selfhood*. New York: Basil Blackwell.

Snell-Hornby, Mary. (1988) *Translation studies*. Amsterdam: John Benjamins.

Tavakolian, Susan L. ed. (1981) *Language acquisition and linguistic theory*. Cambridge, MA: MIT Press.

Twain, Mark. (1953) *The adventures of Huckleberry Finn*. New York: Dodd.

Venuti, Lawrence. (1986) The translator's invisibility. *Criticism*, 28.

Winograd, Terry and Fernando Flores. (1987) *Understanding computers and cognition: A new foundation for design*. New York: Addison-Wesley Publishing.

Whorf, Benjamin Lee. (1956) *Language, thought, and reality: selected writings of Benjamin Lee Whorf*. Cambridge, MA: MIT Press.

Wilks, Yorick. (1973) An Artificial Intelligence Approach to Machine Translation. *Computer Models of Thought and Language*, ed. R. C. Schank and K. M. Colby. San Francisco: W. H. Freeman.

Wilks, Yorick and Dan Fass. (1983) Preference Semantics, Ill-formedness, and Metaphor. *American Journal of Computational Linguistics*, 9(3-4).

Wilks, Yorick. (1985) Bad metaphors: Chomsky and Artificial Intelligence. *Noam Chomsky, Consensus and Controversy*, ed. Soham Modgil and Celcilia Modgil. New York: The Falmer Press.

Wittgenstein, Ludwig. (1953) *Philosophical investigations*. Trans. G. E. M. Anscombe. New York: Macmillan.

Wittgenstein, Ludwig. (1961) *Tractatus logico-philosophicus*. Trans. D. F. Pears and B. F. McGuinness. London: Routledge & Kegan Paul.

Yngve, V. H. (1986) *Linguistics as a science*. Bloomington: Indiana University Press.

Glossary

algorithmic: Referring to a procedure that ends after a finite number of steps, such that each decision is based on clear-cut criteria.

artificial intelligence (AI): The idea that computers can be programmed in such a way that they are able to represent and manipulate knowledge about the world in meaningful ways, performing intellectual tasks that are normally associated with human intelligence. Computers possessing artificial intelligence would be able to generalize, make meaningful inferences, and learn from their mistakes.

asymmetry: A symmetrical relationship is one which can be reversed without making any false claims. For example, in algebra, addition is symmetrical since X plus Y is always the same number as Y plus X. Thus, an asymmetrical relation is one for which the above condition does not hold. For example, division is not symmetrical, since X divided by Y is not always (indeed usually not) the same as Y divided by X. In translation, an asymmetry between expressions means that one is not always an appropriate equivalent for the other.

batch: When a computer operates in batch mode, the users explicitly enumerate one or more commands which are later executed in series by the computer without human intervention. Contrast **on-line**.

billion: A thousand million in American usage (equivalent to the old British milliard, which is giving way to the American usage of billion).

CAT: See **computer-assisted translation**.

cognitive models: For Lakoff, cognitive models are mental representations of human experience. A model allows human beings to make sense of the world. Some models are linear, some radial, some prototypical.

competence: For Chomsky (and nearly all linguists since), competence refers to the internalized system of rules in the language faculty of a speaker. When a speaker has fully incorporated the rules of syntax and semantics for a given language, the speaker is said to possess syntactic competence for that language. Competence is traditionally opposed to **performance**, which relates to the actual production or understanding of an utterance. A person may possess competence but produce a flawed **performance**, such as leaving out words or using syntax that does not match the mental rules, when excessively tired or inebriated, for example. Chomsky claims that linguistics should isolate and seek to explain competence. A little-discussed aspect of competence in Chomsky's work is pragmatic competence. See **performance**.

compound nouns: A sequence of nouns which collectively form a unit, such as 'integer array function' or 'translators association membership directory'. Many specialized terms are compound nouns.

computer-assisted translation (CAT): A rather vague term which has been used to describe both (a) machine translation with human post-editing and/or pre-editing and (b) human translation with the help of various computer software tools. Also called **machine-assisted translation (MAT)**.

controlled language: An artificially defined sublanguage in which authors learn to constrain their writing to conform to a set of rules about syntax and semantics when writing texts. The purpose of a controlled language is to eliminate most ambiguities and all dynamic metaphor so that the language can be more easily and accurately processed by machine. Xerox corporation uses controlled language in its installation, maintenance, and repair manuals for photocopiers. A procedural programming language such as C or Pascal can be viewed as an extreme example of a controlled language or classified as a formal language. It is a point of contention whether a controlled language is a formal language or a restricted form of **natural language**.

CPU: Central processing unit. The main chip or chips responsible for controlling the operation of a digital computer. Microcomputer CPUs are commonly classified according to interior architecture (i.e., 486, Pentium,

Power PC, etc.), and according to clock frequency (i.e., 66 MHz, 90 MHz, etc.).

DBMT: See **dialogue-based machine translation**.

deconstruction: A view according to which meaning ultimately depends on the interrelationships among all members of a concept system. For example, 'horse' may be defined as the hole in the concept system that is *not* filled by 'cow', 'zebra', and so forth. Concepts therefore derive their essence from contrasts with the rest of the system. Carried to its logical conclusion, this idea suggests that all conceptual systems are ultimately arbitrary, because all concepts depend completely upon all other concepts for definition. They lack a **grounding** that is exterior to (and not dependent upon) the system. Literary deconstructionists therefore refuse to look for *The Meaning* of a text. Instead they pursue textual oppositions, seeking to illustrate how the text creates these oppositions and depends upon them.

deep structure: In Chomskyan linguistics, the deep structure of an utterance is an unmarked, acontextual, logical form of the utterance in question. Deep structures are always complete sentences, always declarative (not questions), always active voice (not passive). Chomsky's generative procedure works as a black box that generates these deep structures and in one way or another modifies them into the utterances that ideally issue from the speaker.

default: In machine translation, the default translation of a word is the target language equivalent that the system will use unless it has a specific reason to do otherwise. In a dictionary of baseball terms, 'run' would have a single default translation for each target language. Each default translation would be the target language term for a point scored in a baseball game. The system would always change 'run' in the English text into its default target equivalent unless it encountered evidence that it was being used as a verb in English.

dialogue-based machine translation (DBMT): A term used by the University of Grenoble to describe an interactive approach to MT. In this approach, the human (generally someone with limited ability in the target language) assists the computer by clarifying the structure and referents of prepositional phrases or other elements in a sentence, and by choosing among a list of possible senses of words. The computer asks a question and acts on the answer before asking the next question; hence the computer and the human enter into a dialogue in the hope that the human/computer team can produce a better and/or faster translation than either could produce alone.

e-mail: Short for electronic mail. A method of sending and receiving paperless messages which normally allows delivery anywhere in the world within hours instead of days.

EC: The European Commission.

electronic brain: A term for the first digital computers. Popularly used during the 1950s and 1960s, the term reflects the (then) common idea that computers were fundamentally similar in function and potential to human brains.

EU: The European Union.

European Commission: The administrative branch of the European Union.

European Union: Formerly, the European Economic Community. A political and economic federation of European states, including most of Western Europe.

Eurotra: A major machine translation funded by European interests in the 1970s and 1980s.

eye of the soul: A faculty postulated by Plato, whereby human beings can acquire ideal forms of abstract ideas through pure intellectual intuition.

file: The most common method of organizing information for manipulation by computer. Files consist of one or more (often physically non-contiguous) groups of bytes that are somehow marked as a single cohesive unit by the computer's operating system.

fifth generation computer: The Japanese government funded a project during the 1980s which focused on the goal of creating a fifth generation computer system (the current generation of computers being viewed as the fourth generation). It was hoped initially that such a computer would accept **natural language** as input, among other things.

formal language: A set of sequences of words, often called sentences, each of which is generated mechanically by a set of phrase-structure rules. A formal language may be superficially similar to sentences of natural language or entirely odd-looking. For example, the set {x, x y, x y y, x z y} could be a formal language.

free translation: A style of translation in which the translator is expected to produce target language which has a meaning equivalent to the source language, but which need not preserve word order, word-for-word parallelism, or syntactic patterns of the original. Contrast **literal translation**.

general/domain distinction: An expression implying that dynamic general language is qualitatively distinct from controlled language defined for use within a narrow domain. The essence of the difference is that dynamic general language involves fundamental ambiguity. The meanings of a particular word or phrase cannot be restricted to a finite list. Domain language, on the other hand, ideally exhibits at most superficial ambiguity. Most texts are a mixture of these two extremes.

Generative Grammar (GG): Generally, Chomsky's approach to syntax. Although specific movements within what linguists call 'Generative Grammar' go by different names (e.g., Government-Binding Theory, Lexical Functional Grammar, Head-Driven Phrase Structure Grammar, etc.), all these approaches share the central tenet that a 'generative procedure' defines syntactic representations for sentences in isolation. In this book they are all loosely called Generative Grammar.

GG: See **Generative Grammar**.

given: In philosophy, that which exists, or is assumed to exist, *a priori*.

GramR: A programming language used by the METEO system for translating Canadian weather bulletins.

grounding: A conceptual system is said to be grounded if it can be anchored to something that is outside the system. The groundedness of language is a philosophical problem which various philosophers have resolved differently. See **deconstruction**.

indicative translation: Translation done to provide someone with a rough idea of the nature of the source text, but not to create a high-quality target text for general distribution or publication.

interactive: In machine translation systems, a process that allows the computer to ask a human questions in order to refine output. Usually applied to applications that permit collaboration during the translation process, as opposed to those that allow the human to modify the raw output only after the MT system has completed its work.

interlinear translation: An extremely rigid form of translation in which the word order of the source text is fully preserved, and each word is translated literally.

interlingua: A representation of the logical and ideational content of an utterance which is presumed to be independent of any **natural language**. Some machine translation systems attempt to reduce each sentence to an interlingua; from there, they can derive natural language representations for many target languages at once. It is not clear that a true interlingua is possible.

Language for Special Purposes: Language that is a mixture of dynamic general language and true domain language. Most texts fall into this category, instead of consisting purely of one extreme. For example, the typical software manual may consist largely of terms when it discusses the navigation of menus, but display dynamic general language when it discusses the reasons why a particular feature might be advantageous to a user.

lexical transfer: In machine translation systems, the substitution of target for source lexical items.

literal translation: A literal translation stays as close as possible to the text being translated. The translation seeks to achieve a nearly 1:1

correspondence between words in the two languages. The grammatical structure of the source text is also preserved as closely as possible. Usually, the word order of the source text is not expected to carry over to a literal translation. This extreme type of translation (word for word in the same order) is often called an **interlinear translation**. Literal translations are usually rather unnatural and difficult to understand in the target language.

logical object: The noun (phrase) that 'receives' the action of a verb. A logical object does not change even if the syntax of the sentence is altered, as opposed to a syntactic object, which may disappear, for example, if the sentence is cast in the passive voice.

LSP: See **Language for Special Purposes**.

machine-assisted translation (MAT): A rather vague term that has been used to describe both (a) machine translation with human post-editing and/or pre-editing and (b) human translation with the help of various computer software tools. Also called **computer-assisted translation (CAT)**.

machine translation: Translation performed algorithmically by a computer, without interaction or input by a human.

markup: Indications of the logical structure of a text. Markup may be presentational, in which case it gives clues to structure by changing the appearance of the text as displayed or printed (e.g., headings are bolded and italicized, a blank line precedes each paragraph, and so forth); markup may also be descriptive, in which case logical relationships are explicitly identified by some kind of meta-text coding. Markup is helpful to MT systems because it enables the computer to identify sentences and other segments of text for processing.

MAT: See **computer-assisted translation**.

METAL: A commercial machine translation system marketed by the Sietec division of Siemens Corporation.

metalanguage: A language used for talking about another subject.

METEO: A system that translates Canadian weather bulletins by computer with notable success. METEO was developed at the University of Montréal as an outgrowth of the TAUM project.

microworld: Used by AI researchers, beginning with Winograd. In this book, an extremely narrow domain composed of well-defined objects and tasks.

morphological analysis: In machine translation systems, the process of analyzing sentence constituents into component morphemes. In particular, inflected forms of words are reduced to their base form.

natural language: Language as it is used in natural settings for general purposes. Informal, colloquial speech is an example of natural language. Contrast **controlled language**.

natural language processing (NLP): The treatment of **natural language** by a computer system. Voice/speech recognition and machine translation are common natural language processing applications.

NLP: Natural language processing.

objectivism: A philosophy that underlies much of Western thinking. Lakoff lists several defining assumptions, which include the following: thought is the mechanical manipulation of abstract symbols; symbols get their meaning via correspondences to things in the real world; thought is atomistic and rigidly logical. Such a view implies that there is no fundamental ambiguity, because at its most basic level, conceptual systems are founded on incontrovertible, unmediated facts and categories.

on-line: If something happens on-line, it takes place while a relevant computer program is running, often over a telecommunications network. On-line interaction with a machine translation system allows the operator to actively improve the output of the system, rather than perform post-editing. Contrast **batch**.

ontology: In the current discussion, an ontology is a means of categorizing the universe or some portion of it, so that each concept has a position in a semantic network.

otherness: The quality of being exterior to one's self. A Levinasian view of language suggests that we implicitly recognize the otherness of speakers and listeners by engaging in linguistic actions, because language presupposes a non-totalized context in which communication is desirable.

parsing: In a machine translation system, the process of identifying the relations among various elements in a sentence.

PC: Personal computer. Sometimes called a microcomputer.

performance: The actual production or recognition of language in a real-life context. Suggested by Chomsky as an opposition to the concept of **competence**, which is a mental representation of the knowledge of a native speaker of a natural language necessary to performance. Performance is susceptible to garbling due to complicating factors such as the physical health and mental alertness of the speaker. Chomsky argues that linguistic investigations should divorce performance from **competence** because performance is not a reliable reflection of the underlying linguistic system. See **competence**.

phrase structure rules: A recipe that allows phrases to be described simply in terms of their constituents. These rules are generally layered, in that simple phrases are used as components of more complex phrases. Many machine translation systems use phrase structure rules to identify syntactic relationships during **parsing**. A significant assumption underlying phrase structure rules is that the sentence is the primary unit of an utterance; rules define no element larger than the sentence. These rules have played an important role in various incarnations of Generative Grammar.

pointing device: In a **GUI** environment, the user must be able to point to objects of the interface, such as icons, menus, and scroll bars. The most common mechanism to allow deictic input is the mouse. Other pointing devices include light pens and touch pads. The physical device is complemented by a virtual pointing device which translates movements of the device to movements of a pointer on the screen.

post-editing: The process of using a human translator or writer to clean up machine translation output, after all MT activity is completed.

Prolog: An extremely high-level programming language developed by Alain Colmerauer. Prolog programs are used by AI researchers. They are more intuitive and less opaque (to the programmer) than programs written in lower-level languages.

prototype effects: In some conceptual paradigms, one member of the set may be considered a 'better' member of the set than another. For example, a rabbit could be considered a 'better' (or more prototypical) mammal than a duck-billed platypus. When a paradigm shows prototypical effects like this, it cannot be easily treated as a simple mathematical set, which objectivism prescribes.

rapid post-editing: A technique for producing quick, rough translations in which human translators scan raw MT output and correct only the most significant errors.

sememe: As used in this book, an atomistic concept, universal and language-independent. If such concepts existed, accurate machine translation could be done by mapping source language words phrases onto the sememes, then mapping sememes onto target language words and phrases. This use of sememe may not be consistent with its use by Sydney Lamb.

somatic: Relating to the (human) body.

source text: In the translation process, the source text is the document that is to be translated.

stone killer: A person who has become thoroughly hardened to the act of killing, and can do so with no compunction or emotional involvement.

storm warning: In the United States, meteorologists issue a storm warning when a storm has been observed and is approaching the area in question.

storm watch: In the United States, meteorologists issue a storm watch when conditions are favorable for the development of a storm.

sublanguage: A set of terms (and corresponding concepts) and syntactic constructions that are restricted in their meanings and style to a specific, narrow domain.

surface structure: In Generative Grammar, the underlying structure before transformations have been applied.

target text: The translation, as opposed to the source text (which is the document that was translated).

tuning: The process of adjusting the algorithms of an MT system to better handle a particular text or type of text.

Subject Index

Author Index

In the BENJAMINS TRANSLATION LIBRARY the following titles have been published thus far or are scheduled to appear in the course of 1995:

1. SAGER, Juan C: *Language Engineering and Translation: Consequences of automation*, 1994.
2. SNELL-HORNBY, Mary, Franz POCHHACKER and Klaus KAINDL (eds): *Translation Studies: An interdiscipline. Selected papers from the Translation Congress, Vienna, 9-12 September 1992*. 1994.
3. LAMBERT, Sylvie and Barbara MOSER-MERCER (eds): *Bridging the Gap: Empirical research on simultaneous interpretation*. 1994.
4. TOURY, Gideon: *Descriptive Translation Studies — and beyond*. 1995.
5. DOLLERUP, Cay and Annette LINDEGAARD (eds): *Teaching Translation and Interpreting 2: Insights, aims, visions. Selected papers from the Second Language International Conference, Elsinore, 4-6 June 1993*. 1994.
6. EDWARDS, Alicia Betsy: *The Practice of Court Interpreting*. 1995.
7. BEAUGRANDE, Robert de, Abdulla SHUNNAQ and Mohamed Helmy HELIEL (eds): *Language Discourse and Translation in the West and Middle East. Selected and revised papers from the conference on Language and Translation, Irbid, Jordan 1992*. 1994.
8. GILE, Daniel: *Basic Concepts and Models for Interpreter and Translator Training*. 1995.
9. REY, Alain: *Essays on Terminology*. 1995.
10. KUSSMAUL, Paul: *Training the Translator*. 1995.
11. VINAY, Jean Paul and Jean DARBELNET: *Comparative Stylistics of French and English: A methodology for Translation*. 1995.
12. BERGENHOLTZ, Henning and Sven TARP: *Manual of Specialised Lexicography: The preparation of specialised dictionaries*. 1995.
13. DELISLE, Jean and Judith WOODSWORTH (eds): *Translators through History*. n.y.p.
14. MELBY, Alan with Terry WARNER: *The Possibility of Language. A discussion of the nature of language, with implications for human and machine translation*. 1995.
15. WILSS, Wolfram: *Knowledge and Skills in Translator Behavior*. n.y.p.